Irish cinema in the twenty-first century

MANCHESTER
1824

Manchester University Press

Irish cinema in the twenty-first century

RUTH BARTON

Manchester University Press

Published by Manchester University Press
Altrincham Street, Manchester M1 7JA
www.manchesteruniversitypress.co.uk

British Library Cataloguing-in-Publication Data
A catalogue record for this book is available from the British Library

ISBN 978 1 5261 3837 8 hardback
ISBN 978 1 5261 2444 9 paperback

First published 2019

Typeset by Out of House Publishing
Printed in Great Britain
by TJ International Ltd, Padstow

To
Willie, Conal, Eoin, Paddy
&
In memory of Anne Barton
(1919–2016)

Contents

Figures

Acknowledgements

This publication is the culmination of many years of teaching Irish cinema. Thank you so much to all my students for making me think about what I was saying. Thank you to my peers for turning any conference session we have been involved in into one about Irish cinema, whatever the ostensible topic; to the libraries of Trinity College Dublin and the Irish Film Institute, to the staff at the IFI bookshop, and to my colleagues in the Department of Film Studies at Trinity College Dublin. Thank you to those filmmakers who gave me access to their work, to the production companies for allowing me to use stills from their films, and authors who sent me hard-to-obtain materials. Funding received under the SPeCTReSS network opened me up to new ideas on cultural trauma, as well as enabling me to spend a semester at the University of São Paulo, where much of this book was written. It was a pleasure to work with Manchester University Press and I am grateful for the feedback from the anonymous readers of the manuscript. As ever, none of this could have happened without the support of my family, to whom this book is dedicated, as ever, with love.

Introduction

In October 2015, *The Lobster* (Yorgos Lanthimos, 2015) opened in Irish cinemas. Owing presumably to its starry cast – Colin Farrell, Rachel Weisz, John C. Reilly, Léa Seydoux, Ben Whishaw and Olivia Colman – and film festival success (it won the Jury Prize at the 2015 Cannes Film Festival), what was evidently a challenging art film played nationally in multiplexes as well as the more predictable Irish Film Institute and Lighthouse cinemas in Dublin. The gambit paid off, with the film being tipped to exceed a box office take of €1million by the end of its second week (RTÉ Ten, 2015). Shot in Sneem, County Kerry, with interiors at the luxury Parknasilla Resort, *The Lobster* is unmistakably a co-production. Its director is Greek and its cast multinational; its setting may be Irish, although Ireland is never named as its location. It was produced by Element Pictures (Ireland), Scarlet Films (UK), Faliro House (Greece), Haut et Court (France), Lemming Film (Netherlands) and Limp (UK). It was financed in part by the Irish Film Board.[1]

To pose the question as to whether *The Lobster* is an Irish film is, under these circumstances, laughable. In earlier critical times, a work such as this would have been written off as a 'europudding', that is, the indigestible outcome of mixing up multiple European funding sources with little or no investment in cultural engagement, and a dilution of the project of building a distinctive national cinema. Writing in 1987 in the seminal *Cinema and Ireland*, Kevin Rockett, for instance, warned of the 'necessary compromises of international co-productions' (Rockett, Gibbons and Hill, 1987: 143). Now, co-productions are the backbone of the Irish film industry and the understanding of what constitutes a national cinema is ever more elusive. Theories of transnationalism provide a positive way out of the damning 'europudding', while theorists of globalisation warn against the continued dilution of the local in the face of the global.

No research exists to prove it, but one may guess that another of the draws for Irish audiences of *The Lobster* was that it was, in some way, Irish. Colin Farrell promoted the film widely in the Irish media, and much was made of the local experience of its shoot.

Figure 1   Colin Farrell in *The Lobster*

Or maybe not? Perhaps because *The Lobster* made no pretence of containing its identity within the boundaries of the national, it did not provoke anything like the furore that followed the release of John Michael McDonagh's *Calvary* in 2014. It is unlikely that much attention would have been paid to that film's qualities of Irishness had its director not stated the following in an interview (Associated Press, 2014):

> I'm not a big fan of Irish movies. I don't find them to be technically that accomplished. I don't find them that intelligent. So, I'm trying to get away from the description of the movie as an Irish film ... It's not an Irish film. It's just set in Ireland with lots of Irish characters ... So when you're making a film there, you're trying to convince the Irish audience, no it's not like all those terrible Irish movies you've seen before.

McDonagh's interview provoked national outrage as well as some considerable soul-searching. I was one of a number of writers on Irish film contacted to comment on his words (Shortall, 2014). What was an Irish film, indeed? According to Michael Phillips, a film critic at the *Chicago Tribune*, the American idea of an Irish film is 'a story that's full of fantastically voluble and cheerily fatalistic characters' (Shortall, 2014). Such comments only serve to remind readers of the transatlantic divide – it would be unimaginable for a local Irish writer to have offered the same definition. No one else, myself included, ventured anything more substantial. Several filmmakers, however, agreed with McDonagh, suggesting that Irish audiences undervalue their own cinema and it takes success in overseas markets to persuade them of its merits. Perhaps, then, it is incorrect to guess that Irish audiences particularly want to see Irish films. They may just want to see good films, or populist films, which is largely what Irish cinemas show.

The cream of non-Hollywood film production is exported, often only showing outside their home territories at film festivals. In this way, canons that may exclude much local work are formed. Hollywood itself is reliant on the export market for profit (and on selling on its product to other platforms). Irish audiences, accustomed to see the most populist or best of other industry's films, find themselves faced, at home, with all Irish films. Of those, they are most likely to select, particularly in the cinema, the releases that most conform to the films they enjoy from other territories. Others they may catch up with on television or alternative domestic viewing platforms. Outside of Ireland, by contrast, the perception of what constitutes Irish cinema largely depends on a limited choice of popular or award-winning releases.

This leaves Irish filmmakers with a conundrum that is far from new. They are much more likely to win audiences if they make films that closely resemble global product.[2] They may have to stand by and watch filmmakers from other markets tell Irish stories that Irish audiences embrace, whereas their own films remain unwatched. Success for Irish filmmakers may be in other markets, working on non-Irish films. Neil Jordan, Jim Sheridan and Lenny Abrahamson all know this. Of these three, Jordan to date has managed best to make one for himself and one for the bank; he has also enjoyed most success with the move into long-form television even if *The Borgias* series (Showtime, 2011–13), which he created, was withdrawn before its final season. The wider Irish audiovisual industry is, as the tables in the Appendix demonstrate, largely geared towards foreign television shows. In years when major television dramas are shot in Ireland (*Penny Dreadful* (Showtime, 2014–16), *Ripper Street* (BBC/Amazon Video, 2012–16), *The Tudors* (Showtime, 2007–10)), foreign direct investment can be in excess of nine times that of local investment. Irish-made films are a small percentage of the industry, as is animation, and Irish documentaries an even smaller percentage. Audiovisual production in Ireland is therefore part of a global industry that is, in the main part, uninterested in local and national affiliations.

The globalisation of Irish production has been matched by the globalisation of Irish talent. Not just Irish actors, but directors and production personnel move easily between territories and cultures. In many ways, this has been a liberating process, and to be celebrated. It also challenges us to find new ways of talking about Irish film and to locate, within this whirlwind of competing voices, something to hold on to that is still national, local and meaningful. All this activity has taken place against a massive transformation of Irish society occasioned by the rise and fall of the Celtic Tiger.

The Celtic Tiger and Irish cinema

In terms of chronology, this book takes up where *Irish National Cinema* (Barton, 2004) left off, in the early years of the twenty-first century. By then, the Celtic Tiger was already the defining influence on Irish life. The period of the Celtic Tiger is usually taken to describe the years from the mid-1990s to 2008, during which there was an unprecedented accumulation of wealth in a country otherwise associated with extremes of poverty and depopulation. In fact, by 2001, the real growth was over and a property bubble followed, which burst with the global economic collapse of 2008. During the Celtic Tiger years, the Irish economy was the marvel of not just Europe but much of the rest of the world. As Peader Kirby (2010: 2) has written:

> During the 1990s, Ireland's economy grew at an annual average rate of around 7.5 per cent and in some years towards the end of the decade surpassed ten per cent growth. Not only was this more than three times the average of European countries at the time but it made Ireland one of the most economically successful countries in the world, rivaling the growth of China.

The Celtic Tiger economy soon came to describe a lifestyle of conspicuous consumption, much of it ascribed to the property developers whose bank borrowings ultimately were part of the reason for the country's crash, when it came. The banking sector in particular came under intense public scrutiny as it turned out to have been dependent on unsustainable loans. The crash and the subsequent International Monetary Fund (IMF) series of bailouts plunged Ireland into austerity, returned it to mass emigration, and threw into the public domain a discourse of resentment and despair. Much of this found a focus in the election of anti-government independent candidates to local councils and the Dáil (Parliament), and a turn to left-wing politics, whose platform coalesced around anti-austerity marches and opposition to the imposition of water charges. In 2013, Ireland returned to economic growth, but the scars of the preceding years were evident, notably in a massive housing crisis, a public health crisis and a crisis in education. Where the Irish situation remains some-what distinctive is that the national question remains that of the border (between Northern Ireland and the Republic). In other territories, a new political swing has seen the rise of far-right groupings and the often unpredicted articulation of a disenchanted nationalism that culminated in the election of Donald Trump to the presidency of the United States in 2016 and the British vote to leave the European Union (Brexit) in the same year. Irish politics remain dominated by the two major Civil War (1922–23) parties – Fianna Fáil (centre-left) and Fine Gael (centre-right). Both tend to be moderately socially progressive and fiscally conservative. Even the rise of Sinn Féin, the left-wing Republican party, has done little to stoke any major upsurge in nationalist sentiments.

Analyses of the Celtic Tiger and its aftermath abound, with most agreeing that the rising tide did not 'lift all ships', but instead exacerbated the gap between wealth and poverty in Irish society. It was during this period too that the defining influence on Irish life, the Catholic Church, also collapsed, not least because of its association with institutional abuse. This period from the Celtic Tiger onwards thus witnessed a radical change in the make-up of Irish life. The economic boom heralded in the first substantial wave of immigration, transforming the ethnic composition of the country. At the same time, the Good Friday Agreement of 1998 saw in the end of the Northern 'Troubles' and the decline in the national question as another of the defining aspects of Irish life. Perhaps the most obvious watershed for the way in which Ireland imagined itself was none of these events, but the passing of the Thirty-fourth Amendment of the Constitution of Ireland, widely known as the Marriage Equality referendum, of 2015, thus legalising same-sex marriage. At this moment, it seemed that the country had at last shaken off its old inhibitions and embraced modernity (a moment of optimism that overlooked the continuing ban on abortion as well as widespread social inequality and the conservative implications of marriage as an institution). In 2018, in another defining moment, the country voted by a vast majority in favour of removing the ban on abortion.

In the same Associated Press (2014) interview that provided McDonagh with the platform to air his opinions on Irish cinema, *Calvary*'s star Brendan Gleeson offered his perspective on the film's meaning and subtext:

> Obviously, I live in Ireland and that too has been central to what the film is exploring, in terms of feelings of betrayal, feelings of disillusionment, and detachment, and feeling there's no particular optimism called for at this point in terms of who you put your faith in any more.

People can rage about various bonuses being given to bankers who have catapulted the country and the people into vast amounts of debt and awarded themselves bonuses and people are talking about the paedophile priests and things like that. So, there's a rage but it tends to be muted and a little bit repressed and kept down. People aren't marching in the streets and burning buildings down the way maybe the Greeks let off steam about their situation.

This commentary on the film chimes with the dominant critical approach to analysing Irish cinema, that is, societal. At some point, most writers in the field, myself included, have asked: what does Irish cinema tell us about Irish society? While the 'cinema as social mirror' model now seems simplistic, we can argue instead that the relationship between cinema and society is based on fantasies and projections of the social order. Gleeson's reading of *Calvary* highlights in particular two of the determining tropes of contemporary Irish cultural discourse – the loss of Church authority following the abuse revelations, and the excesses of the Celtic Tiger.

National cinemas in context

When I wrote my first overview of Irish cinema, *Irish National Cinema,* the abuse revelations were already well publicised, even though more were to come. The Celtic Tiger was still new and the Troubles were apparently over. Digital cinema was making early incursions into film practice and the two dominant auteurs were Neil Jordan and Jim Sheridan. Since then, so much has changed (just as so much has remained the same), so many more films have been made, and so much more has been written on Irish film, that I welcome the opportunity to start over with this new volume. This means not least updating my own thoughts on what constitutes a national cinema.

My monograph, *Irish National Cinema,* was part of a Routledge series on national cinemas that was published from the 1990s into the early years of this millennium (Hayward, 1993; O'Regan, 1996; Street, 1997, etc.). Together, they provided a vital questioning of the concept of the national and its relationship to a cultural medium, that is, cinema. The tensions between film as an industry and as an artform constituted one platform for debate, while the part played by cinema in the production of identities constituted another. National subsidies for film further raised the question as to what extent cinema was being promoted as a tool for articulating certain hierarchies of national belonging. Writing towards the end of this highly productive set of debates around the idea of a national cinema, Valentina Vitali and Paul Willemen (2006: 7) concluded that

> the economic forces sustaining any given film do not necessarily mobilise the available narrative stock in the directions preferred by the state. In other words, films may and may not reflect the ideological trajectory dominant within the nation at any one time. The reason for this potential lack of a reflective fit is that the cinematic strategies on which the hegemony of a political configuration depend always also remain available to, and can be activated by, non-dominant power blocs.

To what extent those non-dominant power blocs (if one could even categorise them so positively) have acquired a voice in Irish cinema is one of the guiding questions of this publication. *Irish Cinema in the Twenty-first Century* also fits in with more recent considerations of the place of 'minor' cinemas within a globalised production and consumption environment. Although the case of Irish cinema is fundamentally different to its Danish equivalent, not least because Irish cinema is at once postcolonial and English-language based, Mette Hjort's (2005: 33) identification of Danish cinema as a 'cultural site par excellence for the negotiation of globalizing processes' resonates with my own analysis of the Irish position.

Indeed, it is exactly the challenges of globalisation, particularly to small nations, that distinguish recent writings on national cinemas from the earlier wave of Routledge publications. Here we might also include the edited collection *The Cinema of Small Nations* (Hjort and Petrie, 2007) and *Scotland: Global Cinema* (Martin-Jones, 2009). As both these latter publications recognise, globalisation may threaten small industries, but the influx of investment by major production companies can often facilitate the making of films whose budgets would have otherwise been prohibitive in the limited funding environments of small national industries.

In his polemical *The Myth of an Irish Cinema*, Michael Patrick Gillespie (2008: 28) advocated a rejection 'of the hegemonic implications of a national cinema without ignoring the importance of Irish identity'. Yet Gillespie himself ignores the very nuanced definitions of an Irish national cinema that have gone before him. Following this line of thought, one might as well ask what an Irish identity is. Despite living in what is currently recognised as the most globalised country in the world (Statista, 2015), or perhaps because of this, what it means to be Irish, and how that is represented by us and to us, is still a hotly contested subject. 'Contemporary Ireland', David Fitzpatrick (2015) observed, revels in its novel reputation as the cosmopolitan hub of a 'global', 'trans-national' and 'imagined community' of those choosing, among other identities, to define themselves as 'Irish'. Being 'Irish' entails flexibility, ambivalence, self-parody, unpredictability and just a dash of the old hypocrisy. (Vote Yes for gay marriage, Yes for marriage as the foundation of the family, Yes for the family as a moral institution antecedent and superior to all positive law.)

While it would be uncommon now for any voice on the topic to limit a definition of who is Irish to those who live in Ireland (and ignore the diaspora), the question of who is entitled to consider themselves Irish was unsettlingly resolved in the referendum of 2004 that amended the 2001 Citizenship Act, which had granted Irish citizenship to all children born on the island of Ireland. Under the provisions of the 2004 Irish Nationality and Citizenship Act (Citizens Information, n.d.),

> children born of other foreign national parents in the island of Ireland on or after 1 January 2005 are not automatically entitled to Irish citizenship. These parents must prove that they have a *genuine* link to Ireland. This will be evidenced by their having 3 out of the previous 4 years reckonable residence in the island of Ireland immediately before the birth of the child. On proof of a genuine link to Ireland their child will be entitled to Irish citizenship and can apply for a certificate of nationality. (emphasis in original)

As will be discussed, questions of Irish identity/identities, whether gendered, racial, ethnic, class determined, place-specific or informed by sexual orientation, remain at the heart of most analyses of Irish films.

In this book, I seek to build on the invigorating new critical approaches to the discipline articulated by a range of scholars, while focusing on my own particular concerns around gender representation, history, and the dynamics of place. One of the most contested of these critical approaches revolves around the deployment of genre in Irish filmmaking, and it is useful to revisit briefly the key arguments around this topic.

Irish cinema and genre

Much of the recent work on Irish cinema has focused on its relationship with genre. Genre filmmaking is not entirely new – Jim Sheridan's *The Boxer* (1997), for instance borrows productively from the conventions of the boxing film, while the gangster film – *Nothing Personal* (Thaddeus O'Sullivan, 1995), for instance, and *The General* (John Boorman, 1998) – provided the means through which to discuss both the political divisions of the Troubles and Dublin criminality in the 1990s (Barton, 2002: 99–122; Monahan, 2007: 45–57; Pettitt, 2004: 25–38). The early years of the Celtic Tiger saw a rise in Dublin-based romantic comedies with the making of *About Adam* (Gerard Stembridge, 2000), *When Brendan Met Trudy* (Kieron J. Walsh, 2000) and *Goldfish Memory* (Elizabeth Gill, 2003), and the romantic comedy genre has continued to flourish with releases such as *Leap Year* (Anand Tucker, 2010), *The Stag* (aka *The Bachelor Weekend*, John Butler, 2013) and *Standby* (Ronan Burke, Rob Burke, 2014). What is new is the sudden proliferation of horror films, which now rate as the most popular genre for Irish filmmakers. This increase in genre filmmaking provided the material for Brian McIlroy's edited collection, *Genre and Cinema, Ireland and Transnationalism* (2007). In her introductory essay in that volume, Christine Gledhill (2007) reminds us that Hollywood genre filmmaking bears a double association, as at once socially conservative and as the medium through which global audiences engaged with modernity. This has been amply demonstrated by cinema historians, notably Rockett, whose *Irish Film Censorship* (2004) catalogues the relentless campaign by the policy-makers of the new Irish state against popular Hollywood cinema for fear of its contaminating modernity. On the other hand, as numerous writers have noted, the tradition of representing the Troubles through the prism of the thriller significantly diminished the potential for any nuanced exploration of the politics of the period (Barton, 2004: 157–8; McLoone, 2000: 64–8). National cinemas, Gledhill (2007: 17) further argues, have consistently drawn on, only to appropriate, generic conventions as a mode of address to local audiences:

> Hollywood's traditional genres are increasingly destabilized in their encounter with other national cinemas. It seems as if genericity has broken free from the master genres to create an international pool of protagonists, actions, icons, and performances, capable of multiple configurations and effects to which the genrified 'national' now contributes.[3]

In an Irish context, then, Irish genre cinema draws on familiar generic tropes, which it then tailors to a local context. This practice has the double function of providing the recognition factor discussed above but also of cuing Irish audiences (and scholars) to recognise in them specific local references: 'In this respect, the public nature of the "generic" – and its operation on the borders between cultural recognition and entertainment, between social objectives and subjective experience – may be particularly useful for a culture that is in the process of remaking itself' (Gledhill, 2007: 3).

Gledhill's intervention is helpful in demonstrating that genre film-making is neither a betrayal of avant-garde or political filmmaking, nor of an imagined 'pure' national cinema, which is a position echoed by many of the contributors to that volume and since. In an essay on Irish horror filmmaking, Emma Radley (2013: 113), for instance, argues that these films, 'do not just copy or mimic generic codes, they resignify them, transforming the monologic and monolithic "body" of Irish cinema as they go'. It is hard to know just why Radley considers Irish cinema before the arrival of the horror genre to be either monologic or monolithic; certainly by the time of her writing it was far from this. Still, it is certainly an important argument. Another useful essay written from the perspective of a scholar/filmmaker, Neasa Hardiman's '"*Once* Won't Happen Twice"' makes the case for understanding the global success of John Carney's *Once* (2007) as successfully playing up its peripherality while still conforming to certain of the generic requirements of the musical. This, she argues, is what *About Adam, When Brendan Met Trudy* and *Goldfish Memory* failed to achieve: 'Despite their poster campaigns, these films are not frothy, optimistic romances with happy endings. In this regard, they deviate significantly from genre type, a factor which may have contributed to their lack of international success' (Hardiman, 2011: 83). In other words, Irish filmmakers may so alter generic conventions that they alienate global audiences; they may be *too* Irish. This is also Diog O'Connell's argument. In her *New Irish Storytellers*, O'Connell (2010: 10) discusses the structures of narrative such films display:

> Irish film-makers appropriate devices from a range of sources – mainstream Hollywood, Independent American cinema and/or European films – and then merge them with idiosyncratic and local approaches to telling stories, creating hybrids which define an evolutionary and developmental phase in contemporary Irish cinema.

In her chapter on the Irish road movie, she focuses on three films: *I Went Down* (Paddy Breathnach, 1997), *Accelerator* (Vinny Murphy, 2000) and *Disco Pigs* (Kirsten Sheridan, 2001). Of these, Breathnach's film played best with Irish audiences and critics but failed to make any impact on the international market. As a road movie, it defied generic expectations in certain key ways. For one, the central characters travelled from one point (Dublin) to another (Cork) but then they returned to Dublin again. As she notes, Irish topography does not lend itself to lengthy road trips, but the conventions of the road movie insist that the destination be the final point of the narrative as well as the journey. In addition, *I Went Down* did not depict its characters' inner, psychological journey, but insisted on viewing them from the outside, distancing itself through comedy. That humour, O'Connell further argued (2010: 56), was too local for exogenous audiences to 'get': 'The phrase "in the bath fella" resounds locally and through the enunciation of internationally recognized actor Brendan Gleeson, but is this enough to appeal further afield?'

The answer to this is more complicated than it seems. Several years after *I Went Down*, Gleeson starred in *The Guard* (John Michael McDonagh, 2011), a police procedural that ripped through generic conventions with comic gusto. Not only did it become the top-grossing Irish film to date with a local box office take of over €4.13m, *The Guard* enjoyed considerable financial success overseas, grossing $5,360,274 in the United States, and $14,200,000 globally (IFB/BSÉ, 2011; Box Office Mojo, 2011). The reason that *The Guard* succeeded overseas, whereas *I Went Down* and another of Breathnach's genre films, *Shrooms* (2007), failed, is not only to do with local humour, but indicates just how difficult it is to find a formula that will appeal to local and global audiences simultaneously. What is certain is that Breathnach's experience of the market is much more representative of Irish filmmaking in general than McDonagh's. Humour is, of course, notoriously difficult to communicate. National audiences may reject local jokes as swiftly as do their overseas equivalents. Yet, for certain local filmmakers, comedy is a distinctively national mode of expression. As the next chapter notes, Irish audiences are assumed to favour this mode as well. In discussing his *You're Ugly Too* (2015), the director Mark Noonan (2015) responded to a comment about his characters (that they don't like to say what they are thinking and keep things buried) as follows: 'This quality I think of as a particularly Irish quality, not saying exactly what's on your mind ... Humour is the conduit to get to these true feelings.'

Globalisation and transnationalism

The critical perspectives outlined above are inevitably informed by debates around the global and the local. The two defining economic events of the period covered by this book brought home these issues in a forceful manner. The first was the Celtic Tiger and the second was the economic collapse, which was followed by a recession. Publications such as Eamon Maher and Eugene O'Brien's (2014) edited collection, *From Prosperity to Austerity: A Socio-cultural Critique of the Celtic Tiger and Its Aftermath* and Conn Holohan and Tony Tracy's (2014) *Masculinity and Irish Popular Culture: Tiger's Tales* have begun the process of looking back on this period of boom and bust through the cultural productions that both reflected and shaped it.

The turn towards theories of transnationalism as a critical term is in part a recognition of the need to reposition the national under conditions of globalisation.

Adrian Athique (2013: 5–6) usefully distinguishes between the two terms:

> Globalization is a term which denotes increasing interactivity and exchange and the collapse of the barriers of distance and ideology which have previously served to frustrate the triumph of a universal capitalist order. The transnational, on the other hand, is seen to denote cultural practices that take place across the national boundaries, which have structured the discussion of human geography for much of the twentieth century. Transnational phenomena do not of themselves necessarily infer, as does the term globalization, any particular ideological cohesion or historical volition.

He continues (2013: 6) that 'it is equally clear that national imaginaries continue to provide key staging grounds for transnational politics'. The concept of the transnational is an important one, in so far as it acknowledges that global cultural exchange is not always a relationship of unequal power, but is just as often defined by straightforward mobility. What, after all, are *The Lobster* or Lenny Abrahamson's *Room* (2016) but transnational films, as the latter originated in Ireland by an Irish creative team (which will be discussed further in the next chapter), but is set in North America? The transnational is particularly useful to this book's project, which aims to recognise the continuing validity of the cinematic national imaginary within the global flow of finance and production.

The spatial turn

In *Space and the Irish Cultural Imagination*, Gerry Smyth (2001: xvi) opened his analysis of the cultural and spatial reconfigurations of the new Ireland of emigrants, the euro, globalisation and sudden wealth, with the observation that: 'Whether it be the Tallaght housewife or the Belfast businesswoman, the Clare farmer or the Donegal musician, the Kerry politician or the Cork hurler, issues of space bear visibly upon Irish people's lives to a greater extent than at any point in the past.'

Irish Studies has followed other disciplines in applying theories of space and place to analyses of identity politics, while film studies usefully has intertwined ideas of the social production of space with the cinematic. In 1977, Yi-Fu Tuan (1977: 6) influentially proposed the following distinction:

> 'Space' is more abstract than 'place.' What begins as undifferentiated space becomes place as we get to know it better and endow it with value ... The ideas 'space' and 'place' require each other for definition. From the security and stability of place we are aware of the openness, freedom, and threat

of space, and vice versa. Furthermore, if we think of space as that which allows movement, then place is pause; each pause in movement makes it possible for location to be transformed into place.

As this book will argue, within the Ireland that contemporary cinema evokes, place is increasingly contingent. Who may make their own place in the national space or how they can do so is a fraught dynamic that calls into play factors of class, gender and race.

The first writer on Irish film to foreground issues of spatiality was Conn Holohan in *Cinema on the Periphery: Contemporary Irish and Spanish Film* (2010). Holohan notes that, unlike imperial and colonial centres, Ireland is noticeable for a lack of monumentality. Dublin is, literally, short of national monuments (with no Eiffel Tower, Big Ben, Colosseum or statue of Lenin) by which the centre announces its identity. Those public buildings and monuments that do exist largely date back to the colonial administration, and thus are no longer valid as expressions of power or national identity. The monument, according to Henri Lefebvre (1991: 220), conventionally both reflected and constructed a collective identity. The monument is not just a concrete articulation of power, but also functions as public control (monumental space). The modern city, Lefebvre argues, is laid out in such as way as to keep separate the various social strata and classes:

> Strategic space makes it possible simultaneously to force worrisome groups, the workers among others, out towards the periphery; to make available spaces near the centres scarcer, so increasing their value; to organize the centre as locus of decision, wealth, power and information; to find allies for the hegemonic class within the middle strata and within the 'elite'; to plan production and flows from the spatial point of view; and so on. (Lefebvre, 1991: 384).

Thus, power and space are inextricably linked. By contrast, Holohan has argued, Dublin's lack of monumentality has opened up its spaces to multiple claims and counter-claims of ownership. Further, the lack of any fixed imagery of the city centre means that it is fundamentally unrecognisable, and many Dublin-set films (*Last Days in Dublin* (Lance Daly, 2001), *Adam & Paul* (Lenny Abrahamson, 2004)) ignore the city's actual topography as they move their characters between periphery and centre. Indeed, most fail to fix the centre as the locus of power and control:

> Thus, the city space, with its weakened central control, can be represented as a space of disorder and danger. However, this weakened control is

also celebrated in many films as an opportunity to break down inherited meanings and imagine new and unexpected alliances within the urban space. (Holohan, 2010: 115)

Rural Ireland by contrast, has conventionally been marked by the institutional expression of power, and rural-based films such as *Korea* (Cathal Black, 1996), *The Ballroom of Romance* (Pat O'Connor, 1982) and *This is My Father* (Paul Quinn, 1998) 'portray a world where space is rigidly ordered by the institutions of church, state and family so as to regulate behaviour according to the expectations of Catholic morality' (Holohan, 2010: 114–15). The rural is equally a place identified with pastness. As John Agnew (2011: 319) writes: 'Place is often associated with the world of the past and location/space with the world of the present and future. From one perspective, place is therefore nostalgic, regressive even reactionary, and space is progressive and radical.' Even these binaries offer no clear ideological fixity, for somewhere between the pastness of place and the intangible of space come what Marc Augé (1995) has defined as non-places – the anonymous shopping mall or architecturally interchangeable airport duty-free area.

As the above terms also reflect, space intersects with time. In their monograph, *Mapping Irish Theatre*, Chris Morash and Shaun Richards underline the importance of understanding perceptions and representations of Ireland as existing in different time/spaces. Thus, the West of Ireland is frequently understood as a 'chronotope', existing out of time, or in another time (outside of modernity) (Morash and Richards, 2013: 41–2). It is, in another familiar theoretical trope, a Foucaultian 'heterotopia', that is, an imagined, idealised site within a given culture. Foucault, they remind us, offered a number of possible meanings for his concept, including (Foucault in Morash and Richards, 2013: 41) that 'their [heterotopias] role is to create a space that is other, another real space, as perfect, as meticulous, as well arranged as ours is messy, ill constructed and jumbled'. In this manner, audiences for the early Abbey Theatre peasant plays could experience on stage what in reality was a vanishing place and way of life. The same paradigms transfer easily to cinema, most particularly in the tourist films, which will be discussed in Chapter 7. Overall, these theoretical configurations offer new opportunities to consider how Irish filmmakers have used space, particularly that of the rural and small-town Ireland, to problematise traditional understandings of authority (which will be discussed further in Chapter 7); and in the case of urban films to explore questions of mobility and identity construction (Chapter 8).

Morash and Richards (2013: 122–44) suggest that Irish theatre no longer represents a place or a space, but a concept, that is, 'Ireland' not Ireland, to paraphrase. Their alternative is site-specific theatre that engages very directly with its locations. In cinema, as this book will argue, Ireland too becomes 'Ireland', as its physical geography and spatial co-ordinates are reimagined from production to production. On a very simple level, financial incentives that encourage runaway productions to use Ireland as a location for non-Irish-set films provide audiences with an uncanny recognition effect, with what is familiar now doubling for a partially recognisable Other. In other instances, filmmakers reorganise the space of the city, or shoot rural Ireland, so as to disorient the viewer, creating visual associations between these and other non-indigenous films that again create a similar uncanny doubling between here and not-here. This is a recurrent trope of the Irish horror film, which will be discussed in Chapter 3.

Questions of space, identity and belonging are all integral to representations of Ireland's new immigrant populations. The sole dedicated monograph on Irish cinema and black identities is Zélie Asava's *The Black Irish Onscreen* (2013), which argues that Irish screen culture in general has struggled with the conflation of blackness and Irishness, insisting instead that to be black is to be a foreigner. Also of interest in widening out this discussion is Sinéad Moynihan's *Other People's Diasporas* (2013), which is an interrogation of the unspoken diktat that the new Irish would be understood best through recourse to old narratives of Irish emigration to the United States. As I will argue in this book, in contemporary Irish cinema, the racial and ethnic Other is defined primarily in relation to the indigenous white population. They are seldom viewed for who they are, rather more for how they can illustrate certain characteristics of white Irish identities.

The past in the present

One of the striking features of the Celtic Tiger cinema was its abandonment of history films. Where the productions of the pre-Celtic Tiger years abounded with historical themes, often as a response to concerns around the origins of nationalism, the gradual ending of the Troubles following the Good Friday Agreement of 1998 signalled the decline of nationalism as a defining trope of Irish filmmaking. Even more, it seemed that, for the new generation of Irish filmmakers, concerns about the past were a thing of the past and it was the Ireland of the present that engaged their attention. Instead, then, as Chapter 5 considers, films about Irish history became dominated by British filmmakers, including

Ken Loach, Stephen Frears, Alan Parker and Peter Mullan. Only in Northern Ireland (Chapter 6) has history remained a live theme, with a number of films revisiting the hunger strikes and other historical events. Yet, as this book will argue, Irish history and the Irish past cannot be ignored, and themes of history and pastness imbue all modes of Irish cinema, including horror films, documentaries, and animation. One of the questions that haunted the Celtic Tiger, no more so than following its demise, was whether 'we' had 'lost the run of ourselves'. Had we been so besotted with materialism that we had lost sight of who 'we' were? This is a hugely problematic discourse that hinges on some 'authentic' pre-Celtic Tiger identity that 'we' shared, yet it is interesting to note that certain films (*What Richard Did* (Lenny Abrahamson, 2012), for instance) consider incidents from the Celtic Tiger as having their origins in much older histories (of class and privilege). This film and many other of the productions discussed presently are indebted to discourses of trauma and post-trauma. For obvious reasons these include any number of the Northern Ireland-set narratives. In even more general terms, as I began to detect in *Irish National Cinema*, Ireland has come to stand in for an all-purpose traumatic space, an idea that will be explored in more detail in the chapters to follow.

Gender and Irish cinema

These arguments intersect with issues around gender, race and difference. In his writings on space and national identities, Holohan has traced a movement away from a vision of rural Ireland as an emblematic home space to one where horror resides, and from the city (most commonly Dublin) as the locale for the playing out of fluid sexualities to one where (Holohan, 2015: 3): 'the disenfranchisement of the Irish male caused by economic recession is directly expressed through an image of precarious habitation'. In this sense, the failure to create place from space is as significant as the alternative. His argument mirrors a further shift, that is, from seeing Ireland as emblematically female (Mother Ireland) to one in which masculinity emerges as the marker of national identity. The volume of writings on Irish masculinity in recent years is testament to the vitality of this sub-discipline. In 2013, Debbie Ging published *Men and Masculinities in Irish Cinema* and Joseph Moser published *Irish Masculinity on Screen: The Pugilists and Peacemakers of John Ford, Jim Sheridan and Paul Greengrass*. Other more general but related works are: Fintan Walsh's *Male Trouble: Masculinity and the Performance of Crisis* (2010), Caroline Magennis and Raymond Mullen's edited collection, *Irish Masculinities: Critical Reflections on*

Literature and Culture (2011), Joseph Valente's *The Myth of Manliness in Irish National Culture, 1880–1922* (2011) and Holohan and Tracy's *Masculinity and Irish Popular Culture: Tiger's Tales* (2014). No comparable body of work has been devoted to issues of Irish women and femininities.

In the autumn of 2015, a storm of protest engulfed the Irish theatre world when the director of the Abbey Theatre, Fiach Mac Conghail, announced the programme for the National Theatre's 2016 centenary celebrations. Titled 'Waking the Nation', the line-up included eighteen men and only two women in the selection of directors and writers. Little had been learned, it seemed, in the twenty-five years since the editors of the Field Day project published their encyclopaedic collection of Irish writing *The Field Day Anthology*, volumes I–III, only to find their efforts diminished by fury over the underrepresentation of women authors. The immediate response to Mac Conghail's error of judgement was an online campaign tagged #wakingthefeminists and a public discussion, hosted by the now contrite director, to air the issues around representation that his decision had raised. In the letters page of the *Irish Times*, Susan Liddy (2015) widened the debate out to the film industry, pointing to her own research findings with regard to the low level of female participation in Irish filmmaking and adding that 'only 24 per cent of all produced films from 1993 to 2011 with a male writer had a female character at the heart of the narrative. In comparison, 63 per cent of produced films with a female writer lead with a female protagonist.' The IFB followed with a statement issued on 12 November (IFTN, 2015) that promised the following:

> Gender inequality is an area of major concern to current board members and has been the subject of discussion at our recent meetings and in a number of external fora, including at the Galway Film Fleadh in July 2015. The IFB is currently developing a new strategy which will declare its strong and heartfelt commitment to gender equality and diversity as a strategic priority.

Liddy has since (2016) published more detailed research on this issue and, as we shall see in the next chapter, the IFB has introduced financial incentives to encourage more work by women writers and directors. Responding to studies such as this, Ging (2013: 13) has argued that male domination of the Irish film industry has not served to promote a patriarchal agenda, but rather its opposite: 'Irish cinema, in spite of being so heavily male-dominated and male-themed, has collectively produced some of the most astutely observed and gender-progressive accounts of Irish men and masculinity available outside of academic research.'

Furthermore, Irish films of the past thirty years have 'eschewed heroic, patriotic and successful male figures in favour of male subjects who are socially marginalised, criminal and underclass, depressed, suicidal, abused, forced into exile, gay, queer or transsexual, violent and variously conflicted or in crisis' (Ging, 2013: 16). Ging's nuanced study of Irish masculinities amply justifies her assertion. It also serves to highlight even more the consequences of a failure to address female subjectivities in the same manner. Why has Irish cinema not attempted to create a corresponding discourse around femininities?

Male filmmakers can, of course, tell female-centred stories (Joss Whedon and Paul Feig are often cited as exemplary in this regard). Female directors, Katherine Bigelow for instance, may favour male-dominated action films. Yet, just placing women at the centre of a narrative, or giving female characters equal narrative weight to male characters, is not enough. If it were, Irish cinema would not be particularly deficient. A survey of feature films supported by the Irish Film Board between 1994 and 2015 (listed on their website) reveals no small amount of such titles. Yet, on closer inspection, many are romcoms, general ensemble pieces and horror films. Films that actually foreground female subjectivities in a complex, thought-provoking manner are few and far between. Carmel Winters' *Snap* (2010) is one; other examples come from documentarians: *His & Hers* (Ken Wardrop, 2009) and *Pyjama Girls* (Maya Derrington, 2010). As this book will further explore, this is a complex issue related to cultural attitudes as much as funding strategies. The Abbey Theatre and Field Day controversies illustrate that white male hegemony remains blind to its own dominance. However, if the argument that film can shape discourse has any traction, then the positioning of women in Irish cinema is a matter of serious concern.

Irish cinema: a political cinema?

As the above examples illustrate, contemporary Irish cinema is above all engaged with identity politics. These may not be the big questions (what does it mean to be Irish?) but certainly reflects concerns around generation, gender and belonging. Few of the films that I will be covering in this volume are either formally or politically radical. In a discussion following the twentieth anniversary screening of *Irish Cinema: Ourselves Alone* (Donald Taylor-Black, 1995) at the Irish Film Institute in November 2015, Kevin Rockett challenged Irish filmmakers to create a more politically engaged cinema in the tradition of the ground-breaking generation of the late 1970s and early 1980s – Cathal Black, Joe Comerford, Pat Murphy and Bob Quinn. This he argued would engage younger audiences in the way in which the writings of Eimear McBride (2014) had reawakened interest in contemporary Irish writing, or experimental plays continued to attract theatre-goers.[4] In a similar vein, McLoone (2015: xiv) has written that it is no longer viable to consider Irish cinema as a national cinema, but rather we should see it as part of an international screen culture: 'the ending of the splendid isolation of the image that characterized much of the 20th century'. Local Irish screen culture thus lives within the international rather than outside of it and (McLoone, 2015): 'It seems impossible now to envisage any way in which the more experimental, politically engaged cinema of the 1970s and 1980s could be accommodated within this culture.'

I am not so sure that Irish cinema is no longer a national cinema. Flynn and Tracy (2017) usefully point to the internationalisation of the industry, both in terms of films part funded in Ireland, such as *The Lobster* and *Room*, but also Paddy Breathnach's *Viva* (2015) a Spanish-language film set in Cuba, written by Mark O'Halloran, and nominated as Ireland's entry for Best Foreign Language Film at the Academy Awards, and films with little Irish thematic content co-produced by Irish production companies. As they argue (which will be discussed in the next chapter), this kind of internationalisation is now clearly official Irish funding policy. Eye-catching as such releases are, the majority of Irish-made films remain Irish set and Irish themed. Many of these films are too flimsy to bear the weight of analysis as emblematic of anything in particular; nevertheless, as I hope to argue in the following chapters, taken together, as a layering of representations, they do indeed provide a fascinating way of measuring how Irishness has been culturally configured on film in this century. Hence, the usefulness of the concept of the transnational, espoused by Flynn and Tracy as best describing the industry, and the possibilities that this term offers for retrieving, rather than dismissing, the national.

To do so, I will be drawing on and developing the issues of globalisation, transnationalism, gender formations, the construction of place and of the past that have informed theoretical approaches to Irish cinema in recent years. For reasons of space, I am confining my analyses (except in my discussion of emigration narratives in Chapter 5) to films made in and about the island of Ireland and reluctantly putting aside recent developments in images of Irish America, or the very compelling images of Irishness in films such as *The Proposition* (John Hilcoat, 2005) or *Jindabyne* (Ray Lawrence, 2006). My opening chapter will place Irish filmmaking within the context of the Irish film industry. Following that, I devote chapters to animation, the horror genre, documentary filmmaking, Irish history on film, post-Troubles cinema, images of the countryside and images of the city. I decided against dedicating one chapter to questions of gender;

it is, however, my intention to foreground representations of women in contemporary Irish filmmaking throughout this book. I have interspersed chapters with a brief analysis of a short film.

I cannot discuss all films made in the period under examination – from the Celtic Tiger through the recession to the recovery – and my selection is intended as representative rather than comprehensive. My omissions are therefore multiple, not least my omission of the vast output of the experimental film sector led by filmmakers such as Claire Langan, Maximilian Le Cain and Rouzbeh Rashidi. Their work follows on the tradition of art cinema associated with the pioneering feminist film-maker, Vivienne Dick, and the reader is directed to the comprehensive discussion of Dick's films in the edited collection, *Between Truth and Fiction: The Films of Vivienne Dick* (O'Brien et al., 2009).

Finally, I want to air a concern that has been creeping into how I see the debates on Irish cinema outlined above and in the following chapters relating to public discourse. That concern is that Irish cinema lacks a robust critical culture. The demise of the journal *Film West*, the fluctuating publication of *Film Ireland*, the supplanting of analysis with interviews, particularly with stars under contractual obligation to promote the film, and the influence of aggregator sites, have seriously diminished the space available to analyse Irish films and film culture in any depth. Without Tony Tracy (and latterly Roddy Flynn's) invaluable 'Year in Review' section in *Estudios Irlandeses*, whose reviews I have cited throughout, no open-access site would exist to catalogue and analyse Irish film releases. Without a critical culture, Irish films are being released into a void and filmmakers remain divorced from their audiences. The politics of neoliberalism sidelined cultural pleasure in favour of a model that advocated that every artefact has, first and foremost, a monetary value. I return to the utilitarian argument in the next chapter; this book, however, reflects my own pleasure and engagement in Irish cinema and if it gives rise to some debate on the film culture out of which it arises, then something will have come of it.

Notes

1 On 18 June 2018, the name of Bord Scannán na hÉireann/the Irish Film Board was changed to Fís Éireann/Screen Ireland.

2 For more detailed box office figures, see the Appendix. The box office is analysed in more detail in Chapter 1.

3 The term 'genericity' was coined by Jim Collins in: 'Genericity in the Nineties: Eclectic Irony and the New Sincerity', in Collins, Collins and Radner (1993: 242–63).

4 The screening and discussion were held on 5 November 2015 at the Irish Film Institute, Dublin.

References

Agnew, J. A. 2011. Space and Place. *In:* Agnew, J. A. and Livingstone, D. N. (eds.) *The Sage Handbook of Geographical Knowledge.* London: Sage.

Asava, Z. 2013. *The Black Irish Onscreen: Representing Black and Mixed-Race Identities on Irish Film and Television,* Oxford and New York: Peter Lang.

Associated Press. 2014. *Gleeson on Ireland: 'There's a Rage'* [Online]. Available: www.youtube.com/watch?v=PkkfSQ5WQa4 [Accessed 30 October 2015].

Athique, A. 2013. Transnational Audiences: Geocultural Approaches. *Continuum,* 28, 4–17.

Augé, M. 1995. *Non-places: Introduction to an Anthropology of Supermodernity,* London: Verso.

Barton, R. 2002. *Jim Sheridan: Framing the Nation,* Dublin: Liffey Press.

Barton, R. 2004. *Irish National Cinema,* London and New York: Routledge.

Box Office Mojo. 2011. *The Guard* [Online]. Box Office Mojo. Available: www.box officemojo.com/movies/?page=intlandid=guard.htm [Accessed 19 September 2017].

Citizens Information. *Irish Citizenship Through Birth or Descent* [Online]. Citizens Information Board. Available: www.citizensinformation.ie/en/moving_country/ irish_citizenship/irish_citizenship_through_birth_or_descent.html [Accessed 6 July 2015].

Collins, A. P., Collins, J. and Radner, H. (eds.) 1993. *Film Theory Goes to the Movies,* London and New York: Routledge.

Fitzpatrick, D. 2015. Paper Tigers? *Irish Times* (Weekend Review), 11 July, p. 12.

Flynn, R. and Tracy, T. 2017. Quantifying National Cinema: A Case Study of the Irish Film Board 1993–2013. *Film Studies,* 14, 32–53.

Gillespie, M. P. 2008. *The Myth of an Irish Cinema: Approaching Irish-Themed Films,* Syracuse, NY: Syracuse University Press.

Ging, D. 2013. *Men and Masculinities in Irish Cinema,* Basingstoke: Palgrave Macmillan.

Gledhill, C. 2007. Genre and Nation. *In:* McIlroy, B. (ed.) *Genre and Cinema: Ireland and Transnationalism.* London and New York: Routledge.

Hardiman, N. 2011. '*Once* Won't Happen Twice': Peripherality and Equality as Strategies for Success in a Low-Budget Irish Film. *In:* Huber, W. and Crosson, S. (eds.) *Contemporary Irish Film, New Perspectives on a National Cinema.* Vienna: Braumüller.

Hayward, S. 1993. *French National Cinema,* London and New York: Routledge.

Hjort, M. 2005. *Small Nation, Global Cinema,* Minneapolis and London: University of Minnesota Press.

Hjort, M. and Petrie, D. (eds.) 2007. *The Cinema of Small Nations,* Edinburgh: Edinburgh University Press.

Holohan, C. 2010. *Cinema on the Periphery: Contemporary Irish and Spanish film,* Dublin: Irish Academic Press.

Holohan, C. 2015. 'Nothin' But a Wee Humble Cottage': At Home in Irish Cinema. *In:* Monahan, B. (ed.) *Ireland and Cinema, Culture and Contexts.* Basingstoke and New York: Palgrave Macmillan.

Holohan, C. and Tracy, T. (eds.) 2014. *Masculinity and Irish Popular Culture: Tiger's Tales,* Basingstoke: Palgrave Macmillan.

IFB/BSÉ. 2011. *The Guard Grosses Over €4.13m and Breaks Irish Box Office Record* [Online]. Irish Film Board. Available: www.irishfilmboard.ie/irish_film_industry/news/THE_GUARD_Grosses_over_euro413m_and_Breaks_Irish_Box_Office_Record/1734 [Accessed 22 July 2015].

IFTN. 2015. *The Irish Film Board Release Statement on Gender Equality in Irish Film* [Online]. The Irish Film and Television Network. Available: http://iftn.ie/news/?act1=recordandonly=1andaid=73andrid=4288741andtpl=archnewsandforce=1 [Accessed 17 November 2015].

Kirby, P. 2010. *The Celtic Tiger in Collapse: Explaining the Weaknesses of the Irish Model,* Basingstoke: Palgrave Macmillan.

Lefebvre, H. 1991. *The Production of Space,* Oxford, UK and Cambridge, MA: Blackwell.

Liddy, S. 2015. Women and the Irish Film Industry, *Irish Times,* 11 November, p. 15.

Liddy, S. 2016. "Open to All and Everybody"? The Irish Film Board: Accounting for the Scarcity of Women Screenwriters. *Feminist Media Studies,* 16, 901–17.

Magennis, C. and Mullen, R. (eds.) 2011. *Irish Masculinities: Reflections on Literature and Culture,* Dublin: Irish Academic Press.

Maher, E. and O'Brien, E. (eds.) 2014. *From Prosperity to Austerity: A Socio Cultural Critique of the Celtic Tiger and Its Aftermath,* Manchester: Manchester University Press.

Martin-Jones, D. 2009. *Scotland: Global Cinema: Genres, Modes and Identities,* Edinburgh: Edinburgh University Press.

McBride, E. 2014. *A Girl Is a Half-Formed Thing,* London: Faber and Faber.

McIlroy, B. (ed.) 2007. *Genre and Cinema: Ireland and Transnationalism,* London: Routledge.

McLoone, M. 2000. *Irish Film: The Emergence of a Contemporary Cinema,* London: British Film Institute.

McLoone, M. 2015. Irish National Cinema – What Have We Wrought? Contemporary Thoughts on a Recent History. *In:* Monahan, B. (ed.) *Ireland and Cinema, Culture and Contexts.* Basingstoke and New York: Palgrave Macmillan.

Monahan, B. 2007. Playing Cops and Robbers: Recent Irish Cinema and Genre Performance. *In:* McIlroy, B. (ed.) *Genre and Cinema, Ireland and Transnationalism.* London and New York: Routledge.

Morash, C. and Richards, S. 2013. *Mapping Irish Theatre: Theories of Space and Place,* Cambridge: Cambridge University Press.

Moser, J. P. 2013. *Irish Masculinity on Screen: The Pugilists and Peacemakers of John Ford, Jim Sheridan and Paul Greengrass,* Jefferson, NC and London: McFarland.

Moynihan, S. 2013. *"Other People's Diasporas": Negotiating Race in Contemporary Irish and Irish American Culture,* Syracuse, NY: Syracuse University Press.

Noonan, M. 2015. *In:* Rocks, S. *Arena.* RTÉ Radio One. 20 July. 19.00.

O'Brien, T., Connolly, M., Garfield, R., Zalcock, B. and Dick, V. (eds.) 2009. *Between Truth and Fiction: The Films of Vivienne Dick,* London and Cork: Lux and the Crawford Gallery.

O'Connell, D. 2010. *New Irish Storytellers: Narrative Strategies in Film,* Bristol: Intellect.

O'Regan, T. 1996. *Australian National Cinema,* London and New York: Routledge.

Pettitt, L. 2004. "We're Not Fucking Eye-talians": The Gangster Genre and Irish Cinema. *In:* Barton, R. and O'Brien, H. (eds.) *Keeping It Real: Irish Film and Television.* London: Wallflower Press.

Radley, E. 2013. Violent Transpositions: The Disturbing 'Appearance' of the Irish Horror Film. *In:* Bracken, C. and Radley, E. (eds.) *Viewpoints, Theoretical Perspectives on Irish Visual Texts.* Cork: Cork University Press.

Rockett, K. 2004. *Irish Film Censorship: a Cultural Journey from Silent Cinema to Internet Pornography,* Dublin: Four Courts Press.

Rockett, K., Gibbons, L. and Hill, J. 1987. *Cinema and Ireland,* London: Croom Helm.

RTÉ Ten. 2015. *Lobster and Panti Reign at Irish Box Office* [Online]. RTÉ Ten. Available: www.rte.ie/ten/news/2015/1027/737810-the-lobster-queen-of-ireland/ [Accessed 30 October 2015].

Shortall, E. 2014. Curse of the Irish. *Sunday Times* 21 September, p. 9.

Smyth, G. 2001. *Space and the Irish Cultural Imagination,* Basingstoke, Palgrave.

Statista. 2015. *Top 100 Countries in the Globalization Index 2015* [Online]. Available: www.statista.com/statistics/268168/globalization-index-by-country/ [Accessed 30 October 2015].

Street, S. 1997. *British National Cinema,* London and New York: Routledge.

Tuan, Y.-F. 1977. *Space and Place: the Perspective of Experience,* London and Minneapolis: University of Minnesota Press.

Valente, J. 2011. *The myth of Manliness in Irish National Culture, 1880–1922,* Urbana, IL: University of Illinois Press.

Vitali, V. and Willemen, P. (eds.) 2006. *Theorising National Cinema,* London: British Film Institute.

Walsh, F. 2010. *Male Trouble: Masculinity and the Performance of Crisis,* Basingstoke: Palgrave Macmillan.

I
How to make an Irish film

Before turning to an analysis of the content of Irish cinema, it is useful to understand how Irish films are funded and why. In common with the situation in other European countries and small national cinemas, nearly all Irish films receive state subvention. In Ireland, this funding comes mainly via the Irish Film Board/Bord Scannán na hÉireann (hereafter IFB), but most productions are equally reliant on tax breaks (Section 481) and international co-productions for equity. Section 481 itself depends on government support for its continuation. Unlike, say, British cinema, Irish cinema has always been too small to consider competing with Hollywood, even if it relies to an extent on Hollywood filmmaking codes. This raises a further question (which will be discussed at the end of this chapter): is Irish cinema 'art cinema'?

How to fund an Irish film

The IFB currently (IFB/BSÉ, 2018a) provides for the following: project development; production funding; co-production funding; documentary production funding; animation funding; completion funding; support for distribution; and short film funding. In certain exceptional circumstances, the IFB will also fund television production. From 2017 onwards, additional funding of €50,000 was made available for projects with a female writer or director and €100,000 with a female writer/ director (IFB/BSÉ, 2018a). In 2007, the IFB announced the launch of a new Regional Support Fund to offset the additional cost of shooting in regional areas. Films including *Breakfast on Pluto* (Neil Jordan, 2005) and *The Guard* received support from this fund, but it seems to have since been dropped. Instead, most local councils also offer some film funding. IFB support, therefore, runs from the initiation of a project through its completion, and allows for producers to market and distribute their own films.

The IFB experienced its own crisis during the recession. In 2008, they received government support of €20 million, which was reduced year-on-year to €11,202,000 in 2014 (IFB/BSÉ, 2016: 36). The budget of

2017 saw the Board receive €18 million, returning it to a figure close to its pre-recession income. In addition, following the economic crash, the McCarthy Report (An Bord Snip Nua) recommended that there was no need for a Film Board:

> The Group considers that continued funding of the Irish Film Board is not affordable at this time in the context of other more pressing spending priorities. Given the scale of tax expenditure (€418m since 1993 and €33m in 2008) via the tax incentive scheme for this sector, and given the level of international competition in this market space, there is no objective economic case for subventing the Irish Film Industry. (McCarthy et al., 2009: 18)

In the end, after extensive lobbying, much of which was focused on the jobs created through inward and local investment, the tourist potential of an Irish setting, and the ancillary spend on hospitality and so forth, the IFB was saved.

Other small pockets of money exist, including the Broadcasting Authority of Ireland's licence fee-derived Sound and Vision fund, which has been responsible for much of the funding for the documentary sector, the Arts Council of Ireland, and European money from the MEDIA and Eurimages programmes. Some producers raise finance through crowd funding (*Atlantic* (Risteard O'Domhnaill, 2016) and *Out of Here* (Donal Foreman, 2013) are examples). Filmmakers and the IFB have long been critical of the lack of television funding for Irish filmmaking but given RTÉ's own financial deficit, this is unlikely to change.

Section 481 (the tax incentive scheme) is crucial to Irish film and audio-visual production. One of the major benefits for Irish producers is that they receive the money up front, rather than after the release of the film or broadcast of the television show. It has been estimated (Department of Finance, 2012: 12) that for every €100 raised under Section 481, the exchequer cost was €34 but that only €19 accrued as a subsidy to the producers with the balance being returned to investors or accounted for in administration costs. Thus, it could be more efficient. It is also constantly in competition with tax incentives in other countries, particularly in the neighbouring UK. When the UK introduced tax incentives of 20 per cent for television shows that cost more than £1m per hour in 2013, Ireland increased their incentives to 32 per cent (effective from 2015). They also amended the regulations to allow, as the UK did, companies to claim for non-EU production and creative personnel, including Hollywood actors, as part of the qualifying expenditure.

If IFB support and S481 constitute the two local pillars of Irish film funding, the other major source of money is through co-production.

European Union rules dictate that a tax incentive can only be claimed on 80 per cent of any budget in one country, so that it is in the interest of Irish producers (and overseas producers) to seek co-productions. It is also in the interest of anyone with ambitions to make an Irish film with a budget of more than €100,000, the maximum awarded by the IFB to 'micro-budget', or fully funded, indigenous films.

In their comprehensive overview of Irish film funding and production, Flynn and Tracy (2016: 38) have traced the increase in co-production funding to the recession, when indigenous funding evaporated:

> the Board established a creative co-production fund to make small investments (circa €200,000 per film) in a variety of projects originating in Eastern Europe, Scandinavia and further afield. Inevitably, this diluted the cultural specificity of the body of films supported: between 2009 and 2011 at least sixteen films with no discernible textual connection (i.e. setting or content) to Ireland were supported by the Board.

Flynn and Tracy (2016: 42) also discern a movement by the IFB towards putting higher sums into more market-oriented productions, notably by high-profile directors, featuring established stars: Neil Jordan's *Breakfast on Pluto* and *Ondine* (2009), John Michael McDonagh's *The Guard* and *Calvary*, *Intermission* (John Crowley, 2003), *Shadow Dancer* (James Marsh, 2012), and *The Wind That Shakes the Barley* (Ken Loach, 2005). Overall, Flynn and Tracy (2016: 50) concluded that the IFB was most focused on productions that displayed market potential, even if they had no Irish theme, in order to sustain industrial activity. In fact, as we see below, this is also the practice of production companies, many of whom seem to be using non-Irish-themed co-productions to maintain cash flow.

The IFB's 2016–20 strategy plan (IFB/BSÉ, 2016) acknowledges the Board's previous reliance on economic arguments to justify its funding and places greater emphasis on the cultural importance of supporting indigenous filmmaking. In this, its hand was very much strengthened by recent Academy Award (and other) prestigious nominations and wins. These include animation: *Fifty Percent Grey* (Ruairí Robinson, 2001), *Give Up Yer Aul Sins* (Cathal Gaffney, 2001), *The Secret of Kells* (Tomm Moore and Nora Twomey, 2009), *Granny O'Grimm's Sleeping Beauty* (Nicky Phelan, 2010), *Song of the Sea* (Tomm Moore, 2015), *The Breadwinner* (Nora Twomey, 2017); short films: *Six Shooter* (Martin McDonagh, 2004), *New Boy* (Steph Green, 2007), *The Door* (Juanita Wilson, 2008), *Pentecost* (Peter McDonald, 2011); and features: *Once, Room, Brooklyn* (John Crowley, 2015). Individual nominations for Saoirse Ronan and Ruth Negga in non-Irish as well

26

as Irish films also enhance the prestige of the Irish film industry, as do three Academy Award nominations for Irish costume designer, Consolata Boyle.

Finding an audience for Irish cinema

The IFB's Strategic Plan also acknowledges the challenges of finding an audience for Irish cinema. Over the years, the greatest praise for Irish films in the media has come in the wake of award nominations and wins, and the greatest criticism in terms of box office performance. The following list shows the ten highest-performing Irish films at the Irish box office to date (figures not adjusted for inflation) alongside their US box office take:[1]

> *Michael Collins* €5,139,473/$11,092,559
> *The Guard* €4.3m/$5,359,774
> *The Wind That Shakes the Barley* €4,134,909/$1,829,142
> *Veronica Guerin* €4,020,924/$1,569,918
> *Mrs Brown's Boys D'Movie* €3.8m (no US release)
> *In the Name of the Father* €3,063,964/$25,096,862
> *In Bruges* €3m (approx.)/$7,800,825
> *Angela's Ashes* €2,798,977/$13,038,660
> *The Commitments* €2,764,963/$13,955,001
> *Brooklyn* €2.6m/$38,322,743
> *Intermission* €2,506,172/$889,857

Certain films performed relatively better in the United States than in Ireland, notably *Calvary*, which was the top film at the Irish box office for 2014 with a gross of €1.5m and took $3,600,000 at the US box office. *Laws of Attraction* (Peter Howitt, 2004) took $2,277,196 at the UK/Ireland box office and $17,871,255 in the United States.

Of the other films that had Irish co-producers, the top performer at the US box office was *Becoming Jane* (Julian Jarrold, 2007), which took $18,663,911, and *Love and Friendship* (Whit Stillman, 2016), which took $14,016,568. Of these, the latter ought to have been profitable for its majority producer, Blinder Films, given its low budget. However, there are no figures that suggest that co-producing a non-Irish-set film (other than *Room*, which will be discussed below) was a particularly profitable venture for Irish production companies, rather more that such films paid for overheads and wages. Far more profitable is the television co-production market and many Irish production companies focus on this for income generation.

What is most difficult to explain in these figures is the massive discrepancy between the performance of *Brooklyn* at the Irish and US box offices. Received wisdom suggests, however, that Irish taste, particularly in recent years, favours comedies. This speculation is bolstered by the relative success of *The Young Offenders* (Peter Foott, 2016), which took over €1m at the Irish box office and is now a television series and *The Hardy Bucks Movie* (Mike Cockayne, 2013), derived from a TV show that itself started online, which took approximately €464,000. The performance of *Mrs Brown's Boys D'Movie* (Ben Kellett, 2014) reflects the massive popularity of the original television show, which, as John Fagan (2015) has interestingly argued, speaks to a little-considered audience that favours broad comedy over cool millennial humour.

If all Irish films enjoyed a box office take like that of *Mrs Brown's Boys D'Movie*, then the contentious debates that characterise so many public discussions in Ireland about the Irish film industry would never take place. The films that provoke such heated responses tend, however, to be those that do not appear in the above listings, are supported by the IFB, and achieve minimal financial returns or receive no theatrical release at all. Responding to a question concerning the poor showing of many IFB funded films, then-director of the Board, James Morris (in McGreevy, 2013) suggested that this was the production's fault:

> If it doesn't hit the spot, it is usually a missed opportunity. You can see the potential that is there and it isn't delivered. The other reason is that the talent wasn't there and that is usually the fault of the director because it is a director's medium. If the director blames the script, it is still the director's fault. It is our job to take risks. Some of the films turned out bad, but to say that you should never have had a go, that's another thing.

One problem faced by small Irish productions is promotion. In a marketplace flooded by Hollywood films that come with ready-made campaigns, getting the news out about an Irish release is challenging, particularly in the current environment of deciding the fate of a film in the cinema on the back of the opening weekend figures, rather than letting it build word of mouth. The IFB (IFB/BSÉ, 2018b) offers some support for this, allowing distributors to apply for 90 per cent, up to a maximum of €75,000, of marketing and publicity costs. They also support 'direct distribution', for films that have not found a distributor, 'capped at 80% of the total distribution budget, up to a maximum amount of €15,000'. Even with this, many Irish films achieve miniscule viewing figures at the box office. The most extreme example of this is *Once* which played for only three weeks in Irish cinemas before disappearing. Following its Academy Award win (for best song), Carney's film took $9.3m (€7.2m) at the US box office. In an article commenting on this, Eithne Shortall (2014: 9) remarked as follows:

> In the past couple of years … a slew of Irish films came and went from cinemas here, putting next to nothing in the coffers. Even when reviews are good, the box-office return rarely is. *Good Vibrations* [Lisa Barros D'Sa, Glenn Leyburn, 2013] was a hit with critics but made less than €72,000 before falling out of the Irish charts. *Jump* [Kieron J. Walsh, 2012], *Earthbound* [Alan Brennan, 2012], and *King of the Travellers* [Mark O'Connor, 2012] did worse.

Performing poorly at the box office is not necessarily a crisis, particularly given that most people now watch films on television or other platforms.[2] On the other hand, a good box office take certainly enhances a filmmaker's likelihood of obtaining financing for their next film. A theatrical release gains publicity for a film, which will transfer to its chances of finding an audience beyond the cinema, while media interviews allow the filmmaker to attempt to influence responses to their film. More than that, a theatrical release signals confidence in a production – that it has audience appeal. Not achieving a theatrical release (the fate of many Irish films, IFB funded or otherwise) is also not unusual in an industry with a high degree of wastage, yet it prompts the following questions: why was the film made? At what point did it become evident that it would struggle to find an audience? Why did it struggle to find an audience? Would an early intervention, perhaps at script stage, have effected the necessary changes to secure wider viewing? Should the IFB support fewer films?

Why make an Irish film?

The reliance on revenue-generation as a justification for funding is not unique to the Irish film industry and reflects the wider neoliberal environment. It is, however, an approach that is increasingly coming under scrutiny for what it omits, primarily issues of pleasure both in making a film and consuming it. Nor does the instrumentalist argument help in any way to consider how films (or television) articulate and address societal concerns or create community. It fails to consider how watching a film can broaden viewers' cultural horizons and introduce them to alternative ways of being and it ignores existing reports that arts and culture make a contribution to health, education, crime reduction and a sense of wellbeing.

In the UK, the AHRC report *Understanding the Value of Arts and Culture* (Crossick and Kaszynska, 2016) set out to explore how people benefited from cultural engagement. In line with other such research projects (Merli, 2002), the AHRC report focused largely on participatory arts to make the case that participation engendered feelings of wellbeing, empathy and reflection, as well as encouraging civic engagement. In an Irish context, John O'Hagan (2016) has also considered the societal benefits of state expenditure on the arts.[3] One of his central arguments is as follows (2016: 251):

> works of arts [sic] sometimes manage to convey what whole communities wish to express but cannot do so as well by any other means. The arts can also be a means by which new 'voices' are introduced to a community, voices that can redefine the fabric of the national or local culture. As such, they can play a pivotal role, if used properly, in integrating excluded minorities or new immigrant communities into the wider society thereby lessening the potential for social conflict and exclusion.

He further points to the potential for the arts of critiquing society, and in so doing contributing to a 'functioning democratic liberal society' (2016: 253).

The AHRC study also included film in its remit but the more film-focused survey for the British Film Institute (British Film Institute, 2011), which included face-to-face interviews and telephone surveys, is the most relevant for this discussion. It arrived at a number of interesting conclusions, including the following: 'people repeatedly spoke about the emotional effect of films' and 'Films are seen as entertaining, thought-provoking, moving, aesthetically pleasing, prompting action, expressing identity and even triggering metaphysical experiences' (2011: 68). Film was also seen as contributing to a 'subjective sense of happiness and well-being' (2011: 69).

Rebranding Ireland

While none of the various lobbying groups for government support have shown any huge interest in considering the societal value of film that was outlined above, cinema has been called upon to play its part in 'rebranding' Ireland, following the country's disastrous loss of international reputation in the wake of the economic crash. Film festivals and related events featured as part of Culture Ireland's 'Imagine Ireland' campaign of 2011 aimed at re-engaging the diaspora (so that they then might feel more disposed towards investment), and Irish cultural ambassador, Gabriel Byrne, was central to promoting 'Imagine Ireland'.[4] The interest in film as a cultural export continued with the publication of the 'Creative Capital' report (Minister for Arts, Heritage and the Gaeltacht,

2011). The report's central thrust was that the future for the Irish audio-visual industry (including gaming) was in creating product for export. While the report acknowledged the low levels of interest within Ireland in seeing Irish films and recommended that the IFB increase Irish audiences for Irish films, it did not go so far as to consider how this might be achieved, other than through greater promotion and distribution supports. Projects, it recommended (2011: 8) should be developed with 'international appeal'. The report (2011: 32) further noted 'There is a strong view that *Irish creativity is a brand* in its own right, and the industry should use this asset to achieve even greater international recognition' (emphasis in original). To emphasise this, the authors argue as follows:

> In an increasingly globalised world, content can become homogenous. The creation of content in Ireland must continue to contain a cultural uniqueness which helps to define what it means to be Irish, to depict cultural diversity and carry that message internationally. Indigenous feature films travel internationally and carry a strong message about our Irish identity. Films such as 'The Wind that Shakes the Barley', 'Once', 'The Secret of Kells', 'His & Hers', all depict a unique view of Ireland to a national and an international audience. (2011: 23)

Herein lies the conundrum: Irish films need to be distinctively Irish and culturally diverse. They need to appeal to the local audience, who it seems is required at least to act as a cultural filter, and to function internationally as a promotional vehicle for Ireland Inc. How this is to be achieved, other than as part of a business model, does not feature in the report.

Whose business is Irish cinema?

Whose business is it then to provide for the cultural component of an Irish film? In effect, this responsibility has devolved to the production companies. It is they who are the gatekeepers of Irish filmmaking and, at this stage, few individuals make films on their own. Rather, they are either commissioned to do so by the production company or they approach the company with a project. The Irish Film and Television Network lists sixty-five such companies on the entire island (IFTN, 2017).

Out of these, one of the most influential is Element Pictures. Established by Ed Guiney and Andrew Lowe in 2001, Element is different to other similar producers in that they are fully vertically integrated. They are the primary production company for Lenny Abrahamson, all of whose films, with the exception of *Adam & Paul*, they have produced and distributed in Ireland, and for Yorgos Lanthimos, whose *The Lobster* and *The Killing of a Sacred Deer* (2017) they produced and distributed in Ireland. Element Pictures Distribution holds the Irish and UK distribution rights to *The Guard*. Element also was the minority co-producer on Jerzy Skolimowski's *11 Minutes* (2016), which originated in Poland, and was one of the co-producers of *This Must Be the Place* (Paulo Sorrento, 2011).

Element has a television arm and co-produced *Ripper Street* (after it moved from the BBC to Amazon) and indigenous Irish television shows, including *Red Rock* (2015–). The company operates the Irish VOD (video on demand) platform, Volta. In 2012, Element took over the Light House Cinema, a four-screen arthouse cinema in Dublin's Smithfield and in 2018 the three-screen arthouse Pálás Cinema in Galway, both of which had been in financial difficulties. In 2017, Element acquired the mobile cinema, the Cinemobile.

As this brief overview of their activities indicates, Element mixes up the production of Irish-themed, and non-Irish-themed films. They produced Gerard Barrett's *Glassland* (2014) and *A Date for Mad Mary* (Darren Thornton, 2016), both of which were fully funded in Ireland. *The Lobster* was an Irish–Greek–UK–French–Dutch co-production. *Room* was an Irish–Canadian–UK production. 'When you're making a low-budget film you can finance it out of Ireland but once you want to do something of any ambition you need to look for financing outside of the country,' Guiney has explained in interview (in Barraclough, 2015: 20). What is also evident is that Element's production activities are focused on arthouse films. They have enjoyed huge success in this area, notably with Abrahamson's *Room,* whose Academy Award win (for Brie Larson as 'Best Actress') and nominations ('Best Picture', 'Best Director', 'Best Adapted Screenplay') in 2016 led to the film having a worldwide box office take of $35.4m (€33.3m) on a $13m budget (Deegan, 2016). By engaging in co-productions, Element not only can extend their range, but spread their risk. That they can also distribute and exhibit their own productions gives them a level of control that has so far eluded other Irish production companies. Being so closely associated with Abrahamson and Lanthimos enhances their reputation as a producer that can win awards and should allow them to attract other arthouse projects.

Irish cinema: arthouse cinema?

Element's positioning as a producer of arthouse cinema raises the question as to whether it is appropriate to consider contemporary Irish

Figure 2 The Pálás Cinema, Galway

film more generally as arthouse. Defining arthouse cinema, as most writers will acknowledge, is a slippery task. Older definitions (Bordwell, 1979; Neale, 1981) looked back at the golden age of the European art film (the cinema of Ingmar Bergman, Federico Fellini and others) to distinguish a mode of production that was auteur-based, realist, distinct from the more politically focused modernist film practice, funded by national institutions, and promoted as other to Hollywood. Neale, in addition, was writing in the wake of the much heralded British-German co-production, *Radio On* (Chris Petit, 1979), which has often been taken as inaugurating a new age of British art film production. Thus John Hill (2000) was able to include the cinema of Peter Greenaway,

Derek Jarman and Terence Davies in his discussion of British art cinema. He also (2000: 27–8) detects a rapprochement between art cinema and genre filmmaking in two works by Neil Jordan – *The Company of Wolves* (1984), *Mona Lisa* (1986) – and others. Hill usefully detaches art cinema from the constrictions of the national, and his discussion of the 'postnational auteur' (2000: 23) could easily be applied not just to Jordan but to the work of Lenny Abrahamson. In 2013, Abrahamson explained that, 'I wanted to make films that were culturally relevant in my own country, that challenged people and that people talked about … But in the past couple of years, I've made a conscious decision to open myself up to bigger stories' (in Dawtrey, 2013). This he did by directing *Frank* (2014) and *Room*. *Frank* may have included Ireland as a setting (for certain sequences) and two Irish actors – Domhnall Gleeson and Michael Fassbender – but it displays no interest in interrogating Irishness in the way that Abrahamson's first three films did. *Room,* of course, has no thematic Irish content, yet it is as much an Irish film as the first films in every other way – with Irish financing, production, a screenplay written by an Irish writer (Emma Donoghue, the book's author), and directed by an Irish director.

Discussing Abrahamson's cinema as arthouse is probably too easy and it would be simplistic to extrapolate wider categorisations of the Irish film industry from his example. One definition of art cinema sees it as oppositional to the dominant culture, as was British art cinema of the 1980s, and certainly many of the films discussed in this book are critical of Ireland's embrace of materialism under the Celtic Tiger. Yet, it is less that they are political films in the way that the much lauded 'first wave' of works by Joe Comerford, Pat Murphy, Bob Quinn and their peers in the 1970s and 1980s are understood to be but that they aim to engage audience empathy with alienated, struggling individuals who have found themselves on the wrong side of Ireland's new economy.

Nor is it useful to categorise by theme alone. Arthouse films tend to require state or institutional funding, are viewed most often in arthouse cinemas and at film festivals, and fall into niche categories on VOD platforms such as Netflix. In the context of another small national cinema, Scottish cinema, David Martin-Jones (2009: 229–30) has argued that there now exists a strain of filmmaking that is purposely made for the external arthouse and festival circuit, a trend that is as prone to self-exoticising as its more mainstream alternative. Rosalind Galt and Karl Schoonover (2010: 7) note that films that are part of the mainstream in their home country may well be exhibited in arthouse circuits abroad. In 2010, however, Element's head of distribution, Audrey Sheils, was quoted as saying, 'Irish films haven't done well in Britain for years.

I don't know what the reason is. They seem to fall between two stools. They are not art house movies, they are not subtitled and they are not obvious multiplex product' (in Molloy, 2010). The recent success on the awards circuit of films such as *Brooklyn* and *Room* and the high-profile work of Martin McDonagh (*In Bruges*, 2008) and his brother, John Michael McDonagh (*The Guard*; *Calvary*) may well have reversed this, and led to expectations of Irish cinema as signifying quality entertainment that is still differentiated from mainstream Hollywood or American indie product. To follow Martin-Jones's train of thought, we might ask if this leads to self-exoticising, particularly given the performative nature of both McDonaghs' work. The flaw in an otherwise persuasive way of considering such films is, however, that the alternative always seems to be some elusive 'authentic' indigenous production model – Irish films for Irish people, if you like.

Galt and Schoonover (2010: 8) write that 'art cinema troubles notions of genre' (a reflection that has already been considered in the Introduction). The common experience of watching Irish genre films (such as the horror films discussed in Chapter 3) and feeling that they are not quite 'right', may well reflect an unease amongst Irish filmmakers about overly conforming to genre requirements. 'As for what exactly "an Irish film" might look or smell like, that's another imponderable', Trevor Johnston wrote in *Sight and Sound* (2011), 'though if you ask around, there's definitely a sense that Irish cinema remains very much indie-focused and, in the broadest sense, a writerly affair, since it's the likes of the McDonagh brothers, [Conor] McPherson and [Mark] O'Rowe who have garnered the attention of late.'

This writerly quality, and the high incidence of writer-directors in contemporary Irish cinema, have fostered an auteur atmosphere and a turn towards individuality in filmmaking that further encourage arthouse labelling. So too does the association of many of the successful Irish actors with arthouse cinema, notably Colin Farrell whose career was reinvigorated by *In Bruges* and his subsequent association with Yorgos Lanthimos, and Saoirse Ronan, who has consistently worked in arthouse cinema, from *Atonement* (Joe Wright, 2007) to *Lady Bird* (Greta Gerwig, 2017).

Yet, there are still qualifications to this argument, particularly in terms of gender representation, both on the screen and behind the camera. One would expect a writerly, indie, relatively low-budget cinema to favour female representation. Ronan's Academy Award nomination for *Brooklyn* in 2016 and *Lady Bird* in 2018 and Ruth Negga's Academy Award nomination for *Loving* (Jeff Nichols, 2016) suggest a much greater population of female stars than actually exists. The IFB's 'six point plan' on gender diversity, launched in 2015 following the events discussed in the Introduction, noted that from 2010 to 2015, figures showed the following (Barry, 2017):

- 16% of production funding applications came from projects with female writers attached.
- 14% came from projects with female directors attached.
- 36% came from projects with female producers attached.

For projects that were completed in the same period:

- 21% had a female writer attached.
- 18% had a female director attached.
- 55% had a female producer attached.

The IFB has backed this up, as we have seen, with targeted funding for projects with female directors and writers. Prior to this, as Susan Liddy (2016) has amply demonstrated, the IFB showed little awareness of their responsibilities in encouraging women to participate in the film industry. The much higher representation of women as producers is also predictable, and as much a case of women organising the conditions for men to work as a real gender breakthrough. As I also discuss, specifically in Chapter 8, the relegation of women-centred narratives to the outer limits of the arthouse spectrum has had the effect of further marginalising such stories. Elsewhere (Barton, 2017), I have examined the role of women in Irish documentary making, a genre that has traditionally favoured women filmmakers but not for the most auspicious of reasons, namely that its low budgets make it less of a risk for producers looking to hire a female director, and its work practices favour family friendly hours. Even less encouraging are the opportunities for members of ethnic minorities to make Irish films. Thus, the expectation that active engagement in arts practice encourages diversity and community building seems to be far from realised in the Irish filmmaking context. Instead, the making of Irish cinema has been officially encouraged more as a distinctive national product within an international cultural marketplace, which, particularly when award-winning, will reflect well on the nation as a whole, rather than as a tool for reflecting (on) the national situation.

Despite these qualifications, it seems to me that Irish cinema is overall an arthouse cinema, however difficult that category is to establish. This does not necessarily mean that arthouse films are the most financially successful model, and indeed, as the table above demonstrates, the highest-earning Irish films are those that most closely resemble international productions, with recognisable stars, mid-range budgets and well-established directors. There is also very certainly a market for locally funded films, particularly comedies, which speak directly to Irish concerns. Although I track market performance throughout this book as a measure of impact, it is far from the most useful method of judging a film's artistry or cultural address. How Irish films, whatever their funding, speak to multiple notions of Irishness is the focus of the remainder of this book.

Notes

1 It is extremely difficult to obtain accurate box office figures for local Irish releases as they appear officially under UK and Irish (including Malta). This table is taken from Sheehy (2008) and multiple other sources.

2 A UK study in 2011 revealed that the home is the most frequent place for film viewing, with 86 per cent watching a film on television, and 63 per cent on DVD or Blu-ray, at least once a month. (British Film Institute, 2011: 6). There is no reason to believe that the Irish situation is different.

3 Curiously, O'Hagan excludes film from his argument on the grounds that it receives little public funding.

4 Byrne stepped down as cultural ambassador after two years. He ran into some controversy when he accused the government of trying to shake down Americans for money when they launched The Gathering in 2012. Minister for Transport, Tourism and Sport, Leo Varadkar, responded that Byrne was only 'popular with women of a certain age group', which generated even more controversy. For an analysis of the Imagine Ireland campaign and government arts policy, see Slaby 2011.

References

Barraclough, L. 2015. Irish Eyes Look Abroad for Funding. *Variety* (commercial supplement), 9 February, pp. 19–20.

Barry, A. 2017. *Where Are the Women? Unconscious Bias Training Planned to Make Irish Films More Diverse* [Online]. The Journal.ie. Available:www.thejournal.ie/unconscious-bias-training-irish-film-board-3185955-Jan2017/ [Accessed 12 November 2017].

Barton, R. 2017. A Female Voice in Irish Cinema: Women Filmmakers and the Creative Documentary. *New Hibernia Review*, 21, 17–32.

Bordwell, D. 1979. The Art Cinema as a Mode of Film Practice. *Film Criticism*, 4, 56–64.

British Film Institute. 2011. Opening Our Eyes: How Film Contributes to the Culture of the UK. London: BFI.

Crossick, G. and Kaszynska, P. 2016. Understanding the Value of Arts and Culture: The AHRC Cultural Value Project. UK: Arts and Humanities Research Council.

Dawtrey, A. 2013. Helmer on the Edge. *Variety*, 5 September, p. 87.

Deegan, G. 2016. Movie 'Room' Boosts Element Pictures Profits. *Irish Examiner*, 24 November, p. 16.

Department of Finance. 2012. Economic Impact Assessment of Section 481 Film Relief. Dublin: Department of Finance.

Fagan, J. 2015. 'It's a man in a f***ing dress' ' – Why 11 Million People Cannot Get Enough of *Mrs Brown's Boys*. *Estudios Irlandeses*, 204–8.

Flynn, R. and Tracy, T. 2016. Quantifying National Cinema: A Case Study of the Irish Film Board 1993–2013. *Film Studies*, 14, 32–53.

Galt, R. and Schoonover, K. 2010. Introduction: The Impurity of Art Cinema. *In:* Galt, R. and Schoonover, K. (eds.) *Global Art Cinema: New Theories and Histories*. Oxford: Oxford University Press.

Hill, J. 2000. The Rise and Fall of British Art Cinema: A Short History of the 1980s and 1990s. *Aura Film Studies Journal* 6, 18–32.

IFB/BSÉ 2016. Bord Scannán na hÉireann/Irish Film Board Strategic Plan 2016–2020. Irish Film Board.

IFB/BSÉ. 2018a. *Funding* [Online]. Irish Film Board/Bord Scannán na hÉireann. Available: www.irishfilmboard.ie/funding [Accessed 12 January 2018].

IFB/BSÉ. 2018b. *Distribution Support* [Online]. IFI/BSÉ. Available: www.irishfilmboard.ie/funding/distribution-loans [Accessed 12 January 2018].

IFTN. 2017. *Feature Film Production Companies in Ireland and Northern Ireland* [Online]. Dublin: The Irish Film and Television Network. Available: www.iftn.ie/production/production_companies/production_sub/feature/ [Accessed 11 November 2017].

Johnston, T. 2011. Green Screen: What's Happening to Irish Cinema. *Sight and Sound*, 21, 46–7.

Liddy, S. 2016. "Open to All and Everybody"? The Irish Film Board: Accounting for the Scarcity of Women Screenwriters. *Feminist Media Studies*, 16, 901–17.

Martin-Jones, D. 2009. *Scotland: Global Cinema: Genres, Modes and Identities*, Edinburgh: Edinburgh University Press.

Minister for Arts, Heritage and the Gaeltacht. 2011. Creative Capital: Building Ireland's Audiovisual Creative Economy. Ireland: Department of the Arts, Heritage and the Gaeltacht.

McCarthy, C., McNally, D., McLaughlin, P., O'Connell, M., Slattery, W. and Walsh, M. 2009. Report of the Special Group on Public Service Numbers and Expenditure Programmes. Dublin: Government Public Sales Office.

McGreevy, R. 2013. Irish Audiovisual Industry Nears Tipping Point. *Irish Times*, 18 January, p. 5.

Merli, P. 2002. Evaluating the Social Impact of Participation in Arts Activities. *International Journal of Cultural Policy*, 8, 107–18.

Molloy, P. 2010. Labour of Love Proves a Box-office Hit. *The Sunday Business Post*, 12 September, p. 6.

Neale, S. 1981. Art Cinema as Institution. *Screen*, 22, 11–39.

O'Hagan, J. 2016. Objectives of Arts Funding Agencies Often Do Not Map Well on to Societal Benefits. *Cultural Trends*, 25, 249–62.

Sheehy, T. 2008. Reaching an Audience. *Film Ireland* [Online], September/ October. Available: http://filmireland.net/2009/01/30/reaching-and-audience/ [Accessed 14 October 2017].

Shortall, E. 2014. Curse of the Irish. *Sunday Times*, 21 September, p. 9.

Slaby, A. 2011. Whither Cultural Policy in Post Celtic Tiger Ireland? *Canadian Journal of Film Studies/Revue Canadienne d'Études Cinématographiques*, 37, 76–97.

Short film
Granny O'Grimm's Sleeping Beauty
(Nicky Phelan, 2008)

In this six-minute short animation, the eponymous Granny (rendered in 3D) is reading a fairy tale to her reluctant grandchild who lies terrified in bed, the sheets pulled up around her ears. Instead, however, of *The Sleeping Beauty*, Granny veers off into her own free-associating version of how slighted the fairy godmother was by her exclusion from the christening of the princess, 'because she was old, and decrepit, and not one bit useful in the eyes of all the younger, more exciting fairies, who still had their muscle tone'. The film moves between Granny and the fairy story, with the latter rendered in the flatter 2D to give the impression of an illustration. Unusually for much Irish cinema, animated or otherwise, the narrative is told by and about an older woman. The interpretation of Granny as a hissing witch with strong glasses, an old woollen jumper, and a grudge against pretty younger fairies may not exactly sound progressive, but she is an empowered figure, who is animated to appear reflective, not simply malicious.

It is surely no coincidence that this film, also unusually, was written by a woman, Kathleen O'Rourke (who voices Granny). At the time of the film's release, O'Rourke garnered considerable media interest as the creative force behind the production. She had migrated from performing as a stand-up comedian to a career as a primary schoolteacher and it was as part of her Froebel training that she encountered Bruno Bettelheim's writings on the fairy tale. Granny O'Grimm first saw the light of day as part of The Fallen Angels Cabaret. In 2005, Nicky Phelan of Brown Bag came across the act and suggested that it would transfer well to animation. The film took approximately a year to shoot, and Phelan has noted that they were forced to sandwich it in among the company's income-earning, commissioned work. His comments emphasise the marginality of Irish-themed animation even within the Irish animation industry. Yet, they also draw attention to the potential of this space to rehearse non-normative versions of Irishness. O'Rourke's performance of femininity through this animation is very much in keeping with the output of many female comedians, with its celebration of bad women, the overweight body, and the re-purposing of older patriarchal renditions of femininity as an expression of empowerment.

2
Animating Ireland

The success story of Irish cinema in the twenty-first century is certainly animation. What was a fringe activity in the early 2000s, producing occasional works by individuals operating on their own, now constitutes a substantial portion of the audiovisual industry's output. As the Appendix indicates, figures vary year-on-year depending on individual projects but the industry is regularly worth in excess of €80m per annum.

The surge in animation production reflects a similar global trend, spurred on by advances in computer-generated content creation. These have in turn led to a dramatic reduction in cost, particularly in processes such as in-betweening and background painting, and a consequent speeding up of production time. Work that was previously farmed out to cheap labour markets, mostly in Asia, can now be done on site. Meanwhile, hand-drawn animation has become the preserve of artisan and independent filmmakers. The revitalisation of the Disney Studios and the success of Pixar have consolidated the US industry's position as the pre-eminent producer of animated family films. More than that, animation is widely acknowledged as the base for video-gaming and for special effects in cinema.

This industrial resurgence has been mirrored by increased academic interest in animation, even though the question of the most appropriate theoretical model of analysis – film studies, graphic art, cartooning – remains unresolved. For our purposes, a further theoretical consideration is the relationship between animation and national (live action) cinema, and animation and national culture.

In more general terms, the relationship between animation and live action cinema has been reinvigorated by the new digital turn in film theory, and specifically the idea that digital cinema's loss of indexicality – its correlation with the real world – renders it akin to animation. The use of computer-generated imagery (CGI) to create imaginary worlds that have no physical presence in front of the camera brings filmmaking closer to the work of the animator than the conventional cinematographer, or as Lev Manovich influentially argued in this context: 'cinema can no longer be clearly distinguished from animation. It is no longer an indexical media technology but, rather, a subgenre of painting' (2001: 294). One could easily dispute this generalising statement, particularly (as we discuss in relation to the documentary) as common sense dictates that there is a real world. On the other hand, to use a local example, one can see the working through of Manovich's intervention with a look at the work of Irish animator, Ruarí Robinson. Robinson's debut animation was the Academy Award-nominated *Fifty Percent Grey*. In this short film, a man dressed in a worn space suit rises from the ground in a grey, desolate environment. Spotting a television set with video recorder, he presses 'Play'. On the first occasion that he does this, a coloured image of beautiful surroundings comes up on the screen, and a voice congratulates him on being dead and having arrived in heaven. He turns, walks, takes out his gun and shoots himself in the head. On the second occasion, he rises again, and is welcomed to Purgatory. On the third occasion, after shooting himself again, he is welcomed to Hell. He shoots the television set and once more turns the gun on himself only to find he has run out of bullets. The production is elliptical and allusive; its tripartite structure recalling the tripartite biblical resurrection narrative (on the third day He rose again from the Dead), but offering its central character an illusion of free will. Its circularity reflects YouTube aesthetics of the loop, while the sense of entrapment within the frame that counters the illusion of free will is a common trope in animation. Its theme of male angst surely resonated with the global viewership that guaranteed its unusual visibility, as did its Oscar nomination.

Robinson followed *Fifty Percent Grey* with *The Silent City* (2006), a live action post-Apocalyptic war film starring Irish actors Don Wycherley and Cillian Murphy. The main speaking part goes to Wycherley who adopts an American accent. The short's special effects are entirely computer generated so that the finished result looks as much like animation as it does live action. This was presumably a calling card for Robinson's feature, *The Last Days on Mars* (2013), about a team of scientists on Mars whose mission becomes jeopardised by a discovery they have made. It stars Liev Schreiber, Elias Koteas and Romola Garai. Although all Robinson's work has received Irish funding, none of it is Irish set or Irish themed. What is interesting, in terms of Mancovich's argument, is how Robinson has moved freely between animation, live action and CGI, retaining a very similar look to his productions. In terms of the wider Irish animation sector, his output reflects the trend towards focusing on non-Irish settings and narratives.

Animation and national cinema

Animation's ability to, as Paul Wells (2002: 69) has argued, 'reconfigure narrative in the representation of time, space, and perspective' does not render it utterly different from live action cinema, which can achieve all those mutations. However, this is the core of animation rather than an ancillary activity. Thus, animation can question otherwise fixed identities, reimagine space and destabilise linearity, while still remaining accessible to the viewer, who will expect these formal strategies. For these reasons, it fits very interestingly into arguments around the function of a national cinema, and offers some considerable potential to destabilise or question paradigms familiar from its live action counterpart.

Analyses of animation within the context of national cinemas remain underdeveloped. Outside of Disney (as an expression of American values), the cinema most associated with a national style of animation is Japan, in part because of its long tradition of manga, anime and graphic illustration (Napier, 2005). In the European context, Richard Neupert (2015: 334) has argued that France is exemplary in developing a national animation industry that, 'like French art cinema in general, is a culturally specific mode'. Neupert's contention is that current French animated cinema looks to a national tradition of animation (dating back to Georges Méliès) but also recognises the formal qualities of Disney and global practices. While they may utilise the most up-to-date techniques to create their films, French animators differentiate themselves from mainstream global practices by mimicking older artisan techniques (2D and hand-drawn figures) to retain an auteurist, national style (Neupert, 2015). Animators such as Michel Ocelot (*Kirikou and the Sorceress/Kirikou et la sorcière*, 1998; *Tales of the Night/Les Contes de la nuit*, 2011, etc.) have been important in targeting 'progressive European family audiences' (Neupert, 2015: 339) with their productions. Ocelot places himself very firmly within a French tradition whereas Sylvain Chomet, director of *The Triplets of Belleville* (Les triplettes de Belleville, 2003), has insisted that his films, because of their multiple funding sources, cannot be labelled uniquely French (Neupert, 2015: 340). The auteur model of writer/animator/director that defines French animation distinguishes it further from Disney/Pixar, which relies on massive creative teams for its productions (2015: 353).

Neupert's argument is important for an analysis of Irish animation production. Just as much of French animation is indistinguishable from global cartooning and made to the same technical standards, so Irish animation's financial basis is in the making of cartoons for global television consumption. A child watching *Foster's Home for Imaginary*

Friends on Cartoon Network (2004–9) would be as little aware of the Irish component of the production (in this case that of Boulder Media) as a child in the 1980s would have been if they were one of the millions of cinemagoers whose attendances ensured that *An American Tail* (Don Bluth, 1986) and *The Land Before Time* (Don Bluth, 1988) outperformed their Disney counterparts, *The Great Mouse Detective* (1986) and *Oliver and Company* (1988) (Pallant, 2011: 90). It is the director of *An American Tail* and *The Land Before Time,* Don Bluth, who is at once the godfather and the bogeyman of today's Irish animation industry, and, most of all, it was his decision to locate his new studios, formed in conjunction with Irish American businessman Morris Sullivan, in Dublin, that introduced industrial animation practices to Ireland and kick-started its commercial phase. In common with the French situation, the current generation of Irish animators creating Irish-themed films distinguishes their product by recreating an artisanal style and relying on art cinema traditions to identify their output. Unlike the situation in France, these animators had to invent their own tradition when it came to making these films.

For the purposes of this chapter, I am focusing on those productions that concern themselves with Irish themes, and in particular the challenge of inventing an animation tradition. This inevitably means ignoring most Irish-made animation. According to one industry report published in 2015: '90% of turnover in Irish animation companies is attributed to exports' (Pumares et al., 2015: 94). This list includes IFB funded shorts such as *Fifty Percent Grey* and Eoin Duffy's award-winning *The Missing Scarf* (2013). Much of the Irish-themed output comes in the form of short films.[1] As with live-action shorts, these animations function both as calling cards for the feature industry and as artistic productions in their own right. Creating short films allows animators to experiment with ideas and, very importantly, to develop their own intellectual properties. Intellectual property (IP) rights are crucial to the future development of local animation, and without these the sector will function as little more than a production facility for the global industry. Constraints of space have further limited my discussion to a handful of key Irish-themed films, with a focus on the features, *The Secret of Kells* and *Song of the Sea.*[2] It is also important to take into consideration the critical success of Irish animation (as noted in Chapter 1). Although this has raised the profile of Irish animation globally, it does not automatically translate into commercial success or further business. *Song of the Sea*, for instance, had an estimated budget of €5,300,000 and grossed $850,043 at the US box office (IMDb, n.d.). Cathal Gaffney commented after the nomination of *Give up Yer Aul*

Sins that it yielded press coverage and created contacts, but had not brought in a deluge of extra work (in Lyons, 2002).

Within academia, Irish animation has enjoyed limited attention. Maeve Connolly initiated a discussion of the new cycle of Irish animated films as literary adaptations, noting that at least one third of the Frameworks productions were (at the time of writing) adaptations (2005: 86). Both she and Tom Walsh (2008) have further related this to heritage discourses in live action cinema (see Chapter 5). However, both also acknowledge that Irish animators have tended to engage critically with the Irish literary heritage, stamping their personal mark on what become new authorial (re)creations. Both for instance, cite Tim Booth's *Ulys* (1998) as a work that productively engages with its literary original, James Joyce's *Ulysses* (1922). In an article on *Ulys*, Walsh links the period of political and social instability that informed Joyce's disruptive modernist writing with the abrupt societal changes of the boom years in which *Ulys* was made. Booth's 'use of the plasmatic nature of the animated form', Walsh argues, mirrors the 'sense of embodiment' that Joyce employed to question the social order (2011b: 95). In common with much Irish-themed animation, *Ulys* has a deliberately artisanal, retro appearance. The characters are hand-drawn to look something like the old seaside postcards of buxom women and leery men. These visual techniques enable Booth to reflect the bawdiness of the original in the idiom of the period. At the same time, his simulated, sweeping camera movements and transitions to events that postdate Joyce's original, including the destruction of Dublin's Nelson's Pillar (in 1966), create a temporal and spatial disunity that challenges the myth of historical progression. The blowing-up of the Pillar is thus bound up with the revolutionary 1920s rather than constituting a new historical moment. Not only that, it emerges out of a chaotic world, where the logics of space and time are undermined at every turn. Wells (2002: 11) argues that animation 'intrinsically interrogates the phenomena it represents and offers new and alternative perspectives and knowledge to its audiences'. *Ulys* both offers a new perspective on a classic novel and reflects the tenor of that novel, reproducing and extending its fascination with modernity and the clash of old and new. It is also a statement about animation itself, a bold claim for the medium's entitlement to take one of the nation's canonical texts and transform it into a new work of art.

The origins of Irish animation

Another key concern in Irish critical writing on animation is its funding base and in particular the consequences of co-funding on the content of the feature films (Burke, 2009; Connolly, 2005; Walsh, 2008). The historical background to the current cycle of Irish animation has been well rehearsed (Burke, 2009; Connolly, 2005; Gillett, 2010; Woods, 2002), identifying as the first wave the early home industry; the second the consequences of Don Bluth's decision to set up an animation studio, Sullivan Bluth, in Ireland; and the third being the current phase discussed here. To summarise this background briefly, the history of Irish animation production before Sullivan Bluth amounts to one iconic film, *Clock Gate Youghal* (James Horgan, circa 1910); a small body of work created for and with RTÉ; a few commercials; and short films by individual filmmakers working on their own as a cottage industry. The latter include Tim Booth (*The Prisoner*, 1983; *Ulys*); Harry Hess, who worked initially out of the National College of Art and Design (NCAD) in the 1970s and subsequently with Ballyfermot Senior College; Aidan Hickey, whose *An Inside Job* (1987) remains his best-known work, and Steve Woods (*Ireland, 1848,* 1997), who now lectures at the National Film School and continues to work in experimental animation. In 1971, Jimmy Murakami (*The Snowman* (1982) and *When the Wind Blows* (1986) set up two studios in Ireland – Quateru Films in 1971 and Murakami-Wolf Films in 1989 – the latter primarily to work on the *Teenage Mutant Ninja Turtles* series. The domino effect of industries following similar industries saw another international production house, Emerald City, also relocate to Dublin in this period.

In 1985, Don Bluth, accompanied by two other former Disney staff, Gary Goldman and John Pomeroy, decamped from America to Dublin and, with Morris Sullivan, established Sullivan Bluth studios. Sullivan was the Executive Managing Director and responsible for business operations. Bluth was the chief animator. He had previously worked on *Winnie the Pooh and Tigger Too* (John Lounsbery, 1974) and *Pete's Dragon* (Don Chaffey, 1977) as director of animation. When he was asked why he moved to Ireland, Bluth gave the following explanation:

> We decided we needed a country where we could turn the clock back, where we could go to art schools and find people who have not yet polluted their thinking in animation so we can start new and fresh. We also wanted a country that speaks English. England had already been taken, Canada had already been taken, Australia had already been taken, and there sat Ireland, isolated in the middle of the water and no one had Ireland. We went to Ireland, talked to the government and asked if they would help us out financially. Their grants were very substantial so we said Ireland is it. (Bluth and Sibley, 1990: 25)

It is worth quoting this response in detail because of what it tells us about the intertwining of commercial incentives and cultural expectations that are embedded in Ireland's pursuit of global corporations. The country's attraction as an English-speaking territory and the financial incentives to relocate are familiar refrains from IDA Ireland's long-established policy of pursuing inward investment. Equally, the availability of a young, educated workforce has been the focus of successive IDA Ireland campaigns. Sullivan Bluth did indeed receive substantial government funding, with more to come. The IDA approved capital and employment grants of £2.2m to set up the studios and a further undisclosed sum for expansion and training of Irish animators (McGrath, 1986). Aside from animation production, Sullivan Bluth was notable for establishing, together with Ballyfermot Senior College, now Ballyfermot College of Further Education (BCFE), The Irish School of Classical Animation, in 1989. This offered a three-year diploma course in animation production modelled on the course at Sheridan College in Toronto, Canada, from which Disney have traditionally hired their animators.

Sullivan Bluth enjoyed mixed fortunes in Ireland. Bluth wanted to recreate the model of animation production of the classic Disney era (of the 1940s to the mid- 1950s), hence his journey back in time to the island in the middle of the water. However, as Tom Walsh has argued, all he achieved was a pale imitation of the Disney original (Walsh, 2008: 55). The studio's first film was *The Secret of NIMH* (Don Bluth, 1982), a critical success but a box office failure. This was followed by *An American Tail*, largely funded, as was their next film, *The Land Before Time*, by Steven Spielberg's Amblin Entertainment. Dogged by chronic funding issues, the studio turned to British production company Goldcrest to fund *All Dogs Go to Heaven* (Don Bluth, 1989) and *Rock a Doodle* (Don Bluth, 1991). When that deal collapsed, Bluth had to look elsewhere for funding for his two final films in Ireland, *Thumbelina* (Don Bluth and Gary Goldman, 1994) and *A Troll in Central Park* (Don Bluth and Gary Goldman, 1994). They also dabbled in early video games, which Bluth had already started on before the move to Dublin, drawing sequences for the laserdisc of *Dragons Lair* (1983) and for *Space Ace* (1984). In 1995, a potential investment deal fell through and the company closed, having lost an estimated $30m (Dawtrey, 1995). Its final film, *All Dogs Go to Heaven 2* (Larry Leker and Paul Sabella, 1996), was released after its collapse. All told, it was estimated that over $100m, much of it Irish Government money, had been invested in setting up an Irish animation industry (Bushe, 1995). Many of the Irish staff and other animation graduates relocated to the United States, with most working for Disney where salaries had doubled since its re-emergence as the world's leading animation studio (Bushe, 1995). By the time of Bluth's departure, Emerald had also folded. In 1992, Murakami-Wolf cut its workforce from 130 to thirty after it failed to secure a second contract for *Teenage Mutant Ninja Turtles*. The company continued as Fred Wolf films and the remaining staff worked on *Budgie, The Little Helicopter*. Murakami stayed in Ireland until his death in 2014. In 2000, Fred Wolf finally closed its Dublin offices (Flynn and Brereton, 2007: 14).

In an extended analysis of Sullivan Bluth's influence on Irish animation, Tom Walsh has argued that it represented a new iteration of the colonisation process: 'The Irish artists involved had to adopt an American commercial style, as did the animation students who hoped to graduate from the industry-linked courses on offer. Assimilation of this dominant style had taken place' (Walsh, 2008: 21). Yet, as influential as Sullivan Bluth was on the future development of Irish animation, it was not until the company crashed that, phoenix-like, a local industry was born. When this did emerge, as we shall see, it was already well prepared by Bluth and the BCFE to create product for the global market. Another grouping of local animators, however, resolved to unlearn the practices of the dominant animation industry, and send Irish animation in a new direction.

Irish animation: a new tradition

Their timing was fortunate in several respects. In 1995, Pixar released *Toy Story*, a film that would return animation to its pre-eminence as family entertainment; locally, the economic boom was beginning to take hold and more funding was available for creative enterprises, including film. In 1995, the Irish Film Board launched the Frameworks scheme in conjunction with RTÉ and the Arts Council with the Northern Ireland Film Council. This was aimed at supporting indigenous, short animated films. In 2001, they followed this with Irish Flash, which funded short flash animations of one to three minutes in length. Further support came with the establishment of the Digital Hub in Dublin in 2003, which, for instance, former Brown Bag animator, Andrew Kavanagh, used as an incubator for his company, Kavaleer. Outside of co-production deals, the sector is reliant on a combination of funding from Section 481, the Irish Film Board, the Arts Council, Enterprise Ireland and the Broadcasting Authority of Ireland. This funding also benefited the older generation of animators, such as Tim Booth, who continued to work as solo artists outside the new mini-company system of the BCFE graduates.

Cartoon Saloon and Brown Bag now count as the preeminent local animation companies. However, they are far from alone. Boulder Media was formed in 2000, and their breakthrough came in 2005 when they were commissioned to make *Foster's Home for Imaginary Friends* for

Cartoon Network. In July 2016, the US toy manufacturer Hasbro (*My Little Pony*, *Transformers*) acquired Boulder, which allowed them to move premises and expand significantly. JAM Media, founded in 2002 by Alan Rice, Alan Shannon and Mark Cumberton, won critical acclaim with their BBC series *Roy* (2009–15), which centres on the trials and tribulations of a cartoon boy who lives in the real world. They followed this with *The Roy Files* (2015–16) and *Little Roy* (2016–). The series originated in a short film titled *Badly Drawn Roy* (Alan Shannon, 2004), a 'mockumentary' that mixed animation with live action. The original production concerned the eponymous Roy (voiced by Shannon) who was not 'cleaned up' during the animation process and thus was destined to remain a crude drawing. The film is structured around a series of interviews with Roy's live action relatives (voiced by the director's family) and is narrated by actor Alan Stanford. With its production background and recourse to old family photographs to reconstruct Roy's childhood, *Badly Drawn Roy* relies on its audience's readiness to forge associative links between a traditional working-class upbringing and close-knit familialism. The television series retained the Irish setting; the family's strong working-class identity, however, was replaced by a more class-neutral identity, and when Roy moves school to 'Sandyford Progressive Learning', his learning environment is depicted as modern and multicultural, or in other words, globally relatable. We can see an echo in this of Brown Bag Films' move towards the mainstream; however, in this instance JAM Media have retained enough of the original project (and their intellectual property rights) to render their contemporary work at once global and Irish.

By 2012, there were more than twenty Irish animation companies across the country (Devane, 2012: 12). The day-to-day business of these companies is organised around the creation of content for international children's TV, for the Web, and for advertising. The production process remains, even in the digital era, slow and expensive. Thirty seconds of animation can take up to a week to create and gestation periods for productions can be several years. Animation remains labour-intensive and these companies are significant employers within the cultural sector.

Brown Bag Films

Brown Bag Films started when its founders, Cathal Gaffney and Darragh O'Connell, grew so disenchanted with the BCFE course, and specifically its American orientation, that they dropped out to set up their own company. Their first production was an animated version of *Peig* (1995), made for RTÉ. One of the foundational works of Irish-language literature, *Peig,* first published in 1936 by the Talbot Press, was the auto-biography of Peig Sayers, edited by Irish-language scholar and activist, Máire Ní Chinnéide. Her son, Micheál, transcribed it from Sayers, who was illiterate. The book swiftly became a core element of the Irish school curriculum and a byword of imposed Irish-language learning for generations of Irish schoolchildren. As Ríona Nic Congáil (2009: 200) has written:

> As a direct result of *Peig*'s prominence on the educational curriculum, as an obligatory text, and stemming from the tone of pessimism which was clear as early as the opening line of the book – "seanbhean is ea mise anois, a bhfuil cos léi san uaigh is an chos eile ar a bruach" [I am an old woman now, with one foot in the grave, and the other on its edge] – *Peig* has come to represent every potentially derisory aspect of the Irish language: its rural base; its proximity to and romanticization of poverty; its unwillingness to embrace modernity; and its insistence on putting the illiterate native speaker on a pedestal, above the educated learner of the language.

In 1999, *Peig* was removed from the Irish school curriculum and replaced with Re O' Laighleis's novel, *Gafa (Hooked)*, first published by Comhar in 1996, about a teenage heroin addict. Anyone seeking a commentary on the shifting cultural touchstones of the new Ireland need look no further.

Peig is a series of seven three-minute animations, using hand-painted acetate cels and shot on a rostrum camera. The central figures of Peig and the pig, Humungus, which she keeps under the table, are created in clay animation for the opening and closing sequences. The dialogue retains much of the original book, opening with its famed lines (in English). However, over the course of the series, Peig (who is voiced by a male, Paul Drumm) increasingly muddles the order of the words and has to be helped out in her confusion by Humungus, who addresses the television audience 'to camera'. The animation abounds with visual and verbal anachronisms, with a Dalek, for instance appearing in the corner of the image accompanying the announcement of her 'match', jokingly mistaken by the animators for a football match.

As a statement of intent, Gaffney and O'Connell could have hardly chosen a more iconic book for adaptation. When the first episode aired on RTÉ's late-night entertainment slot, 'The End', comedian and pre-senter Barry Murphy announced that it would offer a 'touch of nos-talgia ... for anyone who had an Irish education'. Murphy may have intended his comments ironically (who could be nostalgic for *Peig*?), but Gaffney and O'Connell's production laid the foundations for much of the style of Ireland's succession of award-winning animations. Their

version of *Peig* is mocking without being offensive. It is deliberately artisanal, with backgrounds created to look like the slightly washed-out pen
and ink watercolours of the amateur painter. Secondary characters are
often static with only the central character exhibiting even rudimentary
movement. Much of the humour is aural, deriving from the gender mis-
match in the voicing and the thick rural accents of Peig and Humungus.
This joking play on rural Ireland of the past conjures up less the actual
privations of the era than representations of it as a period of hardship
that forged the national spirit. At the same time, its appeal is to an
imagined community, to borrow from Benedict Anderson's (2006) influential formula, of Irish viewers connected through the shared memory
of studying *Peig* at school.

Brown Bag Films were also responsible for *Give Up Yer Aul Sins* and
Granny O'Grimm's Sleeping Beauty as well as a number of successful
Irish-themed shorts such as *The Last Elk* (Alan Shannon, 1998) and
Angela's Christmas (2017). Since the release of *Granny O'Grimm's
Sleeping Beauty*, their output has been more focused on the production of children's animation for global networks and platforms such
as Nickelodeon, Cbeebies, Netflix and Amazon Prime. By 2012, they
employed over 100 people (Devane, 2012: 12). One of their flagship
productions is the award-winning *Peter Rabbit* (2012–). This, however,
was developed by Silvergate Media and Penguin Books and thus Brown
Bag Films's input was largely invisible. Another of their high-profile
outputs is the enormously successful pre-school series, *Doc McStuffins*
(Disney Junior, 2012–). In 2015, they were acquired by Canadian 9 Story
Media Group for €40m (Sexton, 2015). This allowed them to move into
their custom-built 20,000-square-foot base in Smithfield in 2016. Their
income is thus almost wholly dependent on service work, which finances
have dictated they favour over local-themed films.

Give Up Yer Aul Sins is a visual reconstruction of a series of
recordings made in the 1960s of children from Rutland National
School in Dublin's inner city, telling Bible stories. As was the case
with *Peig,* much of the film's humour is aural, depending on the child
narrator's strong accent. The centrality of voice and accent to these
two productions is interesting and speaks directly to issues of the
national. This is the voice of an old urban working class of the kind
that has historically been associated with a down-to-earth authenticity. One could go back to comedian and raconteur, Jimmy O'Dea
(1899–1965), whose act was constructed around the humorous
delivery of wisecracks derived from working-class resistance to hegemonic constraints; or to the character of Agnes Browne, first aired on
screen in Anjelica Huston's film of the same name (*Agnes Browne*,

1999) and recreated with such success by Brendan O'Carroll on television and with *Mrs Brown's Boys D'Movie*. *Give Up Yer Aul Sins* as much as *Peig* (and *Mrs Brown's Boys*) relies on ironic nostalgia for its appeal. As Linda Hutcheon (1998) has written:

> It is the very pastness of the past, its inaccessibility, that likely accounts for a large part of nostalgia's power – for both conservatives and radicals alike. This is rarely the past as actually experienced, of course; it is the past as imagined, as idealized through memory and desire. In this sense, however, nostalgia is less about the past than about the present.

Irony, however, 'is one (though only one) of the means by which to create the necessary distance and perspective on that anti-amnesiac drive [of nostalgic remembrance]' (Hutcheon, 1998). Thus the Brown Bag films recreate the historical moment, while emphasising that this is a fictional reconstruction. They solicit feelings of nostalgia at the same time as they acknowledge that the Irish past was not just a time of simpler pleasures and expectations. In this, their complex relationship with indexicality is important. These films both are and are not indexically linked to the phenomenological world; they rely on historically identifiable figures for their protagonists and, in the case of *Sins* a 'real' aural track, yet by virtue of the caricaturing and cartooning effects of animation, they so disrupt time and place as to release them from their indexical associations and remove them to a fictional and thus safely passed past. In a similar manner, Brown Bag's *Angela's Christmas* (Damien O'Connor, 2017), another literary adaptation, this time of Frank McCourt's eponymous short story, references the hardships of Irish working-class life, which are familiar from McCourt's *Angela's Ashes* (1996), but softens them through its focus on the child, Angela (voiced by Ruth Negga) and its invocation of the mood of nostalgia on which Christmas celebrations are so reliant.

Cartoon Saloon and the Irish animated feature

In 1999, Tomm Moore, Paul Young, Nora Twomey and Ross Murray co-founded Cartoon Saloon. All were graduates of BCFE and their intention in founding the company always was to make the feature that would become *The Secret of Kells*. Cartoon Saloon is unusual in that it is based outside of Dublin, in Kilkenny, which was a decision arising out of Moore's involvement with the youth training organisation, Young Irish Filmmakers.

Like Brown Bag Films and many of the other Irish animation companies, Cartoon Saloon juggles commercial television production with their own original Irish-themed works. They were responsible, for instance, for the animated series *Skunk Fu* (2007–8), which was nominated for a BAFTA in 2009. *Skunk Fu* sold to over 120 countries, including to the Cartoon Network in the United States (O'Brien, 2009) but contains no specifically Irish content. This, together with working on commercials, has enabled the core personnel in the company to develop their skills, not just in terms of artistry, but also in negotiating international financing and co-productions. In February 2017, Cartoon Saloon signed a deal with Canadian animation producer, Mercury Filmworks, to form Lighthouse Studios in Kilkenny with the aim of creating product for Disney and Netflix. The venture promised to create 140 jobs (Kane, 2017).

Before they finally released their first animated feature, *The Secret of Kells*, Cartoon Saloon had also made a number of short, IFB supported films, including *Celtic Maidens* (Nora Twomey, 2003). Twomey's film was financed and produced under the Short Shorts scheme and runs to just three minutes. It is a satire on US advertisements for Irish products, in this case a CD featuring songs from performers in a talent competition that evidently references the annual Rose of Tralee contest. *Celtic Maidens* is a rudimentary animation and needs to be viewed as an apprentice work. In many ways, however, its tone is consistent with a long strain of satire that riffs on the falsity of national identity construction, notably the writings of Flann O'Brien (David Nolan) and RTÉ's *Hall's Pictorial Weekly* (1971–80). In her analysis of this film, Connolly (2005: 87) has suggested that the short film format offers greater opportunities for satire than does the more commercially oriented feature, which 'is more constrained by the conventions of heritage discourse'. The argument that short films potentially enjoy greater artistic freedom, and therefore the freedom to critique the social order, than commercial features is familiar from Martin McLoone's (2000: 151–62) discussion of such films in an Irish context. Yet, as McLoone acknowledges, many of these films function as calling cards for commercial work and the argument has its limitations for analysing animation as much as live action.

The Secret of Kells

Wells (2002: 36) has written that 'the Disney aesthetic makes the fine art conditions of its construction invisible, while all other methods essentially privilege the sense of their process, and its inherent relationship to fine art as their creative endeavour'. Wells's analysis here and his subsequent comments (2002: 38–9) on animation's tendency to integrate the process of artistic creation into its storylines have direct relevance to how the first Irish-themed animated feature, Cartoon Saloon's *The Secret of Kells*, can be critically approached. The story is set in medieval Ireland. The Abbot of

Kells, Abbot Cellach (voiced in the English-language version by Brendan Gleeson), is preoccupied by the need to complete the construction of a wall to protect the settlement against the 'Northmen' (Vikings). Isolated from the rest of the religious community, he spends his time in a lofty workroom, whose walls he obsessively covers in mechanical drawings of his fortifications. His orphaned nephew, Brendan (Evan McGuire), is more interested in the company of the other monks who represent a diverse grouping of nationalities and who accuse the Abbot of taking more interest in warfare than the civilising influence of books. Their numbers are augmented by the arrival of master illuminator Brother Aidan (Mick Lally), who has fled Iona and brings with him the extraordinary skills he exercised on the *Book of Iona,* as well as his cat, Pangur Bán. Brother Aidan takes on Brendan as his pupil and, on a mission to find the materials for a rare ink, Brendan meets the fairy girl, Aisling (Christen Mooney). Later Aisling will come to his rescue when he goes in search of the crystal that is hidden in the underworld of the pagan god, Crom Cruach. When the Northmen attack, the monastery is destroyed and its inhabitants scattered. Many years later, the adult Brendan (Michael McGrath) visits the Abbot on his deathbed and presents him with the *Book of Kells.* The film ends with an animated montage of its illustrations.

The Secret of Kells was co-produced with Belgium and France with the main production partner being Les Armateurs (who had produced *The Triplets of Belleville*). The animation was carried out in Kilkenny, Belgium, France and Kesmet Studios in Hungary. Lightstar Studios in Brazil handled some post-production as did Piste Rouge in Paris. In France, Bruno Coulais composed the score, which was arranged and recorded by Kila in Ireland (Cohen, 2010).

The challenge facing Cartoon Saloon was to create a story that responded to such a nationally significant artefact as the ninth-century *Book of Kells*. On display in the Old Library at Trinity College, it is a major tourist attraction and familiar to many for its elaborate Celtic designs. At the same time, it is a Bible, which makes *The Secret of Kells* not an adaptation but an origins narrative. One of the most interesting aspects of this challenge was the filmmakers' determination to exclude all but the most unavoidable mentions of Christianity, which was a startling omission in a country still identified by its religious adherence. Brendan may recite the Lord's Prayer (in Irish) when he first enters the forest, but this seems more intended to ward off the lurking spirits than as an act of devotion. The monks apparently spend little or no time in prayer and the Abbott is preoccupied with his fortifications.

Instead, the film elevates craftsmanship and learning to the position of cultural identifiers; it is also a celebration of the emergence of Irish

Figure 3 *The Secret of Kells*

animation as a national artform, which returns us to Wells's comments on the intersections between fine art and animation. In the film's opening montage, an ethereal voice (presumably an older Aisling's) speaks of all she has seen and the conflicts she has witnessed. At the same time scenes of nature are interspersed with images of invasion and death. As the title of the film, in glowing Celtic script, emerges on the screen, she reaches a crescendo with 'I have seen the book that turns darkness into light.' The dizzying artistry of this sequence sets up the audience both for a display of vividly (re-)animated Celtic imagery and a thematic explor-ation of the triumph of civilisation over savagery. The Celtic triskele, with its origins in pre-Christianity and its subsequent appropriation as a symbol of the Holy Trinity under Christianity, emerges as a key motif. Impressed on the forest trees, it hints at a pantheistic utopian vision of a time when paganism and spirituality were embedded within a harmonic natural environment. Thus, religion appears as a visual reference point, if not as a belief system. At certain moments the screen splits into three contrasting images, which Brendan can move between, simultaneously referencing art cinema practices and the religious triptych.

In her reading of the film, and in particular the sequences where Brendan journeys into the manuscript itself, Lynn Ramey (2014: 116) notes that the animators have played their own jokes with the text so that by stilling the image:

We can make out 'monachulus rufus,' or small redheaded monk, as well as several pseudo-latinate words, such as 'fabricus' and 'illustro' that refer to the making and illustrating of the book. We are warned, however, of the 'mediocris per latin,' which may be a self-referential claim that the pseudo-Latin in this still is, indeed, mediocre.

As she argues, these jokes were for the animators' own benefit and would not have been intelligible to cinema audiences. Thus, in this analysis, *The Secret of Kells* successfully remediates (Bolter and Grusin, 1999) the original by creating a new media object out of an older artefact. In particular by (literally) drawing Brendan into the text, the film: 'incorporates a medieval, if not post-Renaissance, sense of immediacy, drawing the modern viewer into the text in ways that a printed page might not' (1999: 118).

The backgrounds of *The Secret of Kells* are hand-drawn or painted, while the movement of its characters is animated at twelve frames per second rather than the conventional twenty-four frames per second that animators routinely use to produce a sense of time and motion akin to live action cinema. As a consequence, the film moves less in real time than at an idiosyncratic, slightly dreamy pace. Modulations of light and dark, shade and colour, ripple through it to create an intense sense of dynamism coupled with otherworldliness. The monks are drawn as an assemblage of geometric shapes topped with recognisable faces so that they are not just designers but designs. The sequences in the monastery before the attack play out as a time of prelapsarian innocence, with Celtic spirals and knotwork exploding on the screen against a vivid background of emerald greens. Once Brendan enters the forest, the lighting turns milky white and spectral; there Aisling and Pangur Bán form visual mirrors of each other, swirling and shape-shifting in dance-like moves. Bruno Coulais's score reinforces the Irish theme aurally here and throughout, but with a lighter touch than many contemporary Irish soundtracks. The attack of the Northmen is the only sequence that deploys 3D animation, and its use of menacing Gothic blood reds recalls not just the Eastern European animation associated with Kesmet Studios but also the *mise-en-scène* of the classic Japanese epics of Akira Kurosawa: *Rashomon* (1950) for instance, or *Throne of Blood* (1957). By contrast, the flat look of the 2D animation echoes the style favoured by Japanese anime, particularly the work of Studio Ghibli, whose *Ponyo* (2008) Cartoon Saloon was to displace in the competition for Best Animated Feature at the 2009 Academy Awards. Not surprisingly, Moore has consistently cited Studio Ghibli as an influence. To extend the parallels, it is tempting to see the grand finale, when the designs from the *Book of Kells* return the world to vivid, swirling colour, as an homage to the finale of another film about commitment to religious art in embattled times, Andrei Tarkovsky's *Andrei Rublev* (1966). These multiple cultural influences dilute the Irishness of *The Secret of Kells*, but they also point to the void in Irish animation history. In making the first ever Irish-themed animation feature, Moore and Twomey looked to transnational practices to forge a new visual identity for their film, and did so by merging Irish Celtic tropes with historical references from the history of non-Hollywood, non-Disney cinema.

Reviews of *The Secret of Kells* were uniformly positive, lauding the film not just for its use of 2D and its visual richness, but also for its refusal to create Disney-esque child characters. (One might have wished for a central female character in this or Cartoon Saloon's next feature, *The Song of the Sea*, but audiences had to wait for *The Breadwinner* for this.) Brendan is a conventional enough boy hero – solitary, independent and resourceful, who must learn to be brave to accomplish his mission – to be recognisable to a family audience. Aisling is feisty and loyal (although it would be gratifying if her narrative function were other than ensuring the male hero's completion of his quest). Pangur Bán, the cat, supplies another point of reference in the origins narrative, his name derived from the locally familiar poem of the same name dating back to around the ninth century. Written in Old Irish and presumed to be by an exiled monk on Continental Europe, it is recited in Irish at the end of the film, and describes the pleasures of working on a scholarly tract in the company of a cat whose own skill is chasing mice (Moriarty, 2013).

Much of the academic response to the film has focused on its pan-European production background and the consequences of this for its theme and narrative (O'Brien, 2011; Walsh, 2011a). Walsh, for instance, interprets the avoidance of religious specificity as an attempt 'to create a culturally neutral text designed to play to as broad an audience as possible, thus demonstrating the underlying commercial concerns of feature animation production' (2011: 94). It is interesting in this regard, that Moore himself has explained that the secularism of *The Secret of Kells* was a direct consequence of the co-production process:

> Our initial rendering of the plot was more religious. I was very comfortable working with the themes, character, and motifs, since I'm Irish Catholic, but as we worked on the film, the producer Didier Brunner … felt that we should stress the universality of the story. The film is ultimately about being an artist and being able to fully express your creativity. (in Garcia, 2010)

In Ireland, as Moore noted acerbically, the film performed poorly, running for just three weeks on a release of thirty-five prints: '"We were pretty disappointed with the support locally", he told an interviewer. "We thought Ireland would take it into its bosom. It took winning a few awards over the summer [for that to happen]"' (in Shortall, 2009). Even globally, the film did not make its money back in cinemas, with a total box office of $739,454 on a budget of $8m (Box Office Mojo, n.d.).

Song of the Sea

Despite approaches from major American-based animation studios, Moore stayed with the project of creating local, 2D animated features. Cartoon Saloon's next release was *Song of the Sea*. Based on the Selkie (seal people) myth, the film tells the story of Ben (voiced by David Rawie) and Saoirse (Lucy O'Connell) whose father, Conor (Brendan Gleeson) is the keeper of a remote lighthouse. Their mother (Lisa Hannigan) vanished after giving birth to Saoirse and Conor is bringing them up on his own. On Ben's tenth birthday, the children's grandmother (Fionnula Flanagan) appears and against their will packs them off to live with her in Dublin. Soon, Ben and Saoirse, who is mute, find themselves caught up with a gathering of fairies and flee back to the lighthouse with their dog, Cú. On their way, they face down the sea god, Mac Lir (Brendan Gleeson), and Saoirse begins to fade away. Only the song of the sea can save her.

Song of the Sea is unmistakeably the successor to *The Secret of Kells*. The flat 2D style predominates again, with the drawings now resembling a child's illustrated storybook. The soundtrack is again composed by Bruno Coulais and performed by Kila. Consistent too with the earlier film are the frequent invocations of Ireland's mythic past and intermittent usage of the Irish language, notably in song, but now also in the film's credits. A muted palette lends certain sequences a dream-like look, which then transforms into full vibrant colour for moments of action. What has changed is that this second feature is more recognisably a family film. Its present-day setting, its jaunty pace, its sequence of adventures and its main characters – cheeky young boy, vulnerable girl, lonesome father and cackling grandmother – are familiar from multiple child-oriented narratives. All that it lacks is a thoroughly wicked villain. As with *The Secret of Kells,* Moore's second feature was financed and created via multiple international animation companies. Backgrounds and layouts were produced in Luxembourg while some animation took place in Denmark. These sequences were composited in Belgium with post-production, sound and music completed in France.

Over the opening credits, singer Lisa Hannigan recites lines from W. B. Yeats's 'The Stolen Child' of 1889:

Come away, O Human child!
To the waters and the wild

Figure 4 *The Song of the Sea*

With a faery, hand in hand
For the world's more full of weeping than you can understand.

The recital segues to her singing the title song, 'The Song of the Sea' in Irish and we see her (as Ben's mother) teach Ben the lyrics. Later it is his memory of the song that he will draw on to save Saoirse. This set-up invokes classic signifiers of the Celtic Ireland of the Revivalists, most particularly in its citing of one of Yeats's best-known romantic poems. Not coincidentally, it was the ambition of the Celtic Revival of the late nineteenth and early twentieth centuries to free Ireland of the contaminating influences of the coloniser through the reimagining of old Irish folktales and legends. This is also evidently Moore's intention and he is not alone in deploying Ireland's folkloric tradition to create a new contemporary narrative. Eoin Colfer's Artemis Fowl stories (Colfer, 2002, etc.) are an obvious parallel, the distinction being that Colfer propels his Irish fairy world into a dystopian SF future that mingles magic spells and folkloric creatures with technological know-how and plots to destroy the world. Both Moore and Colfer render Ireland as a chronotope, where time and space intersect; the difference is that Colfer's central male hero (the eponymous Artemis Fowl) is a savvy tech aficionado, where Ben is bound by the rules of pre-modern Ireland. His only tech appliance is an already anachronistic Sony Walkman, which is deployed as a lead to bind the children or a lasso for rescue purposes, thus voiding it of its modern usage. *Song of the Sea* makes few concessions to modernity. Even Granny's car, a Citroen 2CV, seems more like a nod to the film's French and Belgian co-producers than a realistic driving option. Dublin is rendered as a quaint ensemble of classic buildings and it is no reflection on Dublin bus drivers to suggest that it is an unlikely plot device that the driver who picks up Ben and Saoirse as they flee the fairy den in the city centre is happy to take them non-stop to the lighthouse. (This is supposed to be on the Dingle Peninsular, though an image of the Donegal Gaelic Games flag hanging over Ben's bed contradicts the local southern accents to locate it in the North-West.) *The Song of the Sea* plays with time in other ways. Its illustrations recall an era of hand-painted cels. Yet the clarity of colour and movement the film achieves could only have been wrought through the computer animation process, which allows for an infinite layering of images and the inclusion of detail.

These vagaries of time and place do not diminish the visual impact of *Song of the Sea*, which like its predecessor is a celebration of 2D design. It was this virtuoso visual style that drew near-uniform plaudits from global critics, many of whom made comparisons with Hayao Miyazake's cinema, notably certain plot lines in *My Neighbour Totoro* (1988), and the visualisation of the witch Yubaba in *Spirited Away* (2001). Indeed, Moore (2012) cited *My Neighbour Totoro* as an inspiration in his blog; equally significant is his mention, in the same entry, of the influence of *Into the West* (Mike Newell, 1992) the popular Jim Sheridan-scripted family film about two young boys riding in search of freedom and the spirit of their mother to the West of Ireland. The latter film, like *Song of the Sea* blends Celtic mythology with the familiar generic trope of children who are misunderstood by adult society (Barton, 2002: 123–37).

Elsewhere, I have discussed *Into the West* as a heritage film, and *Song of the Sea* offers many correspondences to that earlier configuration of Irish cinematic output (Barton, 2004: 148–56). That is, it recycles archaic images of Irish identity, particular gender identity, and takes place in an Ireland associated with rural values and a gentle, community-oriented people. In particular, the figure of Saoirse (meaning 'freedom' in the Irish language), is a problematic rendering of young female childhood. She is both mute and dramatically disengaged, leaving the forward momentum of the adventure story entirely in the hands of the reluctant hero, Ben. Similarly, having Flanagan voice both the grandmother and the witch invites associative connections between both characters that leaves the depiction of the ageing Irish female far short of that of Granny O'Grimm.

To be fair to Moore, it was not his intention to create a nostalgic artefact, but to fashion a narrative that would reconnect young people to the natural world and to the Irish past. As he has said (in Thill, 2015): 'I felt it important to reinforce that losing folklore from our everyday life means losing connection to our environment and culture. In Ireland, during the Celtic Tiger years, we were losing touch so I wanted to speak about it.'

Conclusion

The new wave of Irish animation deserves more space than one chapter, and this discussion does not do justice to the variety of work being released by local studios, some now major producers with international partners. Space has prohibited, for instance, a discussion of the films of Andrew Kavanagh at Kavaleer: *An Evil Cradling* (1999), *The Milliner* (2002), *The Depository* (2003), or of Geronimo's *Ballybraden*, about a school hurling team: 'Like most teams they never win the championship. They get hammered in the first round every year. If this was a Disney show they'd win' (Gerard O'Rourke in Barter, 2013: 5). Contemporary Irish animation, like most national cinema productions, exists in the shadow of its infinitely better resourced Other; for Hollywood substitute Disney. Where it differs from other national animation practices is that it has few predecessors. This has meant inventing a national style, which for the features discussed here has meant returning to older traditions and narratives of Irish identity and remediating them in a way that is at once anachronistic but reliant on contemporary technologies. This practice has echoes in many of the short films which function as visual hallmarks of old-fashioned skills lost to the post-industrial age. Even making this argument about such a young industry brings its own caveats, most particularly that the only two Irish animation features to date are auteur works, driven by Moore's personal vision and the collective ambition of Cartoon Saloon. His and Twomey's experiences in the commercial animation market suggest, unfortunately, that few will be tempted to follow them if so few financial rewards are on offer.

Returning to Linda Hutcheon's distinctions (above) between nostalgia and irony, we can see many of the key short films deploying irony as an antidote to nostalgia's recreation of the 'past as imagined, as idealized through memory and desire'. If the drive to nostalgia is greater in *Song of the Sea* than *The Secret of Kells*, both recognise the pleasures that older modalities offer within modern culture, not just to that national culture but to others outside it. Certain elements within these films, such as use of the Irish language, visuals that carry specific associations of local places, references to older Irish narratives, and a team that loses, attempt to bind the nation as a viewing entity through common points of reference.

The difference between the short animations and the features is one of intended spectatorship. Cartoon Saloon's features imagine what Neupert (above) identifies as 'progressive European family audiences', but also includes their American and global counterparts. The short films, excepting *Angela's Christmas*, are aimed more generally at an adult audience, which sanctions, though does not necessarily guarantee, greater critical engagement. Defining Irish animation within a national cinema context is limited by what is still barely critical mass, and a feature 'industry' dominated by one producer. What binds the films under discussion here is their negotiation with the dominant industry, both forming part of it, yet insisting on remaining visually distinctive, and their struggle to create national content under conditions that overwhelmingly favour a globalised product.

Notes

1 These can be located on the Film Board's website at: www.irishfilmboard. ie/directory/3.

2 Nora Twomey's *The Breadwinner* (2017) does not have an Irish setting.

References

Anderson, B. R. 2006. *Imagined Communities: Reflections on the Origin and Spread of Nationalism,* London: Verso.

Barter, P. 2013. Making It Look Like Child's Play. *The Sunday Times Magazine,* 6 October, pp. 4–5.

Barton, R. 2002. *Jim Sheridan: Framing the Nation,* Dublin: Liffey Press.

Barton, R. 2004. *Irish National Cinema*, London and New York: Routledge.

Bluth, D. and Sibley, B. 1990. Don Bluth on his search for classical excellence. *Animator Mag,* 26, 24–5.

Bolter, D. J. and Grusin, R. 1999. *Remediation: Understanding New Media,* Cambridge, MA: MIT Press.

Box Office Mojo. n.d. *The Secret of Kells* [Online]. Available: www. boxofficemojo.com/movies/?id=secretofkells.htm [Accessed 14 July 2017].

Burke, L. 2009. Drawing Conclusions: Irish Animation and National Cinema. *Estudios Irlandeses,* 187–91.

Bushe, A. 1995. Redundant Animators Snapped Up by Booming US Studios: Irish Artists Can Earn Up to $2,000 a Week in Hollywood. *Irish Times,* 3 November, p. 20.

Cohen, K. 2010. 'The Secret of Kells' – What Is this Remarkable Animated Feature? *Animation World* [Online]. Available: www.awn.com/animationworld/secret-kells-what-remarkable-animated-feature [Accessed 7 July 2017].

Colfer, E. 2002. *Artemis Fowl,* London: Puffin.

Connolly, M. 2005. Theorizing Irish Animation: Heritage, Enterprise and Critical Practice. *In:* Hill, J. and Rockett, K. (eds.) *Film History and National Cinema.* Dublin: Four Courts Press.

Dawtrey, A. 1995. *Bluth's Toon Town to Close* [Online]. Available: http://variety.com/1995/film/features/bluth-s-toon-town-to-close-99129083/ [Accessed 8 July 2017].

Devane, M. 2012. Animation Nation. *Sunday Business Post,* 12 August, pp. n12–n13.

Flynn, R. and Brereton, P. 2007. *Historical Dictionary of Irish Cinema,* Lanham, MD: Plymouth, Scarecrow Press.

Garcia, C. 2010. A Q&A with "The Secret of Kells" Director Tomm Moore. *Blouinartinfo* [Online]. Available: www.blouinartinfo.com/news/story/34316/a-qa-with-the-secret-of-kells-director-tomm-moore [Accessed 7 July 2017].

Gillett, S. 2010. Sketching Success: Brown Bag Films go to the Oscars. *Estudios Irlandeses,* 5, 235–8.

Hutcheon, L. 1998. *Irony, Nostalgia, and the Postmodern* [Online]. Toronto: University of Toronto English Language (UTEL) Main Collection. Available: www.library.utoronto.ca/utel/criticism/hutchinp.html [Accessed 30 June 2017].

IMDb. n.d. *Song of the Sea* [Online]. Available www.imdb.com/title/tt1865505/?ref_=fn_al_tt_1 [Accessed 25 May 2017].

Kane, C. 2017. Cartoon Saloon Inks Deal With Canadian Firm to Create 140 Jobs. *Irish Independent,* 7 February, pp. 6–7.

Lyons, T. 2002. Drawing on Past Successes to Illustrate the Rise of the'Toon. *Irish Independent,* 28 November, p. 36.

Manovich, L. 2001. *The Language of New Media,* Cambridge, MA, MIT Press.

McCourt, F. 1996. *Angela's Ashes: A Memoir of a Childhood,* London: HarperCollins.

McGrath, B. 1986. £2.5m Expansion by Film Studio Will Create 260 New Jobs. *Irish Times,* 29 November, p. 6.

McLoone, M. 2000. *Irish Film: The Emergence of a Contemporary Cinema,* London: British Film Institute.

Moore, T. 2012. Holy Wells. *Song of the Sea* [Online]. Available from: http://songoftheseamovie.blogspot.ie/2012/09/holy-wells.html [Accessed 11 July 2017].

Moriarty, C. 3 October 2013. Pangur Bán. *Irish Archaeology* [Online]. Available from: http://irisharchaeology.ie/2013/10/pangur-ban/ [Accessed 7 July 2017].

Napier, S. J. 2005. *Anime from Akira to Howl's Moving Castle: Experiencing Contemporary Japanese Animation,* New York: Palgrave Macmillan.

Neupert, R. 2015. French Animated Cinema, 1990 to Present. *In:* Fox, A., Marie, M., Moine, R. and Radner, H. (eds.) *A Companion to Contemporary French Cinema.* Chichester, UK and Malden, MA: Wiley Blackwell.

Nic Congáil, R. 2009. "Some of you will curse her": Women's Writing During the Irish-Language Revival. *Proceedings of the Harvard Celtic Colloquium*, 29, 199–222.

O'Brien, M. 2009. Animated Journey to Success. *Sunday Business Post*, 26 April, p. 30.

O'Brien, M. 2011. *The Secret of Kells* (2009), a Film for a Post Celtic Tiger Ireland? *Animation Studies*, 6, 34–9.

Pallant, C. 2011. *Demystifying Disney: A History of Disney Feature Animation*, New York and London: Continuum.

Pumares, M. J., Simone, P., Kevin, D., Ene, L. and Milla, J. T. 2015. *Mapping the Animation Industry in Europe*, Strasbourg, European Audiovisual Conservatory.

Ramey, L. 2014. Immediacy, Hypermediacy, and New Media in *The Secret of Kells* (Moore, 2009). *Medieval Perspectives*, 29, 109–19.

Sexton, C. 2015. It's in the Bag as Illustrator Gaffney Wraps Up €40m Deal. *Sunday Business Post*, 23 August, p. 23.

Shortall, E. 2009. Irish Film Hopes for Oscar Glory. *Sunday Times*, 15 November, p. 2.

Thill, S. 2015. Tomm Moore on 'Song of the Sea,' Reinventing 2D, and Dodging the Studio System. *Cartoon Brew* [Online]. Available www.cartoonbrew.com/award-season-focus/tomm-moore-on-song-of-the-sea-reinventing-2d-and-dodging-the-studio-system-107389.html [Accessed 11 July 2017].

Walsh, T. 2008. *The In-betweeners: Irish Animation as a Postcolonial Discourse*. Doctor of Philosophy thesis, Loughborough University.

Walsh, T. 2011a. *The Secret of Kells*: Ireland's European Identity in Feature Animation. *In:* Huber, W. and Crosson, S. (eds.) *Contemporary Irish Film, New Perspectives on a National Cinema*. Vienna: Braumueller.

Walsh, T. 2011b. Animating Joyce: Tim Booth's *Ulys*. *Animation – An Interdisciplinary Journal*, 7, 83–99.

Wells, P. 2002. *Animation, Genre and Authorship*, London, Wallflower Press.

Woods, S. 2002. Irish Animation Retrospective. *In:* Fourteenth Galway Film Fleadh (ed.). Galway.

Short film
Foxes (Lorcan Finnegan, 2012)

Ellen (Marie Ruane) and James (Tom Vaughan-Lawlor) are one of the few couples to have moved into a new housing estate built in an out-of-the-way location. The rest of the properties lie vacant, a common sight in Ireland of the post-Crash era, and from which only one possible assumption, that they are in negative equity, can be drawn. Their marriage is evidently feeling the strain of their financial situation. Ellen, a photographer, loses her final client and thus her ties to the world of work and social integration. When James confronts Ellen with the fact that she must gain more work as one income isn't enough, her response is, 'The last time I listened to you we bought this house.' Instead, she is drawn to the trio of foxes who scavenge in their rubbish at night. She starts to photograph them obsessively, to chase after them at night; her appearance begins to take on a wild look. In the manner of *Cat People* (Jacques Tourneur, 1942), *Foxes* never quite explains its central female character's transformation. Is it just the projection of a protective husband, particularly since Ellen's first symptoms manifest themselves in a reinvigorated, snarling sexuality?

Foxes anticipates its director's, Lorcan Finnegan, turn towards eco-horror in his subsequent feature, *Without Name* (2016), by suggesting that Ellen's identification with the foxes is just as easily interpreted as guilt over the destruction of nature to build their unwanted estate. Either way, not long after James finds her sleeping during the day, and she turns on him, Ellen vanishes. James falls into the role of homemaker as well as provider, tidying up her studio and mowing the lawn before donning his work-badge and driving off to his unnamed commuter destination. These glimpses into life after the crash reflect common anxieties around social isolation, marital break-up and the upending of gender roles, which dovetail with the film's other concerns around the loss of the natural environment.

With its focus on middle-class professionals, *Foxes* is unusual in Irish filmmaking, as is its almost lethargic central male character, James. The casting of Tom Vaughan-Lawlor in the part carries particular resonances for viewers more familiar with his sadistic gangster, Nidge, in *Love/Hate* (RTÉ, 2010–14). In *Foxes*, James seems emotionally numbed, holding himself together through his work routine and only occasionally letting rip. Technically, *Foxes* is an accomplished production, with the final shot of the fox/Ellen almost convincing. In particular, the sound design, a mix of natural sounds, enhanced to create a howling, screeching noise in the place of music, adds to the privileging of atmosphere over visualisation. *Foxes* is very much a zeitgeist production, speaking to a particular set of middle-class anxieties around place and gender in the wake of the recession.

3

Ireland of the horrors

Until the late 1990s, no recognisable Irish horror cinema existed. Since then, it has become one of the most prolific genres of contemporary Irish filmmaking, and, in keeping with generic precedent, the one most likely to disturb the boundaries of self and Other, geography, gender and race. The selection of films discussed in this chapter range from conventional Gothic horror to exploitation cinema, to 'revenge of nature' horror, to high-school zombie-comedies and other parodies. There is even an Irish-language horror television film, *Na Cloigne* (Robert Quinn, 2010).[1] Irish horror pops up in films made in other territories, including an Irish banshee in the Australian independent production, *Damned by Dawn* (Brett Anstey, 2009) and the uncanny housekeeper Mrs Mills (Fionnula Flanagan) in *The Others* (*Los Otros*, Alejandro Amenábar, 2001). Of the indigenous productions, some trade on fears that arise out of specific local Irish incidents, whereas others take care to distance themselves, through setting and casting, from any identification with Ireland and Irish characters. Most fall somewhere in-between, positioning themselves both as Irish cinema and as globally recognisable product.

Gothic motifs and influences

The genre ostensibly began with the decision in 1995 by veteran low-budget exploitation director/producer, Roger Corman, to establish a production studio in Connemara, Concorde Anois Teo (Concorde Now Ltd.).[2] Corman had been attracted by a grant from *Údarás na Gaeltachta*, which is the body that was established to develop commercial activities in Irish-speaking areas, and the opportunities offered by the Section 35 (now Section 481) tax break scheme. Employees of Concorde Anois were expected to be able to speak Irish and the few US technicians on site were tasked with teaching the local Irish the requisite filmmaking skills to make a Corman picture. These were, at that point, very low budget, straight-to-video, action, SF, horror and exploitation films.[3]

Despite the local funding, few of the films had any Irish content. Two of the horror films, however, were set in Ireland: *House of the Damned*

(Scott Levy, 1996) and *Wolfhound* (Donovan Kelly, 2002). It is probably unfair to consider them as part of the new Irish horror cycle and, given their negligible storylines and the relish taken in displays of female nudity, they qualify more as late Corman than neophyte Irish. What prompts their inclusion here is, however, their invocation of Irish Gothic and folkloric tropes, and their themes of the return home. *House of the Damned* is a straightforward haunted house narrative about an Irish American family who return home to Ireland only to find that their inherited property has a blood-stained past that quickly manifests itself as domestic terror. The film suggests that the events may equally have been caused by the psychosexual imaginings of the wife, Maura (Alexandra Paul). This offers the production the opportunity to include several fantasy sequences where her husband, Will (Greg Evigan), has sex with the spiritualist's assistant, Amy (Mary Kate Ryan) and another when the spiritualist, Dr Edward Shea (Dick Donahue) has a sudden vision of a writhing naked woman being caressed by an amputated hand. *Wolfhound* follows a similar storyline, with returned emigrant, Colum Kennedy (Allen Scotti) finding himself obsessed with a shape-shifting wolfhound who takes on the form of a seductive female, Siobahn [*sic*] (played by 'Playmate of the Year 1995', Julie Cialini). This allows for extended sequences of SM sex between Colum and Siobahn. Meanwhile, Colum's wife, Stella (Jennifer Courtney), comes across her husband's raunchy drawings and is propositioned by the local self-styled alpha-male, Macroth (Brian Monahan). Tipped off by Siobahn that his family is in danger, Colum runs to the village and fights off Macroth, leaving the film to conclude ambiguously. Can Colum leave his past behind and return with Stella to Manhattan or will he always remain in thrall to the village of Wolfshead?

Corman's productions may be laughable, with special effects that would not have been out of place in the 1950s, but in common with *The Daisy Chain* (Aisling Walsh, 2008) and *Wake Wood* (David Keating, 2010), they invoke the Irish Gothic for narrative and aesthetic purposes. Thus, Father Seamus (Eamon Draper) in *House of the Damned* explains (correctly) that Irish Catholicism had its roots in superstitious practices that facilitate his understanding of the hauntings that are now disturbing the South family.

Given how embedded the Gothic is in Irish literature, particularly Anglo-Irish literature, and in cinema as a whole, it is not surprising that these productions borrow from its aesthetics and narrative formulae. In this, they follow Neil Jordan, who, in his writings and in his cinema, has returned over and again to Gothic themes. His horror films, however – *The Company of Wolves* (1984), *Interview with The Vampire* (1994), *In*

Dreams (1999), *Byzantium* (2012) – are not set in Ireland, and only reference the Irish Gothic tangentially, through incidental Irish characters or flashbacks to Irish settings (Pramaggiore, 2008; Zucker, 2008). His early spoof ghost story, *High Spirits* (1988), has an Irish castle setting, but its failure with critics and audiences was to steer him away from this kind of generic playfulness. Elsewhere (Barton, 2014), I have discussed the influence of the Irish Gothic tradition on the output of silent-era director, Rex Ingram. Although he made no films with identifiable Irish settings or characters, Ingram drew creatively on the conventions of the Anglo-Irish literary Gothic to people his cinema with ghosts and other supernatural beings. His characters lurk in shadowy cellars and strange moon-filled castles, threatened by madness and the horror of past transgressions.

The question that these horror films raise is to what purpose the Irish Gothic is evoked in their narratives and atmosphere. In addition to those mentioned above, *Boy Eats Girl* (Stephen Bradley, 2005) and *Isolation* (Billy O'Brien, 2005), in particular, intersperse Gothic visual motifs and narrative markers throughout their diegeses. Fred Botting and Justin D. Edwards remind us of the following (2013: 16): 'Modernity has always been dependent on the antitheses it invoked and suppressed, on the subjects it constructed and excluded through the demonisations of class, gender and racial difference.' Another aspect of modernity has been its subjugation of the colonised Other, which in the colonial and postcolonial imaginary has returned to haunt its oppressors:

> And a spectre is also conjured in the imagined origins of a 'pure' tradition killed off in the incursion of colonial forces. Though haunting can signal the return in spectral forms of cultures and pasts that have been pushed aside, those revenant pasts return often as sites of loss, nostalgia, guilt or betrayal. (Botting and Edwards, 2013: 17)

As this suggests, the horror genre provides a model for exploring Ireland's colonial inheritance and late modernisation, and the repressions inherent in those modalities. In this vein, Jarlath Killeen has noted (2014: 9) that 'Ireland as a whole is readily identifiable as a Gothic space in popular culture.' This is particularly applicable to contemporary cinema, where the country is understood as a spatial and temporal anomaly, or chronotope:

> Traditionally, horror and the Gothic take place in what has been called the 'outlandish': obscure, out-of-the-way places, usually in the countryside and in villages, or – where the Gothic locates itself in an urban environment – monstrosity emerges from under the stairs, from the attic, out of the cellar, spaces on the edge rather than at the centre. To English eyes, the Celtic fringes were such 'outlandish' spaces, Ireland particularly so given

the link between the geographical term 'outlandish' and the Catholicism dominant there. (Killeen, 2014: 9)

We might quibble with Killeen's understanding of the Gothic as being an exogenous/English mode; nevertheless, his spatialisation is useful. He (2014: 207) concludes his study of the genre/trope by suggesting that, in the post-Celtic Tiger years, it remains a vital medium for interrogating the present:

> The challenge for contemporary Irish Gothic is to move away from a now tired attack on the mid-twentieth century as a site of horror and repression, a view which suggests a contrast with the supposedly liberal and progressive Celtic Tiger of the new millennium, and to find a way to deal with the new realities through a Gothic story set firmly in the present.

Adopting the Gothic as a mode offers contemporary filmmakers the opportunity to draw connections between the Irish past and the present moment. Despite the lack of precedent for the genre, there is also the likelihood that a global audience that already links Ireland with folkloric and mythic traditions will recognise the country as a credible site of horror, as local audiences already do. One useful critical approach that binds together these temporal modalities is that of the eco-Gothic, or in more local terms, the Bog Gothic. In a key essay, Derek Gladwin (2014: 39–40) combines both concepts to argue that Gothic narratives set in the Irish boglands combine the eco-Gothic's understanding of nature and the environment as sites marked by 'fear and anxiety, as well as the sublime and the supernatural', with the Irish penchant for 'depicting bogs as untamed wastelands that resist incorporation into modernity and colonialism'. These combined ideas, of a despoiled nature and an old haunting, inform many of the films discussed in this chapter, linking them productively to contemporary worries around the loss of the natural environment and global eco-concerns.

The revenge of nature cycle

As I indicated in my opening paragraph, it is impossible to treat the contemporary Irish horror cycle as a whole. The productions that most obviously lend themselves to a local reading are the 'revenge of nature' or eco-horror films, notably *Isolation*. *Isolation* followed closely on Conor McMahon's 2004 rural horror, *Dead Meat*. Both films share a common set of references to the bovine spongiform encephalopathy (mad cow disease) scares of the late 1990s and their possible link to new variant Creutzfeldt-Jakob disease (vCJD), diagnosed in humans. On top of that, foot-and-mouth disease (FMD) arrived in Ireland in 2001, leading to the mass slaughter and burning of farm animals. As Radley (2013: 121) and Seán Crosson (2012: 65–83) have discussed, *Dead Meat* contains specific references to contemporary Irish politics, notably during a scene in which the hurling coach, Cathal Cheunt (Eoin Whelan) defends the survivors with his hurling stick and sliotar, ironically parroting the slogan of the then-government party, Fianna Fáil: 'A lot done. A lot more to do.'

Where McMahon's production bears all the hallmarks of non-professional filmmaking, O'Brien's is a visually confident production that reflects its director's background in art college and the work of notable Irish cinematographer, Robbie Ryan. Its influences are classic American SF/horror of the 1970s and 1980s, notably *Alien* (Ridley Scott, 1979) and *The Thing* (John Carpenter, 1982). These references are established from the outset when local vet, Orla (Essie Davis), reaches into the uterus of a calving cow only to withdraw her hand sharply after being bitten by something she has touched. This is the classic *vagina dentata* identified by Barbara Creed (1993) as crucial to the gendered horror of such films. The irruption of the mutant from the calf's carcass also recalls the birth scene in *Alien*, while the sequence where the monster runs amok in bloody havoc in the laboratory is a direct nod to the *mise-en-scène* of the remote science station in *The Thing*. The plot is appropriately rudimentary – a foreign scientist, John (Marcel Iures) has persuaded Irish farmer, Dan (John Lynch), to allow him to implant an experimental fetus into one of his herd. Lynch is in debt to the bank and forced to go along with the plan, even as it goes awry. The calf exhibits the signs of drastically accelerated reproductive capabilities and after dissection is found to have incubated six mutant exoskeletal fetuses. One escapes and the scientist discovers that it can reproduce through implanting itself in a human body. Thus, no one must leave the farm. This includes not only John, but a Traveller couple, Mary (Ruth Negga) and Jamie (Sean Harris), who have hidden on John's land in a bid to escape her family's disapproval of their relationship. The generic formula is further acknowledged by having Mary function as a 'final girl' (Clover, 1993), saving herself and destroying the mutant. In other ways, *Isolation* harks back to an earlier model of horror in that, other than in the sequences where the mutant materialises, it achieves its atmosphere through suggestion rather than exhibition. O'Brien and Ryan alternate between tight close-ups of the characters' faces that deny the bigger picture and the reverse shot that would reveal what they see, and a dreamy, exploratory camera that travels curiously around the half-obscured interiors of the farm and laboratory while still refusing to show the full space. The drip, drip of water, grunting and moaning of the cattle, and

Figure 5 Ruth Negga and John Lynch in *Isolation*

murky pools of slurry are contrasted with the high-tech laboratory with its cold, blue lights and gleaming chrome surfaces.

The effect of this fusion of global horror/SF signifiers is to place *Isolation* more in the global Gothic/techno-horror mode than the Catholic Gothic category. That is, the film does not ascribe its horror to Irish superstitious practices, or locate its horror's origins in the Irish past. This is a horror of the present. At the same time, specific Irish narrative tropes (the financially distressed farmer living on his own, the Travellers, the burning cattle carcasses, the quarantined farm) all lend the film a local recognition factor and push it towards a reading as EcoGothic. The low angles serve to make the space strange, and the conventional vistas of the Irish landscape are denied in favour of tight close-ups and artfully staged sequences where the darkness is broken only by outdoor lamps that pick out farming equipment in triangular downlighting. Dan lives on his own, it is suggested, because of a failed relationship with Orla. The unremarkable interior of his house is cluttered, and, as the condensation from John's breath suggests, inadequately heated. No more than Jamie's van, it is a male space, an inversion of the conventional associations of the feminine with the domestic. There are further suggestions that Dan is in some way emasculated causing him to flinch and look away when Orla shoots the infected calf.

When the horror strikes, the once-whole images of the establishing sequences become fragmented. The Gothic darkness increasingly absorbs and overwhelms the farming and laboratory equipment as the action moves from the farmhouse and the caravan into these other spaces. The symbol of biotechnology, the ultrasound scanner, fails not once but twice to detect the monster, and when it comes to delivering the calf, Dan has to deploy a pulley that clanks and grinds like a medieval rack. The effect of this fragmentation is to lose sight of the pastoral, the traditional and the domestic as if they had simply been eradicated.

Irish horror: race and reproduction

The common thread that runs through these Irish horror films is fear of reproduction. It is, of course, the thread that binds it to global horror, which has traditionally derived its grand guignol effect from the visualisation of the female reproductive organs and childbirth as uncanny and abject. What is particularly interesting in the Irish context, is that two of the films bracketed under the Irish horror category foreground mixed-race female heroes, or 'final girls'.[4] Thus, Ruth Negga in *Isolation* is joined by Samantha Mumba in *Boy Eats Girl*. The latter is a fusion of the high-school teen romcom with the zombie attack movie (rom-zom-com) and concerns a group of middle-class Dublin school-goers, one of whom, Nathan (David Leon) is saved from accidental suicide by his mother, Grace (Deirdre O'Kane), thanks to a voodoo ritual that she discovered in the local church vault. The consequence is to turn Nathan and much of the school, parents and teachers into zombies. The situation can only be rescued by the young woman Nathan fancies, Jessica (Mumba), in combination with Grace and Nathan's geeky/virginal friends, Diggs (Tadgh Murphy) and Henry (Laurence Kinlan) and with some belated adjustments to the pagan ritual by Grace.

The casting of Negga and Mumba as the pure-of-heart heroes who face down the monster was an interesting decision. Irish-Ethiopian Negga had not yet achieved global recognition for her Academy Award-nominated role in *Loving* but was familiar to Irish audiences for a plethora of film and television roles, often playing non-Irish parts. Mumba is Zambian Irish and has moved between a career in pop music and acting. Neither Negga nor Mumba is a recent immigrant and by virtue of being mixed-race could arguably be considered less Other than, say, a black immigrant actor. This has implications for how the films are read if we take on board Kinitra Brooks's (2014: 467) point that the 'strong black woman' is a byword for monstrosity. Her discussion of the characters of Michonne in Robert Kirkman's ongoing comic series *The Walking Dead* (2003–) and Selena in *28 Days Later* (Danny Boyle, 2002) considers the extent to which both texts subvert and complicate this stereotype by positioning these 'strong black

Figure 6 David Leon and Samantha Mumba in *Boy Eats Girl*

woman' characters as identificatory figures. Mary and Jessica are also identificatory figures but in a less radical way, not least because of their mixed-race identities.

Both films are ostensibly colour-blind in the sense that no plot points or narrative strands involving these characters are presented as having been inflected by their racial identification. A white actor could have occupied either role without any alteration to how the story played out. Mary and Jessica are 'as-if'/'but not' white. Colour-blindness as a narrative and aesthetic strategy is problematic for critics in so far as against-the-grain analyses that read colour back into such texts are potentially regressive. At the same time, colour-blindness negates the persistence of race-based inequality in Irish and other Western societies. Zélie Asava's (2013: 88) analysis of both films reads race back into them, as she argues that 'these actresses and their protagonists represent Irish identity, but also symbolize foreign corruption and invasion – particularly in the case of pregnant [as she is at the film's ending] Mary in *Isolation*'. However, she (2013: 86) also acknowledges the availability of progressive readings of both films, particularly in their repositioning of 'the mixed race female as heroine rather than "tragic mulatta"'.

As far as intentionality is concerned, the casting of Mumba in *Boy Eats Girl* is in keeping with its aspirations to identify with new models of

Irishness. In a classroom exchange, schoolteacher Craig (Denis Conway) initiates the following discussion:

Craig: Samson, who are you?
Samson (Mark Huberman): Irish
Craig: Irish, OK. So you identify yourself by your nationality. Now what does being Irish mean to you?
[Samson looks confused]
Craig: Anyone else? Yes, Bernard?
Bernard (Domnhall Gleeson): Myths and legends. Scholars and writers. Joyce, Beckett and Yeats.
[The classroom sniggers]
Craig: Mr Digges, how does being Irish make you feel?
Digges: Suicidal.

It is hard to imagine an equivalent American film pausing the action to deliberate on issues of national identity. *Boy Eats Girl* seems to do so for two reasons, the first to demarcate the Irish literary tradition as passé, the second to suggest that for a younger generation assumptions of what constitutes Irishness have radically altered. This now paves the way for the film to embrace a new model of addressing national identity (the zombie film) and new ways of being Irish (survivors, not victims; suburban; mixed race; middle class; secular).

Having a non-white central character from a wealthy suburban background allows *Boy Eats Girl* to follow through on its ambitions succinctly. Mumba makes the film look more global and less traditionally Irish. Yet below its apparently colour-blind surface (no one references Jessica's mixed-race identity), the film's Gothic conventions hint at other racial motifs that lend it the historical, culturally specific depth it seems at pains to deny. The Pandora's Box that Grace opens at the film's beginning is an old book that she stumbles across when carrying out restoration work on a church. The film travels swiftly from the stained-glass windows, pausing only to emphasise the positioning of the serpent entwined in the artwork, to the vault where an ancient text is stored. Opening its pages, Grace comes across a section entitled 'La Réanimation'. As she pauses on it, the priest, Fr Cornelius (Lalor Roddy) suddenly looms up behind her, warning her fiercely against entering this space: 'The resting place of the missionaries who have strayed from the path. To disturb them is to rouse their blackened hearts.'

Grace will soon deploy that magic to re-animate her son Nathan and thus, as references to the serpent in the Garden of Eden support, confirm woman as both the giver of life and the mediator of evil. But she does not create this evil; that is the responsibility of the Irish Catholic Church's missionaries. They in turn, did not formulate the incantations that will reanimate Nathan, they learned them from the native peoples, whom they were supposed to convert. The disruption of the natural order that drives *Boy Eats Girl* is thus located far back in Ireland's Catholic history. Its origins lie in blackness and the white man's tampering ways, and hint at one of the least explored aspects of the Irish orders – what exactly did white Irish missionaries get up to in African and Caribbean countries? Once disturbed, the evil can only be righted by two of the least empowered representatives of Irish society, a middle-aged mother and a young woman of unnamed black origins.

The intersection between mutant reproduction and fear of blackness may be implicit in *Boy Eats Girl*, but it coalesces more explicitly, albeit in a highly confused manner in *Isolation*. As Asava reminds us (2013: 3) and as we saw in the Introduction, the referendum of 2004 (the year before the release of *Isolation*) concluded with the Irish people voting to revoke the right of all children born on the island of Ireland to automatic entitlement to Irish citizenship. The amendment followed an overwrought public narrative of black women travelling to Ireland in the last stages of pregnancy in order to give birth to children who would be Irish.

Although one may guess that the public discourse around black pregnant women infiltrating the body politic informed *Isolation*, its confusion arises out of the positioning of Ruth Negga's character as – possibly – a Traveller. When Dan encounters Jamie and Mary, the latter explains to him that she comes from a big family. 'How does it go with the Traveller boy? Do they like him? Are you popular with his crowd?' Dan asks her in turn.

This doesn't actually establish her as a Traveller; in fact, it suggests otherwise. Later, however, when the guard (policeman) visits the farm, he explicitly refers to Mary as a Traveller. If she is supposed to be a Traveller, then the casting of Negga is inexplicable. While it is not out of the question that a Traveller woman be mixed-race, it is highly unlikely. Even if Mary's family is from the settled community, her casting remains problematic. For someone who, in an Irish context, is visibly marked as Other, to be in a relationship with a member of an ethnic grouping that is consistently defined as Other, is at best overdetermined. An early, brief sequence hints at an essentialist positioning of her character. Coming into the byre just after the cow has given birth, Mary looks at, then kneels and touches the animal who is lying exhausted on the ground. Not only is it evident that it she is not named Mary by chance, her empathy for the cow suggests a maternal bond, which the film will come

76

good on at its conclusion, as both will have incubated a monster. This doesn't make Mary a monster, but hints that her natural (animalistic) maternal instincts render her vulnerable to mutant reproduction.

The mutant's bloody pursuit of the humans, particularly a human vessel to appropriate as a host for the procreation of further mutants, proceeds in a predictable manner. One by one the secondary characters meet their doom, including Jamie, although not before he has been attacked. This leaves Mary, as the 'final girl' to dispatch the monster and save the human race. A coda to the action sees her, in a nod to the necessity for pregnant Irish women to travel to Britain to obtain an abortion, in an English hospital undergoing an ultrasound. As the radiologist declares the fetus to be normal, an abrupt close-up to the screen hints strongly that this is far from the case.

The ending raises the question, why did Mary have to be mixed-race? Asava (2013: 99) argues as follows:

> As fantastical stories, *Boy Eats Girl* and *Isolation* allow for the dominant social politic to be decentred, and for marginalized voices to be heard. Their framing of mixed-race women alongside zombies and monsters is representative of the fear of mixing, which Mary and Jessica attempt to overcome.

While both films' policy of colour-blindness suggests a utopian vision of Irish society, it remains difficult to ignore the implications of their casting mixed-race women as the female leads. In *Isolation* in particular, a lurking and particularly insidious essentialism seems to inform the suggestion that Mary may be a Traveller. Certainly, if she and Jamie had successfully escaped, she would have become a Traveller, as if all Others are the same. Foregrounding strong, central female characters and casting Irish female actors is commendable, particularly given the conspicuous failure of much contemporary Irish cinema in this regard. Yet, one way or another, both films' marginalised subjects become the bearers of a horror that is strongly linked to motherhood, coupling and reproduction. In both films, the uncanny and the abject are coded female. The conclusion of *Boy Eats Girl* affirms the triumph of the feminine over the monstrous, while *Isolation* hints at the alternative as its outcome. At the same time, *Boy Eats Girl*'s positioning of Mumba's Jessica as economically privileged empowers her in a manner denied Negga's Mary. Furthermore, Jessica, unlike Mary, remains virginal at the film's end, which could be read as rewarding chastity (and the containment of her blackness) over Mary's sexual activity. Thus, if the mixed-race female is to thrive in Irish society (and Irish cinema), we might extrapolate, it helps if she is middle class and chaste.

Irish horror – whose home?

In an early sequence in *The Daisy Chain*, Martha (Samantha Morton) walks into the bedroom of her new home in Ireland, the house in which her husband, Tomas Conroy (Steven Mackintosh) grew up. She is pregnant, and the film soon reveals that their first child died a cot death in England. In the room, a crucifix is hanging over the bed. Martha lifts it off and disposes of it, leaving behind its trace on the wallpaper. Once ridded of the iconography of Catholicism, the Irish home, the film seems to suggest, can function as a healing space for the English woman. The small local village (with an inexplicably modern swimming pool and hospital) is already home to many young women and children, further associating the Irish home space with maternal plenitude. Indeed, the film's opening echoes numerous Sunday newspaper profiles of young urban couples 'getting away from it all' to raise their families in the West.

As it was in *House of the Damned* and *Wolfhound* the motif of the return home that drives the tourist films is soon rendered horrific. Indeed, at the moment in which Colum announces to Stella, in the latter film, 'This is what it's all about, hun. Clean air, normal people, simple needs', we know that their sojourn is doomed. This re-envisioning of the comforting image of Irish domesticity recalls Freud's (2003: 124) classic analysis of the uncanny as 'the class of the frightening which leads back to what is known of old and long familiar.' 'Heimlich' and its opposite, 'unheimlich', describe the unease at the heart of that familiar space, the home, and the fear that something uncanny lurks there. Or, as Elisabeth Bronfen (2004: 23) argues in her study of the use of the home in Hollywood cinema: 'Because it compels the subject to recognize that he or she never was and never will fully be master of his or her own house, the uncanny emerges as the privileged trope for psychic dislocation.' Freud, further, saw the uncanny as a relic of primitive fears lurking in human consciousness, and this idea is echoed in many of the Irish horrors. *The Daisy Chain* is just one example, hinging as it does on folkloric fears of the changeling. The orphaned child, Daisy (Mhairi Anderson), attaches herself to the young couple, but, as the villagers sense, there is something uncanny about her and her provenance. Unfortunately, the film's ethical positioning is highly compromised as Daisy is apparently autistic, which renders her characterisation as the monstrous child nothing less than offensive.[5]

That this is an 'outlandish' space, riddled with superstition, is left to Tomas to explain to Martha: 'It's a small place. Things don't change. People really believe that stuff.' Later, after a string of fatal accidents and unexplained events apparently caused by Daisy, the local doctor (Ron

Donachie) reassures Martha, 'It's not your fault, love.' 'I know,' Martha replies, 'It's this place.'

Martha is English and thus positioned as the rational Other to the superstitious locals, particularly their elderly male neighbour who chases Daisy away whenever he sees her and, towards the end of the film, tries to burn her (to release the baby for whom the fairies substituted her). The signifiers and spaces of Catholicism – the crucifix, a wayside memorial, the Church that Daisy won't enter – are layered over an almost hysterical paganism. These moments, combined with shots of ominously crashing waves and dark skies, suggest that the West is not just 'outlandish', it is *unheimlich*.

Over and again, these films position Ireland as an uncanny space. It is implicit in the Corman productions, and continues through this film to others such as *Wake Wood*, in which a couple, Patrick (Aidan Gillen) and Louise (Eva Birthistle), who have lost their only daughter Alice (Ella Connolly), relocate from the city (where Alice was mauled to death by a dog) to the countryside, in an attempt to move on from their loss. Neither the city space (of elegant Georgian buildings) nor the rural space is identified. *Wake Wood* was largely shot on the border between Pettigo in the Republic and Fermanagh in Northern Ireland (where the rebirthing rituals that will form the central horror narrative of the film take place). In keeping with the plot requirements of such horrors, Patrick and Louise may not trespass beyond the borders of this uncanny space or Alice will die again. Like *The Canal* (Ivan Kavanagh, 2014 (discussed below)), *Wake Wood* is both identifiably Irish and not-Irish. Gillen has a career history of moving between playing non-Irish and Irish parts and is now a recognisable global star. The production was intended as a revitalisation of the Hammer Horror label, and its plot points, combined with the casting of Timothy Spall as an English-sounding landlord, draw on the English folkloric tradition of witchcraft and magic incantations more than on the conventions of the Irish/Catholic Gothic. At the same time, Patrick, Louise and many of the secondary characters are identifiably Irish and it is likely that audiences assumed that the film was Irish-set. It is thus not just a film that is diegetically concerned with boundaries (between life and death, between the uncanny space and the normative, between the urban and the rural, between the Irish Gothic and the English folkloric), but one whose own production history is defined by border-crossing.

Irish horror and global horror

The films discussed in this chapter number, alongside Irish animation, amongst the most globalised of Irish productions. Works such as the

Corman films, *Wake Wood* and *The Canal* position themselves deliberately as global generic product. They may be set in Ireland (and even this is not always a certainty), but their aesthetics and narratives belong to an international circuit of horror releases. Just how productive this is varies from film to film. Very certainly, the globalising tendencies of *Boy Eats Girl* allow it to foreground female and non-dominant racial identities. Even that, a key feature of the genre, is no guarantee of a progressive outcome. The tensions between conservatism and modernising alluded to by Christine Gledhill (and referenced in the introduction) remain constantly in play, no more so than in Paddy Breathnach's *Shrooms*. The story of a group of college students who travel to Ireland to trip on magic mushrooms, Breathnach's film is visually indebted to Asian horror and narratively to the American scream queen tradition. Neither could rescue a production that became one of the most critically derided films of the era.[6] Certainly, its vision of the Irish (as *Deliverance*-style (John Boorman, 1972) hillbillies) or its depiction of its central female characters (axe-wielding hysterics), did little to suggest that the introduction of exogenous influences could usefully revivify local traditions of representation. More than anything, *Shrooms* illustrates the point that simply referencing local characters and events does not endow a film with substance. Part of its confused and scattergun attempt to blend the local and the global was a storyline built around two threatening older men, who lurk in the woods and turn out to be former inhabitants of a religious institution. Kathleen Vejvoda (2015: 49) argues convincingly that 'From an ethical standpoint, the representation of abuse survivors as monstrous and doomed is deeply troubling, especially given the wide distribution and popularity of horror films.' This is the dilemma that faces the local horror film as it treads that fine line between reflecting (on) and exploiting specific social issues.

That more can be achieved than *Shrooms* proved capable of is borne out by the recent spate of Spanish horror films such as *El Espinazo del Diablo/The Devil's Backbone* (Guillermo del Toro, 2001) and *El Orfanato/The Orphanage* (J. A. Bayona, 2007). These films are routinely analysed as commentaries on the traumatic past of Fascism and the Civil War (Delgado, 2008; Lazaro-Reboll, 2012). This extends to Alejandro Amenábar's *Los Otros*, which, although ostensibly stateless like *The Canal*, can convincingly be read as an allegorical commentary on the 'Pact of Forgetting' (el pacto del olvido) that became official state policy following the death of Franco in 1975 (Acevedo-Muñoz, 1998: 203–18). Similarly, Japanese and Korean horror cinemas offer themselves to social and historical interpretations that have not impeded their successful distribution to overseas territories whose audiences are unlikely to interest themselves in uncovering the same meanings (Shin, 2009: 85–100).

Shrooms would have probably received less critical attention were it not for the fact that its director is a respected figure within the Irish industry. Breathnach has made a career out of adapting local narratives to global genres, starting with the art film *Ailsa* (1994) and continuing through *I Went Down* and the crime caper *Man About Dog* (2004). His Cuban-set *Viva*, as we have seen, earned global critical success. Perhaps *Shrooms* was, like *I Went Down*, 'too national', but it seems more that it was neither national enough nor global enough to find an audience (the film performed dismally on international release and a glance at the comments on the IMDb illustrates just how badly it played with horror aficionados).

It is tempting to believe that when Ivan Kavanagh turned to making *The Canal*, he bore Breathnach's experience in mind. *The Canal* is one of the most globalised of the recent Irish horrors and watching it is a disorienting experience in more ways than one. On the surface, this is a conventional horror film, opening with a young couple purchasing an old house that turns out to be haunted by the perpetrator and victims of a gruesome murder that took place there in the early twentieth century. The husband, David (Rupert Evans), is a cinema archivist. His wife Alice (Hannah Hoekstra) has an unspecified but apparently glamorous occupation and, unbeknownst to David and their child, Billy (Calum Heath), a lover, Alex (Carl Shaaban). David begins to suspect that all is not as it seems and follows his wife one night. He witnesses her making love to Alex and shortly afterwards she disappears. Her body is found in the canal that links their house with Alex's place and apparently also with the city location where they work. The detective, McNamara (Steve Oram) informs David that he will be the police's main suspect. By the end of the film, as David becomes increasingly unhinged by visions of the Victorian murderers that he believes he has captured on old film stock, the audience is left to decide whether to believe his version of the murder or that of the law.

The themes and narrative structure of *The Canal* render it internationally legible. Although Kavanagh has spoken in interview of the influence of Ingmar Bergman on his work, and this is certainly detectable in his previous film, *The Fading Light* (2009), this film is clearly indebted to the Japanese Gothic horror cycle, especially *Ringu/The Ring* (Hideo Nakata, 1998). The poster for the film, an image of a ghostly female figure rising out of the water with her back to the camera and long dark hair tumbling down her bridal gown, firmly positions Kavanagh's film within the Japanese tradition, extending back to the classic *Kwaidan* (Masaki Kobayashi, 1964). In one sequence, David tries to persuade his colleague in the archive, Claire (Antonia Campbell-Hughes) that he has captured a ghostly woman, whom he spotted on the far side of the canal, on his old movie camera. Claire is at first disbelieving, assuring David that she sees nothing. Then, slowly the ghost appears on the screen, gliding upwards from the canal bank and, as Claire begins to take in what she is witnessing, the apparition, in a direct nod to *Ringu*, breaks the boundaries of the screen, irrupting into the room where they are viewing David's footage. Other sequences featuring ghostly children suggest the influence of the contemporary Spanish horror cycle, particularly *The Devil's Backbone* and *The Orphanage,* while the filmic referencing recalls the plot of Alejandro Amenábar's *Tesis/Thesis* (1996), which is a horror film partly set in a film school. In this, *The Canal* shares much with *Shrooms*, although it is a more assured and coherent production than the latter.

An accomplished soundtrack that blends sophisticated digital effects with an eerie score by Ceiri Torjussen heightens the film's tension, but it is the refusal of the specifics of place and identity that is, from a local perspective, truly disorienting. *The Canal* is a Welsh/Irish/Dutch co-production with financing coming from the Irish Film Board, Film Agency Wales, Section 481, the Welsh production funding company, Gennaker Ltd, and the Benelux production company, A-film. This presumably accounts for the casting of Dutch actors, Hannah Hoekstra and Anneke Blok (as Alice's mother, Marie). Just what influence the Welsh involvement bought is harder to determine. Critics routinely referred to *The Canal* as Irish and most identified its setting, if they did, as Dublin. As a branding device, neither its national identity nor its location seemed to have been worthy of further comment, with reviewers focusing on its value as a genre offering. As his last two films had received almost no distribution, Kavanagh was pretty much unknown, meaning that *The Canal* was also not discussed as an auteur work.

Although *The Canal* marks a departure from Kavangh's previous low- to no-budget works, it does in fact bear authorial traces. The sophisticated soundtrack is one, the complex visual set-ups and use of multiple camera angles, another. In an early sequence in the film archive, a poster for the director's *The Fading Light* hangs on a wall, inviting connections that only an informed fan of Kavanagh's cinema will make. Even the multiple allusions to other films (which are discussed above and further expanded in interviews and reviews) function not just as cinephiliac gameplay, but locate the director within an inner circle of auteurs. The cinephiliac inheritance is reinforced with Kavanagh's much publicised decision to shoot the fake early cinema newsreel with a real camera dating from 1915. The result is an uneasy commingling of low-budget art film and global entertainment form. In particular it is hard to escape the feeling that the actors were not quite in tune with Kavanagh's arthouse sensibilities. Their performances, particularly the lead's, are those of generic, mainstream cinema, to the point that they often seem overwhelmed by the film's complex visual *mise-en-scène*.

Kavanagh (in Hennessy, 2015) has explained his casting and location decisions thus: 'I wanted an international cast as I didn't want the film to be grounded in any one country to keep the dream construct attached. If it's set in Ireland it's not an Ireland people would be accustomed to, it could be in London.' Dublin features include the 'film archive' where David and Claire work. The building is in fact that of the easily identified National Archives of Ireland, with its red-and-black banners advertising the institution's name in English and Irish, rather than the home of the Irish Film Archive, which is at the Irish Film Institute. The eponymous canal that links David's period home and the modern apartment building where Alex and Alice make love looks familiar from Dublin's network of canals but the location of the two houses and their apparent proximity to the city centre make no topographical sense. They are not so much non-places as 'any places'. As Kavanagh notes, it could as easily be London. The police who comb the canal area for Alice's body bear the words 'police' on their blue uniforms, instead of the Irish 'garda'. The child actor, Calum Heath, is a redhead with a Dublin accent, and his childminder, Sophie, is played by Kelly Byrne, and is also identifiably Irish. Why an Englishman with a foreign wife should have an Irish child remains unanswered by the film's narrative and unquestioned by its critics. None of the local reviews queries these details.

Earlier Kavanagh films, notably *Tin Can Man* (2007) and *The Fading Light,* were quite different in this regard. The latter is, as mentioned above, the film most indebted to Bergman but also the contemporary European arthouse tradition. A minimalist narrative, with an almost unbearable realism, it follows the death of the mother of three adult children, one of whom, her son, has special needs. Although set in a nondescript suburban home, the Irishness of the siblings is never in doubt nor is the Irish location. On top of this, perhaps not coincidentally, their strong sense of kinship is fatally disrupted by the one English character who, in effect, sets in motion the destruction of the family. *Tin Can Man* is another horror film, although in this case its influences are clearly early David Lynch and specifically *Eraserhead* (1977). Shot with Kavanagh's characteristic skewed angles, visceral soundtrack and black-and-white imagery, the film describes the surreal encounter between an English stranger and a young Dublin man and what transpires when the stranger encourages the Dubliner to take his downtrodden life into his own hands.

How important was this 'any place', non-identifiable setting to *The Canal's* dream construct? In truth, the oneiric effect could have been as easily achieved by other techniques. It seems more that it was the associations that came with an identifiable Dublin, or even Irish, location that would have worked against the film's aesthetic ambitions. The Irishness that films such as the Corman productions or *The Daisy Chain* invoke to lend their narratives a recognition factor is that of folklore and myth and belongs to the idiom of the rural past. It was these very specific national identifiers that Kavanagh seems to have been so keen to avoid. Dublin thus had to become an 'any place' global city.

One immediate payoff for Kavanagh and the production team was that *The Canal* became the first of the Irish horror films to be acquired by Netflix (US). It was picked up for distribution in the UK, the United States, Australia and New Zealand, Germany, Austria, France, Switzerland, the Benelux countries, Scandinavia, Taiwan, South Korea, Singapore, Malaysia and the Middle East. While it is reductive to divide films into categories of global versus transnational, Kavanagh's refusal of geographic and cultural specificity places *The Canal* very firmly in the former category.

Conclusion: the instabilities of place

In her essay on the Irish horror film, Radley (2013: 117) argues that the genre has transformed Irish cinema as a material form and as a critical category: 'the dialectic that is established in Irish horror films between a disruptive, semiotic generic sensibility and an established, symbolic national sensibility works to deconstruct and rearticulate the post-colonial bias in the discourse of Irish national cinema'. Radley further posits (2013: 123) that these films reflect a 'crisis in/of the representable in the wake of the more general transformation in the landscape of Irish subjectivity post-Celtic Tiger'. Central to her argument is the notion that such films constitute the abject of the national cinematic project and thus facilitate the emergence into that project of characters and topics for whom hitherto there was no representational space.

This sense of discomfort around the genre as a whole and its positioning within the traditions and evolution of Irish cinema are very interesting. One could as easily ask whether deploying a genre with underlying conservative tendencies to address the new social formations of the Celtic Tiger era and its aftermath offers any real opportunity for change. To echo concerns raised elsewhere in this book, is representation in itself enough? As we have seen with Negga's casting as a mixed-race/Traveller woman (possibly) in *Isolation,* or the depiction of the autistic child in

The Daisy Chain as monstrous, or the foregrounding of hysterical killer women and monstrous victims of institutional abuse in *Shrooms*, new modes of representation are in themselves not always progressive. The horror film is often even guiltier than other genres of reinforcing rather than questioning Otherness.

At the same time, these films radically disrupt other representational conventions, notably of Ireland as a recuperative space (Negra, 2007: 143). The journey to Ireland, or from the Irish city to the Irish countryside, no longer facilitates psychic healing (as it does in the tourist films) or the return to a safe past, but instead becomes a voyage into terror and death. Through their constant recourse to fragmentary images, half-seen spaces, and unrecognisable locales, these films refuse to imagine Ireland as a defined territory. Its boundaries are always subject to rupture, as are the boundaries between the human and non-human, the spiritual and the pagan. As Morash and Richards (2013: 121) observed of the contemporary Irish stage, 'nothing is familiar … all is terrifying', so the chaos that other and older cinematic narrative forms managed to contain now erupts onto the screen.

Killeen's challenge to Irish cinema to 'find a way to deal with the new realities through a Gothic story set firmly in the present' (2014: 207) has been answered not so much by one discrete film, but by fragments of many. Formally, these works are less concerned to acknowledge the inheritance of the Irish Gothic than to incorporate elements of global Gothic, including eco-Gothic, into Irish (or somewhat Irish) narratives and settings. Their address is more commonly oriented outwards to consumers of Asian or Spanish horror than backwards to the Anglo-Irish writerly tradition. At the same time, they readily deploy familiar figures – shapeshifters, revenants, werewolves, monks and changelings – from Irish myth and legend that serve to locate these films within Irish narrative traditions and to mark them with a measure of cultural distinctiveness. To this they add new emblematic figures, many of which are oriented around reproductive horror, such as the mutant cow and the suburban zombie. Yet others, as we have seen, trade on the interchangeability of the globalised Irish urban space to create works that could take place in any territory or location.

This instability of space reflects its resistance to being appropriated as place. Morash and Richards draw their analysis of Irish theatrical space from Yi-Fu Tuan's (1977: 6) argument that 'From the security of and stability of place we are aware of the openness, freedom, and threat of space, and vice-versa.' Yet in the horror film, the binaries of openness and freedom versus threat (and chaos) no longer hold. Nor does that most traditional of safe places, the domestic, offer sanctuary. At the same time, the films find themselves struggling to create a sense of place for another reason. Despite its Gothic literary tradition, and the recent spate of releases, Ireland remains a void within horror cinema, with few points of recognition, even now, for audiences.

One response to this generic vacancy is to foreground the incongruity of Ireland as a horror film location. This is the strategy of the final film of this chapter, *Grabbers* (Jon Wright, 2012). Another co-production (between the UK and Ireland), *Grabbers* has acquired cult status for its successful deployment of comedy, encouraging its audience to enjoy the premise that the inhabitants of a remote Irish island would find themselves the victims of the eponymous, gloopy, bloodsucking monsters who have fallen onto the shoreline from the sky. Its characters are an alcoholic guard, Ciarán O'Shea (Richard Coyle) and his overly conscientious rookie partner, Lisa Nolan (Ruth Bradley), the town drunk, Paddy (Lalor Roddy), the dedicated scientist, Dr Smith (Russell Tovey) and the local pub landlady, Una Maher (Bronagh Gallagher). As these cursory descriptions suggest, the islanders might have sprung from the pages of any British-Irish comedy, *Oh Mr Porter!* (Marcel Varnel, 1937), for instance, or the Ealing community-comedies, particularly *Whisky Galore!* (Alexander Mackendrick, 1949). In this tradition, *Grabbers* mocks the workings of official authority, while resolving its central crisis through celebration of the Celtic fringe's Otherness – here, consumption of alcohol in excessive quantities repels the monsters. Its play with recognisable Irish character types locates it further within the comic tradition of *The Guard*, while the incongruity of alien forms landing on a remote island such as this recognises the continuing low profile of the Irish horror genre. Global audiences might have been less attuned to the wavering accent of Sheffield-born Coyle than local filmgoers, but otherwise, unlike *The Canal*, *Grabbers* is very much rooted in an Irish space, and dependent on that for its comic effect.

There is no one workable summary of Irish horror cinema. As this chapter has demonstrated, this burgeoning genre is, alongside Irish animation, the most unbounded of Irish production categories. Again, in common with Irish animation, although for different reasons, this is in most cases a deliberate strategy. The films draw on, only to problematise, local representational traditions. This dilution of the local, in some but not all of the films, comes at the expense of any sustained engagement with the specificities of identity politics, never mind national politics. Yet, identity politics seep into their narratives, if more at a referential level than as a critique. So, too, do concerns around ecology and tampering with nature. Equally, while the films may reference the Irish Gothic tradition, they do so in passing, rather than as a way of lending their narratives historical depth. Overall, as a category, they are more interested in placing themselves in the global Gothic tradition, alternating between referencing classic Hollywood horror and Asian horror. Taken together, one has a sense of a genre that is fired by an energy and iconoclasm that are often absent from other Irish productions. At the same time, they are more conservative in their social outlook than they seem at first glance, and what appears to be a rethinking of conventional gendering often ends up as predictably normative. Even as I write, more are being made and released, and there is a sense with these films of a genre in the making, with an as yet undetermined ending.

Notes

1 For more on this, see Crosson (2011).

2 Setting a date on the beginnings of the cycle is confused by definitions. For instance, Crosson (2011) argues that it begins with *The Eliminator* (Enda Hughes, 1996) or possibly *Zombie Genocide* (Andrew Harrison, 1993).

3 For more on Concorde Anois, see Fennell (1997) and Linehan (1997). Corman was also the producer of *Dementia 13* (Francis Ford Coppola, 1963), another Irish-set horror film.

4 The term is taken from Clover (1993). In fact, the final girl – the virginal heroine who ultimately would dispatch the monster – was already out of fashion as a horror trope by then.

5 The problematic associations between autism and monstrousness were commented on in reviews of the film. See Asava (2010) and Clarke (2010).

6 *Variety* pronounced *Shrooms* to be as follows: 'Ok vid fodder with few real scares and not an ounce of originality' Elley (2007). The *Sunday Times* critic wrote: 'Conceived as a relentless Irish horror, the film ends up a mid-Atlantic cadaver' (Barter, 2007). The *Irish Times*'s verdict was 'Shrooms – appropriately enough for a film in its genre – remains an ugly Frankenstein's Monster poorly constructed from other men's discarded organs' (Clarke, 2007).

References

Acevedo-Muñoz, E. 1998. Horror of Allegory: *The Others* and Its Contexts. *In:* Jordan, B. and Morgan-Tamosunas, R. (eds.) *Contemporary Spanish Cinema.* Manchester and New York: Manchester University Press.

Asava, Z. 2010. Myth and Murder in the Daisy Chain. *Estudios Irlandeses,* January, 209.

Asava, Z. 2013. *The Black Irish Onscreen: Representing Black and Mixed-Race Identities on Irish Film and Television,* Oxford and New York: Peter Lang.

Barter, P. 2007. Paddy Breathnach Is a Fun Guy. *Sunday Times* (The Culture), 18 November, p. 13.

Barton, R. 2014. *Rex Ingram: Visionary Director of the Silent Screen,* Lexington: University of Kentucky Press.

Botting, F. and Edwards, J. D. 2013. Theorising Globalgothic. *In:* Byron, G. (ed.) *Globalgothic.* Manchester and New York: Manchester University Press.

Bronfen, E. 2004. *Home in Hollywood: the Imaginary Geography of Cinema,* New York: Columbia University Press.

Brooks, K. D. 2014. The Importance of Neglected Intersections: Race and Gender in Contemporary Zombie Texts and Theories. *African American Review,* 47, 461–75.

Clarke, D. 2007. The Unspeakable and the Inedible. *Irish Times* (The Ticket), 23 November, p. 13.

Clarke, D. 2010. Turn and Face the Strange Ch-ch-changeling. *Irish Times,* 16 April, p. B13.

Clover, C. J. 1993. *Men, Women, and Chain Saws: Gender in the Modern Horror Film,* Princeton, NJ: Princeton University Press.

Creed, B. 1993. *The Monstrous-feminine: Film, Feminism, Psychoanalysis,* London: Routledge.

Crosson, S. 2011. Na Cloigne *Estudios Irlandeses,* 6, 202–4.

Crosson, S. 2012. Aspects of Contemporary Irish Horror Cinema. *Kinema: Journal of Film and Audiovisual Media,* Spring, 65–83.

Delgado, M. 2008. The Young and the Damned. *Sight and Sound,* 18, 44–5.

Elley, D. 2007. Shrooms. *Variety,* 3–9 September, p. 57.

Fennell, N. 1997. Roger Corman and the Irish Film Industry. *The Irish Review* Autumn–Winter, 57–65.

Freud, S. 2003. *The Uncanny,* London: Penguin.

Gladwin, D. 2014. The Bog Gothic: Bram Stoker's 'Carpet of Death' and Ireland's Horrible Beauty. *Gothic Studies,* 16, 39–54.

Hennessy, S. 2015. Interview: Ivan Kavanagh, Wri/Dir of 'the Canal'. *Film Ireland* [Online]. Available: http://filmireland.net/2015/05/07/interview-ivan-kavanagh-wri-dir-of-the-canal/ [Accessed 18 May 2015].

Killeen, J. 2014. *The Emergence of Irish Gothic Fiction: History, Origins, Theories,* Edinburgh: Edinburgh University Press.

Lazaro-Reboll, A. 2012. *Spanish Horror Film,* Edinburgh: Edinburgh University Press.

Linehan, H. 1997. Corman Uncovered. *Irish Times* 22 August, p. 13.

Morash, C. and RichardS, S. 2013. *Mapping Irish Theatre: Theories of Space and Place,* Cambridge: Cambridge University Press.

Negra, D. 2007. Fantasy, Celebrity and 'Family Values' in High-End and Special Event Tourism in Ireland. *In:* Balzano, W., Mulhall, A. and Sullivan, M. (eds.) *Irish Postmodernisms and Popular Culture.* Basingstoke and New York: Palgrave Macmillan.

Pramaggiore, M. 2008. *Neil Jordan,* Urbana and Chicago: University of Illinois Press.

Radley, E. 2013. Violent Transpositions: The Disturbing 'Appearance' of the Irish Horror Film. *In:* Bracken, C. and Radley, E. (eds.) *Viewpoints, Theoretical Perspectives on Irish Visual Texts.* Cork: Cork University Press.

Shin, C.-Y. 2009. The Art of Branding: Tartan "Asia Extreme" Films. *In:* Choi, J. and Wada-Marciano, M. (eds.) *Horror to the Extreme: Changing Boundaries in Asian Cinema.* Hong Kong: Hong Kong University Press.

Tuan, Y.-F. 1977. *Space and Place: The Perspective of Experience,* London, Minneapolis: University of Minnesota Press.

Vejvoda, K. 2015. Beyond Horror: Surviving Sexual Abuse in Carmel Winters' *Snap. In:* Monahan, B. (ed.) *Ireland and Cinema, Culture and Contexts.* Basingstoke and New York: Palgrave Macmillan.

Zucker, C. 2008. *The Cinema of Neil Jordan: Dark Carnival,* London: Wallflower.

Short film
The Herd (Ken Wardrop, 2008)

The shortest of the short films included here, Ken Wardrop's *The Herd* runs to under five minutes. In this time, his brother, Trevor, and mother, Ethel, speak to camera about the appearance of a fawn in their herd of Limosin cattle. Between interviews, Wardrop gradually reveals the fawn, at first glimpsed behind one of the cattle, then springing into full view. Trevor takes a tough position on the intruder, now seen attempting to suckle from a cow, while Ethel threatens vengeance should he make any attempt on the animal. As discussed in the next chapter, Wardrop is an openly gay man. For these early films, he returns over and again (see also *Useless Dog* (2004)) to his family farm and rural background for his settings. His out-of-place animals, both wild and domestic, queer these most conventional of spaces. At the same time, his interviewees consider the consequences of difference. In *Useless Dog*, Trevor is reconciled to the presence on the farm of the idle sheepdog and her offspring despite their poor work ethic, and one suspects his threats to the fawn are issued more tongue-in-cheek to rile his mother than to pose any serious danger to the visitor with the 'identity crisis'. Like *His & Hers* (which will be discussed in the following chapter), *The Herd* is a film of great charm. Scored by Denis Clohessy to sound like the accompaniment to an early cinema short film, Wardrop's production is edited (by the director) to spring like the fawn itself from sequence to sequence. Here, as in *Useless Dog*, rural life is a place of simple concerns, a perspective that overlooks the considerable challenges of modern farming. This very particular auteurist vision carried through to Wardrop's feature length *His & Hers*, where his insistence that the audience share his take on women's lives in the Irish Midlands won over the public in large numbers but left him open to criticism for what could be interpreted as regressive gender politics. Wardrop's rural Ireland is a space at once within and outside of modernity; the dialogue borrowing ironically from popular cultural concepts around societal contribution. Here, as elsewhere, his deceptively ordinary topics are a cover for a very particular vision of Irish life.

4
Documenting Ireland

In common with other countries, Ireland has seen a flowering of documentary making in recent years. Documentaries now routinely receive limited theatrical releases, and in the period since 2006 the *Guth Gafa* (meaning 'Captive Voice' in Irish) documentary festival, located initially in the small village of Gortahork (Gort an Choirce) in the Donegal Gaeltacht and more recently in Kells in County Meath, has showcased both local and international productions. The Irish Film Institute also runs an annual documentary festival, initially titled 'Stranger than Fiction' and now simply the IFI Documentary Festival. Documentaries enjoy repeated broadcasts on TG4, make regular appearances on the RTÉ schedules, and have won prestigious awards at international festivals.

Unlike their fiction film counterparts, however, Irish documentaries remain very local in their funding and address. Most receive some level of financing from the IFB whose advice to prospective applicants that their emphasis 'is on feature-length, creative documentaries with high cinematic production values which are capable of reaching an international audience through theatrical and festival exposure and on new platforms' strikes a more optimistic than practical note (IFB/BSÉ, 2018). Setting aside the near impossibility of defining a 'creative documentary' (when is a documentary not creative?), few of the films discussed in this chapter reached any theatrical audience other than an Irish one. Many do find viewers via the Irish VOD platform, Volta, though again this limits their reach to local audiences (who live in high-speed broadband areas). Continuing their advice, the Film Board notes that 'BSÉ/IFB is keen to encourage documentary filmmaking that expresses a view of the world – past, present and future – that is both strongly personal and creatively Irish' (IFB/BSÉ, 2008). Here they are on safer ground. In fact, so focused are Irish documentaries on exploring Irish places and identities, both in the past and now, that it would not be a stretch to argue that they are the true claimants to the mantle of a national cinema.

Irish documentaries are formally diverse and resistant to categorisation. Most documentary theorists now agree that Bill Nichols's (1991: 32–75) original four modes – direct-address/expository, verité/observational, interactive and self-reflexive – no longer hold, yet most also return to Nichols's foundational theorisation of documentary as a starting point for further analysis. Few now would argue that cinema verité can be understood as editorially neutral, or that it provides unmediated access to its material. At the same time, many documentarists, including some discussed in this chapter, work within an observational mode, retaining a sense of objectivity and detachment from their material. Others produce more essayistic and personal works, closer perhaps to the nebulous 'creative documentary', defined by one handbook as offering a more subjective approach, driven by an authorial voice and indicating a specific ideological position (de Jong, Knudsen and Rothwell, 2013: 3).

In common with the fiction sector, many of the documentaries share an interest in geographically and socially marginalised identities. It is these films that form the focus of this chapter. I omit home movies and amateur work uploaded on to YouTube and similar platforms.[1] Nor do I cover reality television. This is not to denigrate such work, or to privilege what might be seen as the 'official' sphere over the multiplicity of voices emerging from other spheres. It is simply an attempt to establish some boundaries around the discussion, which can only ever be incomplete.

Documentary as truth

Scepticism about truth claims made on behalf of the documentary image has always accompanied critical analysis of the form, but the rise of digital production has forced theorists to re-examine the relationship between signifier and signified. No longer is it possible to state, as does Bill Nichols in his canonical, *Representing Reality*, that 'There is indeed, a distinctive bond between a photographic image and that of which it is a record. Something of reality itself seems to pass through the lens and remain embedded in the photographic emulsion' (Nichols, 1991: 5). Yet, still, there remains something to be retrieved from the documentary. There is a mutual understanding between it and its audiences that it can make truth claims, reveal injustices and cover aspects of life neglected or subject to bias by other image makers. In taking this position, I follow Stella Bruzzi's lead in her *New Documentary: A Critical Introduction*, where she argues that the extreme scepticism of various theorists towards documentary's truth claims neglects the commonsense understanding that reality exists. As she writes (2000: 9), documentary is 'a perpetual negotiation between the real event and its representation'.

The suggestion that documentary 'flourishes in the midst of crisis' (Arthur, 1993: 109) is worth bearing in mind. One such crisis may the ontological crisis of the image occasioned by the rise of digital culture, but another crisis of equal proportions is the crisis wrought by neo-liberalism and globalisation. The failure of the vast majority of fiction films to address the social consequences of neoliberalist policies has certainly contributed to the rise of the documentary as a voice of discontent. The popularity of the genre among younger audiences in particular may be explained by the anti-establishment attitudes of its high-profile practitioners (Nick Broomfield, Andrew Jarecki, Michael Moore, Errol Morris and Louis Theroux) and the sense that it speaks for society's otherwise voiceless outsiders. These documentary auteurs emerged from a post-direct cinema/*cinema verité* revision of the ethics and aesthetics of the genre. Where direct cinema proposed that the ideal documentary unfolded without any authorial intervention to reveal a/the truth, these later practitioners, by inserting themselves into the narrative, drew attention to the role of the documentarian as opinion-maker. At the same time, as this list indicates, the voice of much documentary remains white and male and even these often self-deprecating works can appear voyeuristic and patronising vis-à-vis underclass subjects. In Ireland the documentary took a turn away from state-sponsored production to critical intervention with the release of Peter Lennon's *Rocky Road to Dublin* (1967) and confirmed its anti-establishment credentials with *The Road to God Knows Where* (Alan Gilsenan, 1988).[2] One difference between then and now is the new visibility of the genre within public culture. Ironically, this is reliant on its appearing in that old-fashioned space, the movie theatre. As with the feature film, it remains the goal of most documentary makers to achieve at least a festival screening if not a theatrical release for their production.

Documenting community

A number of documentaries – *Pyjama Girls* (Maya Derrington, 2010), *The Pipe* (Risteard Ó Domhnaill, 2010), *Ballymun Lullaby* (Frank Berry, 2011), *Broken Song* (Claire Dix, 2013) *Atlantic* – draw on local communities and very specific geographic locales for their material. Although what constitutes 'community' is widely contested, I use the term here to refer as much to ties of place as to groupings of people with shared concerns. Regrettably, space prohibits me from discussing community films, which were defined by Eileen Leahy, in her study of the Irish community film (2014: 161), as commissioned or invited by the community, made through participation with the community and funded through community channels. Thus, such films exist 'in the interstices between commercial and experimental cinema, as well as between socially conscious film, which engages with communities, without necessarily being produced by them, and grassroots media, often produced by activist groups or on behalf of them' (2014: 20). My focus here is, however, on the representation (and construction) of community in mainstream Irish documentary filmmaking.

Dublin communities

The Dublin suburb of Ballymun has long functioned as a symbol of social disadvantage. Built in the 1960s as part of a policy to rehouse Dublin's inner-city inhabitants, its tower blocks were eventually demolished (2004–15) as part of a multi-million euro urban regeneration project. *Into the West* opens in the area around the flats; the Roddy Doyle-scripted television series *Family* (RTÉ/BBC, 1994) is set there, and other films set in working-class districts, such as *Bloody Sunday* (Paul Greengrass, 2002) have been shot there. Since then, community initiatives (including making the community film, *Leisure Centre* (Joe Lawlor, Christine Molloy, 2007)) have focused on issues of social development through education and opportunity.[3]

Frank Barry's *Ballymun Lullaby* shares with the community films an awareness of the importance of countering the negative imagery that has accumulated around Ballymun. At the same time, it offers a clear political message about the relationship between place and identity. The driving force at the heart of the film is music teacher, Ron Cooney, whose mission is to engage the local primary school children in music practice. It is his idea to approach the RTÉ chamber orchestra with a proposal to perform with the Ballymun youngsters and, working with some of his older success stories (lyricists and performers), they release an EP (extended play record), the eponymous 'Ballymun Lullaby'. Like Berry, one suspects, Cooney believes firmly in the community's potential, and his opinions are echoed not just in the song's lyrics but by local interviewees and better known 'talking heads' such as campaigner Father Peter McVerry and singer Glen Hansard, himself from Ballymun. The EP is a local success and leads to a live performance in the Helix at Dublin City University, though Cooney is left musing that it could have travelled further.

Following a shot of young girls singing, *Ballymun Lullaby* opens with newsreel footage of the 1963 housing protests (over the lack of accommodation in the inner city for working-class families) and moves on to the construction of Ballymun. Interviews with inhabitants testify to the locality's sense that they have been abandoned by the centre and misrepresented by the media. Continuing to cut back to the song, which is upbeat and anthemic, further newsreel footage brings the viewer to the destruction of the Towers. As the film progresses, the audience will learn that the song that punctuates the documentary is 'The World Is Your Oyster', composed by Daragh O'Toole:

Going out the door
I put my coat on
'Bye' to my mother
And out I go
Walking down the road
I see the changes that are happening
I wonder to myself
Which way I'll go
There's so many ways that I can go
There's so many ways that I can go
As my mother says "The world is your oyster"
Enjoy this great life!
So many ways to go
So many ways to go
As my mother says "The world is your oyster"
Enjoy this great life!
So, 1, 2, 3, 4. Now Go!

Ballymun Lullaby has none of the punishing competitiveness of reality television and Berry downplays the potential for a tense narrative of 'will they, won't they' (the choir) make it. As much as the film is about the performers, it is equally interested in exploring the consequences for this generation of moving out of the Towers into new low-rise housing. One of the interviewees, Darren, echoes the general consensus when he says 'some people can adapt to a new place but some people just can't forget old Ballymun. They can change Ballymun from old to new as much as they want but they will never, ever change the people.' Interviews with Cooney's pupils follow them as they walk through the locality, often alongside railings fencing off derelict open spaces. This repeated shot is an evocative one; the interviewees have to turn their heads to speak to the camera, which is positioned to one side of them. They frequently break off to answer an off-camera question or to banter with passers-by. These unseen interlocutors and the glimpses of the background beyond the railings suggest a tension between on- and off-screen spaces, or, as theorised by Noël Burch (2014: 17–31), a dialectical relationship between the two.

In one such sequence, Darren is talking about his song-writing when he stops, says 'Hang on', turns around and looks at someone out of frame. The camera stays on him as he challenges the unseen individual: 'What's wrong with you?' The camera then follows a black car driving away and past Darren as he resumes his walk. Darren shrugs. Off-camera, we hear one of the filmmakers ask, 'What did he want'? 'I don't know,' Darren responds, 'he just asked if I was all right, turned around and went back.' Denied a reverse shot, the viewer can only imagine those other worlds beyond the control of the frame. Who is organising Darren's space – the filmmaker, the car-driver or Darren (who is temporarily directing the camera) himself – is reflexive of a wider dialectic between seen and unseen that structures the film. Ron Cooney concedes that he loses most of his choir when they move on to secondary school and the temptations of street life. Despite the positivity of so many interviewees about the people of Ballymun, most recognise that a lurking criminality still exists there, unseen in the film, even as they insist that it should not define their area.

Making performance its theme allows *Ballymun Lullaby* to foreground processes of creativity that are at once textual and consistent with its own practice. It is even more prominent in another work set in Ballymun, Claire Dix's *Broken Song*, a film that was more obviously conceived as a creative documentary. Unlike *Ballymun Lullaby*, Dix's film was funded by the Arts Council under its 'Reel Art' scheme, and is shot in black-and-white interspersed with moments of colour photography. *Broken Song* is concerned with the rap scene coming out of Ballymun and another working-class Dublin suburb, Finglas. James Costello, one of its subjects, has just launched his first album and acts as a mentor to younger men in the area, notably Willa Lee. The latter is on the cusp of recognition but also facing prison time for an assault he committed when he was younger. The decision to shoot in black-and-white and the occasional shifts into abstraction, notably a repeated shot (in colour) of what seems to be a sunken underwater housing estate, allow the documentary to play more like an artist's music video than a work of reportage. The stylisation of *Broken Song*, specifically the underwater scenes (with their somewhat primitive CGI), creates allusive connections between this particular street music, artistry and the instability of place. This is nowhere more apparent than in the pre-credit sequence, which is a beautiful and moody, three-minute-long, slow-motion study of three of the young men jumping into the sea off Dublin and floating in the water. As each one plunges in from the pier, the camera enters the sea with them, the water churning until they rise to the surface. Predominately in black-and-white, the scene shifts into colour randomly during the underwater shots. This sequence will be reprised later in the film when the young men meet on a pier to rap together and swim. Conventionally in Irish cultural representations the journey to the sea signals an escape from the confines of the urban to the freedom of the ocean, usually the west of Ireland. *Broken Song* remaps that spatial dynamic just as it replaces the voice of traditional Ireland with the idiom of the American inner city.

Dramatic confrontations such as the clash between Willa Lee and his mother punctuate the more abstract sequences, as does Lee's own slightly self-exculpatory account of the assault for which he is now facing trial. The filmmakers are careful not to take a position on Lee's criminality, though perhaps *Broken Song* might have been stronger if they had.

Documenting gender

Embedded in the lyrics of 'The World Is Your Oyster' is a faith in the Irish mother as the enabler of her children's futures. It is interesting to note that she remains indoors while seeing her child off, as if the lyrics imagine change, but not quite yet. Similarly, the scenes between Willa Lee and his mother reflect very conventional associations of motherhood with the domestic space. As I have discussed elsewhere (Barton, 2017), documentary making is an area that has offered women filmmakers in Ireland better work opportunities than has fiction filmmaking and many recent Irish documentaries have been produced and/or directed by women. The reasons for this are not entirely flattering: women tend to be trusted more with low-budget, human-interest films than high-profile, larger-budget productions; and documentary shooting schedules are usually more manageable for a director trying to balance family life and a career than the fiction film equivalents. It is ironic, then, that one of the most widely seen films about Irish women's lives, *His & Hers*, was made by a male director, Ken Wardrop, and another very successful work, with particular focus on performing gender, *The Queen of Ireland* (2015), was directed by Conor Horgan.

To start, however, with another film that garnered widespread media attention: Maya Derrington's *Pyjama Girls* serves as a reminder that class may be as determining or more determining than gender in the production of a documentary. *Pyjama Girls* follows two teenagers, Lauren Dempsey and Tara Salinger, as they share cigarettes together and hang out with their friends in Dublin's Basin Street Flats and at Lauren's grandmother's house in Ballyfermot. Lauren's voice-over structures much of the film as she recounts her mother's addiction, their fights, her phone call, aged six, to her aunt to come to collect her and her baby sister,

Danika, and her subsequent life with her grandmother, Peggy. Peggy also supplies further generational history, reminiscing about visiting her own mother when she worked on the barrows on Thomas Street, in Dublin's inner city. The voice-over closes with Lauren's hopes that she will be the parent to her sister that her mother never was. *Pyjama Girls* led to a flurry of newspaper articles and broadcasts with the fashion for young, usually working-class women to wear pyjamas as outdoor dress achieving ethnographic levels of interest.

There is very little to tie together the two strands of the film – pyjamas as street fashion and Lauren's family background – other than a shared interest in narrating young working-class women's lives. Of all the productions discussed here, this is the least structured, with very little sense of a drive towards a conclusion, something that Derrington has mentioned in interview (in Whittaker, 2010):

> I have to admit that I didn't think I had an ending. The girls we were following kept joking that they were going to get themselves arrested to give us an ending. It was in the edit that we found the ending. It says something about the open-ended nature of life.

In the same interview, Derrington speaks of her shock when she first saw young women wearing pyjamas on the street and how this prompted

Figure 7 Tara and Lauren in *Pyjama Girls*

98

her to make the documentary. This (shocked) gaze at Lauren, Tara and their friends has been critiqued by writers on the film for its class-based dynamic. Sinéad Molony (2014: 197), picking up on this and other comments by Derrington – that she used to walk past the Charlemont Street flats on her way to work and wondered about stepping over the boundary that frightened her – concludes that the filmmaker presents 'the pyjama girls through a voyeuristic middle-class frame that reasserts a dominant class relation of pride and shame'. Derrington has, however, also argued that pyjama wearing is a subversive act:

> There is an underlying revolt there. It seems like a statement against the excess of the boom. Then there is the statement of, 'You know I'm not working, I know I'm not working, let's none of us pretend that I am in the working population'. (in Battles and Dunne, 2009: 7)

In a more nuanced discussion of *Pyjama Girls'* ethical and class positioning, Jenny Knell (2011) poses the question: 'does the film give an authentic voice to its working-class subjects or simply appropriate their voices in order to challenge ways of thinking about Dublin's urban space and the divisions wrought by social class?' This question might as easily have been posed around any number of other Irish and non-Irish fictions about working-class life. It is a fraught problem for documentary filmmakers, many of whom share an ambition to provide a platform for underrepresented members of society to speak for themselves while at the same time using their subjects to highlight social disadvantage. Derrington herself has spoken of her desire that middle-class viewers would better understand the lives of pyjama girls (in Clarke, 2010: 8). Whether the outcome has to be an either/or is debatable; *Pyjama Girls* ultimately achieves both but the two modes (of education and observation) sit uncomfortably alongside each other, particularly given the strength and poignancy of Lauren's multi-generational narrative which, one suspects, emerged organically in her encounter with the filmmaker. In common with the other films discussed in this chapter, another tension arises between place and character. Not unlike *Broken Song*, the camera punctuates the subjects' narratives with composed shots of the location. Visually, these sequences recall an earlier release from the same production company, the documentary on asylum seekers, *Seaview* (Nicky Gogan and Paul Rowley, 2007). Rowley also shot *Pyjama Girls* and while his camerawork and the film's editing provide a rhythmic counterpoint to the voice-overs, they work to aestheticise the Basin Street flats, notably when the camera picks out the familiar iconography of working-class spaces (trainers suspended in the air from their knotted laces, an upturned stroller in a tree and walls covered with graffiti), framing them as it might a gallery photograph. As in *Seaview*, which was filmed in a former Butlin's Mosney holiday camp that had been converted into a centre for asylum seekers, the photography invites the viewer to look differently at spaces that through mainstream news coverage have become metonymic for degradation. Yet, here as in *Broken Song,* this aestheticising gaze risks transforming such places into abstractions.

Both *Pyjama Girls* and *His & Hers* raise further questions about the use of setting in women's narratives. One of the interesting comments that Lauren makes in *Pyjama Girls* is that the flats are like your house, so that wearing pyjamas in their outdoor spaces is the same as wearing them at home. As explanations go, this is slightly disingenuous as they don't just wear their pyjamas around the flats, and one of the public discourses that fed into the film was a discussion held over the air-waves about the propriety or otherwise of young women wearing their pyjamas in shopping centres and labour exchanges. The suggestion that women are most confident occupying domestic spaces is reinforced by Derrington's favouring of extended sequences where the generations mix easily together in bedrooms, kitchens and living areas. This is where Lauren appears to relate her own life story, although, as her voice-over is played out of synch with the image, there is no evidence that she actually did so. The domestic space is also the setting for *His & Hers*. Seventy women (this figure includes a baby, a toddler and an older woman who bookend the documentary, and none of whom speaks) from the Irish Midlands recount an aspect of their lives to camera and as voice-over. *His & Hers* is very much a concept film, made by a director/auteur. Ken Wardrop's graduate film from IADT (the Institute of Art, Design and Technology), *Undressing My Mother* (2004) comprised a startling inter-view with his mother where she undressed to camera while talking about her feelings of loss following the death of her husband.[4] *His & Hers* echoes a theme of *Undressing My Mother*, women's relationships with men, with the interviewees offering approximately one to two minutes of observations on their fathers, boyfriends, sons and husbands. Each interviewee is older than the last so that by the end of the film, many of the women are widowed, as is Wardrop's mother, who appears in this film too. Wardrop has been clear that she is also the inspiration behind *His & Hers*: 'It's a celebration of my mother's life, it's the longer form of *Undressing My Mother* … It's a celebration of a very ordinary woman though to me she's extraordinary' (in O'Connell, 2012: 142). To that end, he chose women from the Irish Midlands and filmed them in their homes, apart from the final shot, which is in a nursing home. He deliber-ately excluded any disturbing personal information that emerged in the preliminary interviews:

Figure 8 Interviewee in *His & Hers*

A character who had had her child taken from her as a kid when she had been in one of the work houses, all these stories that they wanted to tell me because they needed to express themselves and they thought that's why I was interested. But I was interested in the ordinary. (O'Connell, 2012: 139)

His & Hers, which cost €100,000 to make, was the most successful domestically released Irish documentary of its day, taking in more than €300,000 at the Irish box office. This made it the highest-grossing documentary since Michael Moore's *Fahrenheit 9/11* in 2006. The previous highest-grossing Irish documentary was *Waveriders* (Joel Conroy, 2008) which took €114,000 at the Irish box office (Molloy, 2010: 6). Strategically, Wardrop's film was released against the World Cup, anticipating a non-football viewership. Its release was significantly augmented with distribution through the Access Cinema network of film societies. The film also benefited from strong reviews, a number of international awards and an endorsement from Michael Moore.

It is a film of considerable charm that bespeaks an empathy between the interviewees and its small production crew, notably Wardrop himself. The effect of the stationary camera, which carries over from the shorts, and the very careful placement of the speakers – indoors in kitchens, bedrooms, living rooms and staircases mostly – underlines the authority of the filmmaker. The camera does not follow the interviewees, they have to walk into frame; they may even be partially cut off and occluded from view. In this sense, and because of his readiness to discuss his documentary and even to intervene in readings of it, Wardrop's position as director/auteur is as evident as if he had appeared within or out of frame, which he does not. Critiques of the film then have to take into account the personal drive behind it (Wardrop's desire to honour his mother's life through exploring lives such as hers) and the consequences of his universalising of her experience. For Patricia Neville (2015: 101), this exclusive positioning of women within domestic spaces as well as the emphasis on their relationships to the men in their lives is a limiting, even regressive perspective and the film 'clearly advances a conventional, heterosexual and sanitized version of female–male relationships'. Wardrop, on the other hand, has explained that the making of the film was in part informed by his identity as a gay man (in O'Connell, 2012: 143). In the film, the women are repeatedly interviewed as they carry out chores: peeling potatoes, ironing, folding clothes and cutting the lawn. This insistence on the repetitiveness of female domestic labour, and the sense of entrapment engendered by the framing of the women by doors and through windows offers the film up to quite a different reading to Neville's (and possibly even to Wardrop's), as a commentary on women's internalisation of conservative gender norms.

One might add in a further reservation about the film's final shot. From having placed the camera indoors, occasionally looking out, it suddenly appears on the outside looking in to the care home, and for the first time a man is glimpsed, slowly walking out of the room on a Zimmer frame, as if its elderly female subject were no longer entitled to a voice, or a space of her own. Possibly in response to this, and to equal public acclaim, Alex Fegan released *Older Than Ireland* in 2015, in which he interviewed a selection of centenarians, male and female, urban and rural, about their lives over the 100 years of the Irish state. The upbeat tone of most of the respondents suggested that there was much to celebrate. Such a message might have come as some surprise to the many critics of the direction taken by the state, particularly in social affairs, since its foundation.

Campaigning documentary

If there is one binding concept behind the documentaries discussed so far, it is an approach that favours personal narratives over public affairs. At the same time, the filmmakers repeatedly invite the viewer to come to wider conclusions about public issues through these personal stories.

Irish documentarians, overall, have been less interested in making local equivalents to *Super Size Me* (Morgan Spurlock, 2004), *Fahrenheit 9/11* or *Enron, The Smartest Guys in the Room* (Alex Gibney, 2005) that address global issues (if from an American viewpoint).

One exception is Risteard Ó Domhnaill, whose *The Pipe* and *Atlantic* best match Mike Wayne's (2008: 91) claim: 'The emergence of feature film documentary as a prominent player within the sphere of public opinion formation has evidently crystallized around the great assault on corporate capitalism, consumerism and globalization of market relations.' Both are campaigning films; *The Pipe* follows a group of Mayo inhabitants in their efforts to prevent oil company Shell from laying a pipe through their local bay and under their land to an inland refinery and *Atlantic* documents the changes wrought by over-fishing and oil exploration on three remote fishing communities in Ireland, Newfoundland and Norway. *The Pipe* makes its point through a focus on local activists (from the Shell-to-Sea campaign), who speak to camera, and one of its central tensions is around the fissures within the community that emerge as the campaign develops. In the end, the small victories over Shell, and the admiration that the viewer is likely to feel for those who stand up for their principles in the face of that corporate behemoth is mitigated by a sense of loss. Will this community ever retrieve the bonds of friendship that once defined it? That same sense of loss accompanies the Irish interviewees of *Atlantic* in particular. In Newfoundland and Canada, the focus is on tensions between the economic benefits of oil production versus the damage to fishery and the environment of the underwater explosions used to detect oil. In Ireland, it is equally on EU fishery policies and the Irish Government's part in allowing large trawlers to empty the oceans of the fish traditionally caught by small local fishing communities. In its questioning of government policies, *Atlantic* is more overtly political than was *The Pipe*, where, in the absence of representatives of Shell or the political establishment, the local guards constitute the only visible opposition to the protestors. Because they are also from the locality, these segments play to the film's message that this controversy has ruptured the community's cohesiveness.

Ó Domhnaill's focus on the local and his interweaving of people and place are consistent with Irish documentary's wider concerns. In this, the films engage with a greater range of spaces and identities than do their fiction equivalents even as they share Irish fiction film's concern with narratives of marginalisation. At the same time, the documentaries, with the exception of *Atlantic*, seem more concerned with documenting the social than transforming it. It is as if the business of imagining other realities was not within their remit. Faced with the spectre of pushing

Figure 9 *Atlantic*

beyond the immediate realities of their subjects' lives, or moving outside of the 'ordinary', the response seems to be to resort to abstraction (underwater housing estates) or aestheticisation (a stroller lodged in a tree). The assumptions around gender and space fall into similar categories, as if presuming that their audiences would resist a radical re-imagining of these social/spatial relationships. As I have discussed elsewhere in relation to another highly successful local release, *One Million Dubliners* (Aoife Kelleher, 2014), about Glasnevin cemetery, this film ultimately offers its viewers the comforting proposal that, in a society where entitlement to a place of your own is no longer guaranteed, at the end of your mortal life, it is (Barton, 2015a). Kelleher followed *One Million Dubliners* with *Strange Occurrences in a Small Irish Village* (2016) about the village and shrine of Knock where in 1879 the Virgin Mary was supposed to have appeared to fifteen of the villagers. The film interviews pilgrims, tourists, merchandisers, the shrine 'handmaids', a woman who allegedly experienced a miracle cure, the local priest, and others, to reveal an array of opinions about the shrine's history and its meaning in the modern world. In exploring a narrative of faith in miracles, Kelleher is careful to refrain from judgement, or to pursue the references that emerge to pro-Life beliefs or clerical scandals. Despite the inclusion of individuals such as the handmaid who is looking for gender parity in her work, the overall mood is one of gentle nostalgia. Here, as in so many of the Irish documentaries, one has a sense that the intention is literally to document – a moment, a place, a way of being, a forgotten corner of Ireland – that has survived the ravages of modernisation, globalisation and the homogen-isation of contemporary culture.

More radical subject matter, as is Horgan's portrait of drag artist and LGBT campaigner, Rory O'Neill (aka Panti) in *The Queen of Ireland,* can veer in surprisingly conservative directions. This film concludes with O'Neill's return home to the village of his birth and the emotional moment of his reintegration to the community through their acceptance and celebration of his drag act. In these films, community is paramount, and most end up, one way or another, celebrating the personal, profes-sional and spatial configurations that identify belonging to a particular grouping of people.

This is not to dismiss all Irish documentary as socially irrelevant, but to recognise its limitations. Few Irish documentary makers encourage their viewers to question what they are seeing or offer conflicting perspectives on their topics. Instead, they propose an unmediated account of their subjects that leaves those viewers in a safe place. These subjects tend to be portrayed so as to elicit a specific response, usually with the socially marginalised individual. In this manner, they suggest a contract between maker and viewer – an expectation that they share a common social and political sensibility, which is fundamentally liberal in outlook. Whether the greater involvement of women in documentary making in Ireland has any relevance to these conclusions is very difficult to deter-mine without adopting essentialist positions. I have discussed in detail (Barton, 2017) Neasa Ní Chianáin's experience of making her documen-tary, *Fairytale of Kathmandu* (2007), about poet Cathal Ó Searcaigh and his relationships with young men in Nepal. It may well be that the hostility she experienced, and the gendered criticisms of her ethical approach, served as an object lesson, not just to her, but to her peers.

Irish documentary has produced its own auteurs, whose work comes from an identifiable ideological perspective. This chapter concludes with a discussion of one of the most consistent and challenging of these.

The films of Pat Collins

Filmmaker and former editor of *Filmwest* magazine, Pat Collins follows in a tradition of critics turned auteurs familiar from the *Cahiers du Cinéma* era of Jacques Rivette, Jean-Luc Godard, Claude Chabrol and François Truffaut. John Corner (2008: 21) writes that 'one might, with some caution, speak of "art documentary"', and certainly Collins's films fit within this category. That is, they address social issues but still, in Corner's (2008: 21) words, require 'the kind of imaginative engagement and textual sympathy' that certain modes of fiction films elicit. Another approach is to categorise Collin's work as essayistic. In his discussion of the essay film, Timothy Corrigan (2011: 4) writes as follows:

> Straddling fiction and nonfiction, news reports and confessional auto-biography, documentaries and experimental film, they [essay films] are ... practices that undo and redo film form, visual perspectives, public geographies, temporal organizations, and notions of truth and judgment within the complexity of experience.

Such a definition fits well with these films. Even if Collins himself does not appear in them, his organising, authorial presence is inescapable, as are his concerns with issues concerning landscape, memory and modernity. Some, such as *Fathom* (2013), were wholly funded by the Arts Council, whereas others, including *Silence* (2012), were co-produced with South Wind Blows, the Dingle-based events organiser. His main sources of funding have been the Irish Film Board, RTÉ and TG4. In interview Collins has been clear that he makes his films because of his interest in their subject matter: 'I never work on something that I'm not very interested in. To make a documentary just for money wouldn't work out well for anyone concerned. I would prefer to do almost any other job than trying to manufacture enthusiasm to make a film' (in Gildea, 2008).

For someone whose output is dependent on public funding, Collins has been surprisingly prolific. His first documentary was *Michael Hartnett: A Necklace of Wrens* (1999) and he continues to produce work at the rate of usually two or more films a year, some short, others feature length, with *Silence* being his first non-fiction release (although as we shall see, it is not so easily categorised). He has won numerous awards and his productions are consistently well received by critics. At the same time, his name remains largely unknown outside of cinephile circles, and screenings of his films are restricted to festivals, television and art cinemas. Few of Collins's productions have a life beyond a short theatrical run or a one-off screening. *Tim Robinson: Connemara* (2011) and *Silence* are available on commercial DVD, while others of the films are sold directly from the Harvest Films website. Unusually, he directed part of the RTÉ/BBC co-production with the Keough-Naughton Institute for Irish Studies documentary, *1916 The Irish Rebellion* (2016). Collins's documentaries can be loosely divided into: profiles of writers and artists – *John McGahern: A Private World* (2005), *Nuala Ní Dhomhnaill – Taibhsí i mBéal na Gaoithe* (2007), *Gabriel Byrne – Stories from Home* (2008) and others; profiles of places – *Oileán Thoraí* (2002), *Cathair Chorcaí* (2005) and others; and explorations of Irish history – *The Great*

Irish Famine: Remember Skibbereen (2009), *Living in a Coded Land* (2014) and others. Some are made in English, some in the Irish language. Such divisions, however, achieve little more than illustrating the reductiveness of categorising. I want to focus here on three of Collins's later films that technically and thematically best exemplify his auteur practice: *Tim Robinson: Connemara, Living in a Coded Land* and his semi-fiction feature, *Silence*.

From his earliest works, Collins has drawn on archival footage to lend historical depth to his portraits of people and places. Although this is a commonplace documentary practice, it has taken on a more abstract and ontologically nuanced expression as his work has developed. In *Oileán Thoraí,* the Tory islanders speak to camera, many of them reminiscing about the past, recalling older ways of life, and telling stories of fairy revelries and other supernatural occurrences. These memories are intercut with photographs and historical footage of the island, and, although the rhythm of the film's edit lends it a somewhat dreamy tone, there is nothing particularly remarkable about its construction or its content. Such reflections on the past, coupled with a suspicion that modernity is only achieved through loss, are unexceptional, even predictable, when articulated by the inhabitants of this remote island off the Donegal coast. Subsequent films were to return to these themes, but in a more complex manner and utilising less obvious settings. We can detect in Collins's work a movement between the didactic and the poetic that is not a movement between two opposing poles but the intersection of the two.

Tim Robinson: Connemara and *Silence* offer the viewer the traditional point of access of a single enunciating subject (the cartographer, Tim Robinson, in the first, and the sound recordist, Eoghan Mac Giolla Bhride, in the second). At the same time, these are authored films, doubly authored in so far as Collins the director/auteur has selected two subjects whose own perspectives – on landscape, the past and loss – closely mirror his own treatment of the same topics in earlier works, and would be reprised in *Living in a Coded Land*. In this regard, Corrigan (2011: 30) has noted the following:

> An expressive subjectivity, commonly seen in the voice or actual presence of the filmmaker or a surrogate, has become one the most recognizable signs of the essay film, sometimes quite visible in the film, sometimes not. Just as the first-person presence of the literary essay often springs from a personal voice and perspective, so essay films characteristically highlight a real or fictional persona whose quests and questionings shape and direct the film in lieu of a traditional narrative and frequently complicate the

documentary look of the film with the presence of a pronounced subjectivity or enunciating position.

Born in England, with a degree in mathematics from Cambridge, but
a long-time resident in Connemara, the artist, cartographer and writer,
Tim Robinson, is a highly regarded public figure. Very certainly his
views on the landscape as a repository of memory struck a chord with
Collins. Robinson's Connemara is at once despoiled by modernity, just
as is Collins's contemporary Ireland, but it is still capable of inducing
moments of epiphany. In *Tim Robinson: Connemara,* Robinson recalls
one such moment, when the passengers of a bus in which he is travelling fall silent as they witness the beauty of the sun setting over the
lakes. That film opens with his words: 'Without the occasional renewal
of memory and regular rehearsal of meaning, place itself founders into
shapelessness, and time, the great amnesiac, forgets all.' Over images of
the people of Connemara and its landscapes and seascapes, Robinson
recalls his reasons for settling in the region and his practice of cartog-
raphy, his attempts to mesh his feelings about the place with the dots
representing it on his maps. The camera follows him on his walks around
Connemara, leaving him occasionally and following its own route, with
rushing Steadicam shots through the woods interspersed with medita-
tive tracking shots down the bark of trees. The loss of the Irish language
with its richness of expression, and the anglicisation of place names,
have contributed, Robinson proposes, to the desecration of place. This
evocation of Connemara as the embodiment of a lost or dying Gaelic
culture has left the cartographer open to accusations of romanticism.
'The danger is', as Gerry Smyth (2001: 54) has written, 'that the "primitive" landscapes of the west are romanticised vis-à-vis other, somehow
more mundane, less human (or sometimes all *too* human) landscapes,
thus contributing to the notion of that region as a haven of authenticity
in a world swamped with simulacra.' Collins, too, might face the same
critique. His depiction of the Atlantic coast and its islands suggests that
the abandonment of these former heartlands of Irish-speaking culture
constitutes an irreparable loss. Visually, the repeated motif of the ruined
cottage set alongside archival footage of thriving rural and small village
life of the past is in danger of fostering a similar discourse. Collins's
camera insists on the purity of the Irish countryside (no dumped rubbish
or modern bungalows) versus the anonymity of the globalised city space
where men in business attire rush past.

This kind of regressive nostalgia is countered by Collins's highly
mobile camera, particularly his use of Steadicam. In fact, as the opening
sequences of *Silence* illustrate, he tends to draw attention to the place

of technology in his works. Following a quotation from the poem, 'Insomnia in Southern Illinois' by John Burnside, the film moves to a shot of reels of analogue tape playing a recording of a female voice (that of Nellie Nic Giolla Bhride) singing 'The Breeze and I', and to a partially seen image of a curtain flapping beside a broken frame of glass in a rural landscape (an image that will be contextualised later on in the film). It cuts to a man walking through fields at dusk; as the singing continues, it mingles with the sound of seabirds calling in the background. Before the image has faded, industrial sounds replace the traditional song and the seabirds. The film then moves to the same man (whom the end credits identify as Eoghan Mac Giolla Bhride but who is referred to throughout only as Eoghan), recording the clatter of a city street as trams pass around him. A voice indistinctly murmurs the names of German tram stops and transport announcements. Shortly afterwards, we see him explaining to a young woman that he is going for work, 'purely work'. The rest of the conversation is drowned out by the sound of a train on the tracks below. Over the credits, we then see Eoghan driving down the motorway interspersed with a collage of images showing a map of Donegal, archival footage of men launching a boat and a sequence of worn photographs – of two men in front of an old kitchen dresser and other family and group snapshots. In a hotel bar, the barman tells him about a story he heard on the 'wireless' of an abandoned island off Scotland where the starlings still, fifty years on, mimic the sound of the mowing machines that used to be there. 'Would that be the kind of story, you're …', he asks. Eoghan responds that he is not really collecting stories, 'it's more quiet'. 'Be careful of that,' the barman (Andrew Bennett) warns him. 'Too much quietness would drive a fella mad.' These opening sequences establish much of what is to come. *Silence* is at once an exploration of the Irish landscape and history and an antidote to conventional depictions of Irish identity (still current in documentaries such as *The Irish Pub* (Alex Fegan, 2013)).

Eoghan travels through Ireland, interviewing people along the way and discussing with them his project – to record areas that are away from man-made sound. As he nears Tory, so he becomes increasingly solitary. He lights a fire in the darkness and sits singing a traditional Irish song. In another sequence, he runs his hand across the mossy bark of trees and through the water of a stream, then across the cracked plaster of a wall. The filmic journey includes old footage of people packing up and leaving one of the islands. The specific reference becomes clear when Eoghan discusses the evacuation of Inishbofin with a boatman. By this stage, he seems distracted from his initial challenge and caught up with a personal quest, the return to his old home on Tory. To complete his

Figure 10 Eoghan MacGiolla Bhríde in *Silence*

journey, he must listen to the landscape, and to those voices of the past that speak through it. Subjectivity is thus bound up with history and place. Still, *Silence* denies its audience the kind of Eureka moment that more conventional filmmaking relies on. Eoghan's quest does not end on a triumphant high of self-fulfilment, or celebrate the journey home to Ireland. Instead, it concludes with Eoghan sitting at the broken window looking out at the island's ruins. Whether or not he will return to Berlin and the young woman remains unknowable; at the very least, he seems to have come to terms with the rejection of home that is implicit in the act of emigration.

To what extent *Silence* is a fiction is complicated by the fact that the man who plays Eoghan is Eoghan Mac Giolla Bhride, and that he is also credited as co-writer. Mac Giolla Bhride, an engineer turned writer and filmmaker, is from Gweedore in mainland County Donegal, and the recordings are of his mother singing traditional, unaccompanied Irish songs or 'Sean Nós'. In an interview, he has said the following about the film: 'The themes that are explored are subtle things like loss, our attraction to landscape, reconciling with the past, and language' (in Brady, 2012: C4). Not only did *Silence* draw on these recordings, it also used old reel-to-reel tapes of Mac Giolla Bhride's grandfather talking in traditional Donegal Irish, which is a way of speaking that is now virtually lost. Further, Mac Giolla Bhride worked with Collins on the production of *Oileán Thoraí*, which prefigures many of the concerns of *Silence*, notably the depopulation of the Irish-speaking islands and the accompanying loss of the islanders' traditions.

The idea of filmmaking (and sound recording) as an act of preservation is consistent with Collins's wider practice. His interviews with conservationists and ecologists (such as Michael Hartnett) and his explorations of place function as records of those people and places. At the same time, they are guided by his own concern over the loss of tradition under globalisation and the erosion of the past by colonisation. These twin concerns inform *Living in a Coded Land*. The film opens with Collins's trademark collage of images, juxtaposing newsreel footage of people going about their lives in rural and small-town Ireland of the past and of today. The archival footage relates to the present-day footage loosely and is more suggestive of continuity – in so much as the activities are not particularly different in the past and in the present – than radical change. Following the announcement of the film's title, the tone alters and a succession of interviewees appears. Some have been interviewed for the film, while others, such as writer and politician Conor Cruise O'Brien (1917–2008) are selected from archival footage. At this point too, the footage takes on a more overtly political tenor, featuring in succession: a historical documentary about the Williamite invasion, wreath-laying commemorations, images of Republican funerals, Orange Order parades. Throughout the remainder of the film, these voices will comment on key Irish historical events and their consequences for the development of Ireland as a colonised society. Their comments float over images of the countryside, often at dusk, and are interspersed with other archival images, such as of Séamus Ennis (1919–82) playing the pipes. Other interviewees consider what it means to live a coded life, which most agree means being part of an establishment biased towards the managerial classes and new entrepreneurs, and one that is fundamentally opposed to implementing the democratic aspirations of the Republic. In later sequences, scenes of rural plenitude give way to urban dereliction and the film takes up the theme of emigration, interspersing footage of families taking leave of each other at the airport, with an interview with the playwright John B. Keane who describes leaving Ireland with throngs of others on the way to England, with documentary footage of tenement families destined to emigrate. The film ends with Patrick Kavanagh's poem, 'Prelude', written to then-Taoiseach, John A. Costello, as a reminder that the latter had promised to find him employment:

> Walk on serenely, do not mind
> That Promised Land you thought to find
> Where the worldly-wise and rich takeover
> The mundane problems of the lover.
> Ignore Power's schismatic sect
> Lovers alone lovers protect.

Where Collins's practice differs from conventional documentary making is that the inclusion of archival footage does not act as a guarantee of truthfulness, rather it endows the image with temporality. This is particularly evident in the later films where the sharply focused digital image gives way to the slightly degraded celluloid insertion. Past and present are at once embedded in the same space (of the local and the national) but they are not the same. As Collins's collage of images and interviews suggest, events are not ordered consecutively but in clusters determined by place. Place is also the keeper of memory, which in turn operates outside of official history.

It seems safe to ascribe these ideas to Collins even if he does not directly articulate them himself. Within the films, his, in Corrigan's words, 'pronounced subjectivity or enunciating position' remains a constant. Whether through his portrait of Tim Robinson, which relies so heavily on the latter reading from his books, or his decision to frame *Silence* around a character whose quest reconciles him to his past and to the landscape of that past, or through the choice of interviewees included in *Living in a Coded Land,* or indeed its precursor, *What We Leave in Our Wake* (2010), Collins has created a body of work that is distinctive both visually and intellectually. Furthermore, his recycling of key interviewees (Michael Hartnett, John McGahern, Tim Robinson) from documentary to documentary endows his work with thematic consistency.

Whether this recourse to the past as a time/place of authenticity aligns Collins with romanticism is another question. Certainly, there are elements of that discourse in his lingering shots of ruined buildings, extended long takes of the Irish countryside, and his critique of modernity. There is something of the romantic wanderer in Eoghan's journey in *Silence,* which, in common with the other films, only in passing addresses the issues of isolation, lack of opportunity, lack of infrastructure and poverty that have contributed to rural depopulation. Where other works discussed in this chapter, including the auteur films such as *His & Hers,* offer very little by way of a vision for change, Collins displays an intellectual sense that going back to the past involves a return to a place of radical alterity. How that might effect change in the present or the future remains, however, unclear.

Notes

1 For more on home movies, including Irish home movies, see Rascaroli, Monahan and Young (2014).

2 For a discussion of these films see and their context, see O'Brien (2004: 170–8 and 208–21). For essays on Alan Gilsenan and *The Road to God Knows Where*, see O'Brien (2015) and Barton (2015b).

3 Leahy (2014: 138–65) discusses Ballymun community filmmaking in detail.
4 For a selection of short articles on *Undressing My Mother*, see the dedicated section of *Short Film Studies*, 1(1), 2010, pp. 57–111.

References

Arthur, P. 1993. Jargons of Authenticity (Three American Moments). *In:* Renov, M. (ed.) *Theorizing Documentary.* London and New York: Routledge.

Barton, R. 2015a. Every Plot Has a Story. One Million Dubliners (Aoife Kelleher 2014). *Estudios Irlandeses,* 10, 197–9.

Barton, R. 2015b. "More Sax, Less Clannad" *The Road to God Knows Where. In:* Pettitt, L. and Kopschitz Bastos, B. (eds.) *The Road to God Knows Where/ A Estrada Para Deus Sabe Onde.* Florianópolis, SC: Universidade Federal de Santa Catarina.

Barton, R. 2017. A Female Voice in Irish Cinema: Women Filmmakers and the Creative Documentary. *New Hibernia Review,* 21, 17–32.

Battles, J. and Dunne, S. 2009. Life's Just a Pyjama Party for City Girls. *Sunday Times,* 30 August, p. 7.

Brady, T. 2012. The Quiet Man. *Irish Times,* 27 July, pp. C4–5.

Bruzzi, S. 2000. *New Documentary: a Critical Introduction,* London: Routledge.

Burch, N. 2014. *Theory of Film Practice,* Princeton, NJ: Princeton University Press.

Clarke, D. 2010. So, What Are Pyjama Girls Really Like? *Irish Times,* 14 August, p. 8.

Corner, J. 2008. Documentary Studies, Dimensions of Transition and Continuity. *In:* Austin, T. and De Jong, W. (eds.) *Rethinking Documentary, New Perspectives, New Practices.* Maidenhead, UK and, New York: Open University Press and McGraw-Hill Education.

Corrigan, T. 2011. *The Essay Film: From Montaigne, After Marker,* Oxford and New York: Oxford University Press.

De Jong, W., Knudsen, E. and Rothwell, J. 2013. *Creative Documentary: Theory and Practice,* New York and London: Routledge.

Gildea, V. 2008. *An Interview With – Documentary Filmmaker Pat Collins* [Online]. Dublin. Available: http://filmbase.ie/an-interview-with-documentary-filmmaker-pat-collins/#.V3TjlVczPzI [Accessed 21 August 2017].

IFB/BSÉ. 2018. *Documentary* [Online]. Available: www.irishfilmboard.ie/ funding/production-loans/documentary [Accessed 2 February 2018].

Knell, J. 2011. Pyjama Girls (Maya Derrington 2010). *Estudios Irlandeses,* 6, 207–10.

Leahy, E. 2014. *Community Filmmaking in Ireland.* Doctoral thesis, Trinity College Dublin.

Molloy, P. 2010. Labour of Love Proves a Box-office Hit. *The Sunday Business Post,* 12 September, p. 6.

Molony, S. 2014. House and Home, Structuring Absence in Post-Celtic Tiger Documentary. *In:* Negra, D. and Tasker, Y. (eds.) *Gendering the Recession, Media and Culture in an Age of Austerity.* Durham and London: Duke University Press.

Neville, P. 2015. Mediating between His & Hers: An Exploration of Gender Representations and Self-Representations. *In:* Monahan, B. (ed.) *Ireland and Cinema, Culture and Contexts.* New York and Basingstoke: Palgrave Macmillan.

Nichols, B. 1991. *Representing Reality: Issues and Concepts in Documentary,* Bloomington and Indianapolis: Indiana University Press.

O'Brien, H. 2004. *The Real Ireland,* Manchester: Manchester University Press.

O'Brien, H. 2015. Alan Gilsenan: The Life of the Mind. *In:* Pettitt, L. and Kopschitz Bastos, B. (eds.) *The Road to God Knows Where/A Estrada Para Deus Sabe Onde.* Florianópolis, SC: Universidade Federal de Santa Catarina.

O'Connell, D. 2012. Dióg O'Connell interviews Ken Wardrop, Director of *His & Hers* (2010). *In:* MacKeogh, C. and O'Connell, D. (eds.) *Documentary in a Changing State, Ireland Since the 1990s.* Cork: Cork University Press.

Rascaroli, L., Monahan, B. and Young, G. (eds.) 2014. *Amateur Filmmaking: the Home Movie, the Archive, the Web,* New York: Bloomsbury Academic.

Smyth, G. 2001. *Space and the Irish Cultural Iimagination,* Basingstoke: Palgrave.

Wayne, M. 2008. Documentary as Critical and Creative Research. *In:* Austin, T. and De Jong, W. (eds.) *Rethinking Documentary, New Perspectives, New Practices.* Maidenhead, UK and New York: Open University Press and McGraw Hill Education.

Whittaker, R. 2010. *Spotlight on 'Pyjama Girls'* [Online]. Available: http://filmireland.net/2010/08/17/pyjama-girls/ [Accessed 20 August 2017].

Short film
Pentecost (Peter McDonald, 2011)

Actor Peter McDonald's *Pentecost* (which was nominated for an Academy Award in the same year as *The Shore*) may be set in a different time and place, but it still plays out recognisable tropes of Irishness that must account in part for its nomination. The short film is set in 1977 and opens with altar boy, Damien Lynch (Scott Graham), swinging the incense burner with excessive vigour and knocking Fr Hanley (Don Wycherley) off his feet. His mortified father, Pat Lynch (Michael McElhatton), bars him from watching soccer for three months, a particularly cruel punishment given that Damien's team, Liverpool, are shortly to play in the European Cup final. Damien is offered a chance to redeem himself when the Archbishop (Des Nealon) comes to celebrate Mass and the parish finds that he is the only available altar boy trained to swing the thurible.

Written with a relish in the richness of the spoken word, *Pentecost* speaks to memories of growing up in Ireland in an era when Catholicism was at the heart of family life and the parish revolved around the Church. It is also a classic rendering of boyhood football infatuation. The film is crisply edited, with a cast who was well accustomed to playing comedy, an assured child performance from Graham, and an eye for the detail of 1970s decor, particularly Damien's multi-patterned bed clothing and his wall of football posters. It is also unashamed to render the past of Catholic life as a time marked by well-intended paternalism. The elision of the paternalism of Church and family is most telling in one brief response, when Damien assents to his father's admonishments to behave with 'yes, father', a choice of wording more commonly reserved for addressing a priest.

Most of all, with its turn to surreal slapstick and its invocation of popular cultural markers, *Pentecost* recalls the hit comedy series, *Father Ted* (Channel 4, 1996–8). A key sequence takes place ahead of the Archbishop's Mass, where Fr O'Toole (Eamonn Hunt) drills the altar boys in their routine in the manner of a football coach in the locker room before a big match – a scene that will ring true to anyone who has played schoolboy team sports.

In this scenario, it is perhaps no surprise that Damien's mother, Marie (Valerie Spelman) is reduced to the role of onlooker. Her part in the short film is simply to register silent support for her husband; still, it is remarkable that she doesn't have one line of dialogue other than to repeat the grace after her husband at table. This is a film that is absolutely about innocent memories of Irish boyhood, a recasting of the Irish past as a time of simple dreams and benign social structures.

5
Irish history and trauma

The movement away from historical filmmaking that coincided with the flowering of the Celtic Tiger had its origins, as we saw in the introduction, in the new ideological imperatives of the boom years. Focusing on contemporary Ireland allowed the younger generation of Irish filmmakers to distinguish themselves from their predecessors and what often seemed like an unhealthy obsession with the past. Technology too played no small part in this shift: early digital cameras were unsuited to the historical drama and its tradition of perfectly composed images. The lower budgets of the digital era were another consideration, given the cost of shooting period dramas. As well as signalling the waning of the history film, the late 1990s and early twenty-first century also saw the cycle of local heritage films that had accounted for much of the filmmaking of the preceding years come to a close.

Irish heritage cinema – *Hear My Song* (Peter Chelsom, 1991), *Into the West, War of the Buttons* (John Roberts, 1993), *Broken Harvest* (Maurice O'Callaghan, 1994), *The Run of the Country* (Peter Yates, 1995) and others – was distinctive for being structurally and thematically conservative, particularly in terms of gender representations. These films tended to be rural-based and many centred their narratives on children, whose state of innocence became a palimpsest for Ireland of old, and by extension, the innocent Irish people of bygone times. They share this nostalgic mode with heritage cinema from other territories, particularly the pastoral nostalgia of works such as *Jean de Florette* (Claude Berri, 1986) and *Manon des Sources* (Berri, 1986). By locating their narratives in the countryside and in the past, or even in a version of the countryside defined by pastness, the Irish productions were able to make a break with the traumatic imagery of the Troubles and the impression of a country defined by lawlessness and violence. In this, the films had much in common with Irish Tourist Board (Fáilte Ireland) campaigns designed to persuade tourists that a visit to Ireland was a visit to a country of timeless and ancient beauty, populated by welcoming natives who had no axe to grind with foreigners (particularly the lucrative UK tourist market). Drawing on theories of the tourist gaze, it was evident that many of the films replicated such a gaze as part of their aesthetic (Barton, 2004: 148–56).

As we will see in Chapter 7, the tourist film did not entirely disappear. *P.S. I Love You* (Richard LaGravenese, 2007) and *Leap Year* (Anand Tucker, 2010) continued in the heritage tradition of suggesting that to travel to Ireland was to travel back in time, with the new attraction of a handsome Irishman as a reward. Heritage practices have lingered on in other productions – in *Song of the Sea* for instance. On television, as Anthony Mcintyre (2016) has discussed, *Moone Boy* (Sky, 2012–15) recreated a 1980s rural childhood that was at once nostalgic for older spatial configurations, specifically the mother in the home, but more progressive in its depiction of new formations of homosocial friendships. In cinema, Thaddeus O'Sullivan's *Stella Days* (2012), about Fr Daniel Barry's (Michael Sheen) attempts to open a cinema in a small Tipperary village in the late 1950s, is typical of the Irish version of the heritage film in its combination of mild social criticism, here the narrowmindedness of the Catholic hierarchy, with a seductively photographed vision of small-town Ireland in the era of rural electrification.

The release of *Stella Days* was more of an anachronism than a trend, with few contemporary Irish filmmakers interested in replicating its aesthetic. Instead, the early twenty-first century witnessed the release of a series of high-profile history films that revisited the past as a site of trauma. A number of these dealt with the Troubles (and are discussed in the next chapter). Of the remainder – *The Magdalene Sisters* (Peter Mullan, 2002); *The Wind that Shakes the Barley*; *Philomena* (Stephen Frears, 2013); *Jimmy's Hall* (Ken Loach, 2014) – it is worth noting how many were the work of British filmmakers. The most prominent emigration narratives of this period, *In America* (Jim Sheridan, 2002) and *Brooklyn*, however, came from Irish directors and the local industry was responsible for several lower-key releases, including *Song for a Raggy Boy* (Aisling Walsh, 2003); *Kings* (Tom Collins, 2007); *The Secret Scripture* (Jim Sheridan, 2017).

Why this group of British filmmakers should have been attracted to the telling of Irish history cannot be easily explained. The most convincing argument is that in the early twenty-first century, Irish history came to be widely understood as the locus for the depiction of trauma, not for reasons of postcolonality alone or the lengthy tradition of forced emigration, but because of the more recent revelations of abusive Church power. Anchored by their guarantee of factuality, these films invited global audiences to relate their own personal/national traumas to the Irish stories, while also reassuring them that the events depicted were over and safely in the past, indeed in someone else's past. That these films were in the English language certainly aided their circulation; at the same time their focus on Irish characters rendered them both 'us' and 'Other', part of the dominant culture but at the same time its white, underclass Other. Only for Irish audiences were these stories native, yet, I suggest, the local audience could claim the same viewing position as the global audience, watching these films as offerings from another time and place.

Personal trauma in these productions is consistently deployed to invite associative connections with the wider concept of cultural trauma. Cultural trauma (whether as a result of war, genocide, terrorism, political crisis, economic crisis, or other, such as institutional abuse) is endemic to contemporary society. Piotr Sztompka (2000: 458), for instance, argues:

> I believe cultural trauma is most threatening, because like all cultural phenomena it has the strongest inertia; it persists and lingers considerably longer than other kinds of trauma, sometimes over several generations, preserved in collective memory or hibernating in collective subconsciousness, and occasionally gaining salience when conducive circumstances arise.

In an important attempt to define film's relation to cultural trauma, E. Ann Kaplan (2001: 204) has distinguished four main positions for viewers of trauma films: they are introduced to the traumatic theme, but comforted by the film's closure; they are vicariously traumatised by the intensity of the image and may recoil in horror; they are positioned as a voyeur; and they are addressed as a witness. As we will shortly see, these distinctions very usefully help to understand how the history films discussed in this chapter can undercut the comfort of narrative closure through moments of intense emotional engagement.

Narrating abuse

The Magdalene Sisters takes its place amongst a series of exposés concerning the Catholic Church and institutional abuse. Most writers on the Irish scandals agree that child sexual abuse entered the public domain with the Kilkenny incest case of 1993 when a father of two was sentenced to seven years imprisonment on pleading guilty to rape, incest and assault against his eldest daughter. Extensive media coverage of the case, including interviews with Mary, the man's daughter, ensured that this became a turning point in Irish public discourse. Prior to that, the physical abuse of children was common knowledge but also common practice. Starting with *Dear Daughter* (RTÉ, 1996), the role of the Church in covering up physical and sexual abuse and the treatment of children in religious-run institutions was exposed in a series of television documentaries: *Sex in a Cold Climate* (Channel 4, 1998); *States of Fear* (RTÉ, 1999); *Suing the Pope* (BBC, 2002); *Cardinal Secrets* (RTÉ, 2002); *Deliver Us From Evil* (Amy J. Berg, 2006). The release of two high-profile fiction films, *Doubt* (John Patrick Shanley, 2008) and *Spotlight* (Tom McCarthy, 2015) created further associative links between the Irish Catholic Church and child abuse, as did the popular television series, *Ray Donovan* (Showtime, 2013–) and the Netflix documentary, *The Keepers* (2017).

Shortly after the release of *The Magdalene Sisters* came the global success that was Dan Brown's *The Da Vinci Code* (2003), a novel that relished the potential in portraying religious faith as devious, violent and sinister. Globally, Catholicism has become shorthand for a medieval adherence to a hegemony of evil-doers shrouded in the mystery of ritual. The close associations between Irishness and Catholicism have in turn elevated Ireland to a test case par excellence for the deconstruction of Catholic hegemony certainly, but also of authority generally.

James Smith's interpretation of the success of *The Magdalene Sisters* in America reflects this point:

> The film's American release … coincided with an ongoing two-year media frenzy that pursued revelations of clerical child sexual abuse across every Catholic diocese in the United States … These international scandals thus became the interpretative prism through which audiences viewed and understood Mullan's film. (Smith, 2007: 139)

Since Smith's writing, *Spotlight* dramatised the real events of the Boston abuse scandal, much of it perpetrated by Irish priests. Constructed to reflect the conspiracy thrillers of the 1970s, *Spotlight*'s popularity among viewers certainly could be ascribed to a general satisfaction in seeing these old pillars of authority taken down.

Based closely on the stories told in the earlier documentary, *Sex in a Cold Climate,* as well as on other sources such as Patricia Burke-Brogan's play *Eclipsed* (first produced in 1992), *The Magdalene Sisters* is set in County Dublin in the early 1960s and follows the fates of four young women, Margaret (Anne-Marie Duff) who has been raped by her cousin; Rose (Dorothy Duffy) and Crispina (Eileen Walsh), who are single mothers, the latter being mildly intellectually disabled; and the orphan, Bernadette (Nora Jane Noone), who is deemed a liability because of her openly expressed sexuality. Incarcerated in the Magdalene Asylum run by the Sisters of Mercy, the young women experience sexual, physical and mental abuse. Crispina is removed to a psychiatric hospital after an episode where Margaret takes her revenge on the abusive priest by placing stinging leaves in his underwear in the laundry; the other three eventually escape.

Mainstream cinema most commonly addresses issues of cultural trauma via narratives of personal trauma, encouraging audience identification with the victims, and offering hope of a better future, or resolution of the traumatic events. We can see this at work very clearly in *The Magdalene Sisters*. Mullan has spoken in interview of how his film was more spectacle-driven than that of his former director, Ken Loach: 'It's [*The Magdalene Sisters*] a rainy-day, sit-down-and-see women's drama that happened to be about something important' (in James, 2003: 17). The melodramatic effect of Mullan's directorial approach reaches its apogee in the sequence in which Margaret orchestrates the young women's escape. Facing down the evil Sister Bridget (Geraldine McEwan) as she grapples for the keys to the safe, Margaret screams, 'Let go, you fucking twisted bitch, let go!' Shortly afterwards she yells behind her at the wakened nuns, 'Don't you fucking think of coming after us.' Evidently this sequence provides its audiences with the kind of cathartic release that melodrama promises. Yet, its use of language and its enactment are completely implausible, nor are they consistent with the conclusions to the interviews in *Sex in a Cold Climate* where the narrators remember how they variously left the Laundries.

Although both *Song for a Raggy Boy* and *Philomena* end on more downbeat notes, the sense of closure remains. The former, adapted from the memoir of the same name by Patrick Galvin who also wrote the original screenplay, is set in a fictional Christian Brothers reform school, St. Jude's, in Cork. Its director, Aisling Walsh, had already made the television film *Sinners* (BBC, 2002), set in a Magdalene laundry and, like Mullan's film, starring Anne-Marie Duff. *Song for a Raggy Boy* thus functions as a male counterpart to the Magdalene narrative. It opens in 1939 with the arrival at the school of its first lay teacher, William Franklin (Aidan Quinn). Franklin suffers from traumatic flashbacks to his days fighting with the communists in the Spanish Civil War where he witnessed the executions of his wife, Rosa (Simone Bendix) and comrade, Preston (Danny Sapani). Once at the school, Franklin discovers a brutal regime, engineered by the sadistic Brother John (Iain Glen). What he does not realise is that there is also a concealed culture of sexual abuse.[1] Franklin befriends a number of the boys and introduces them to poetry. Despite his interventions on their behalf, the brightest of the boys, Liam Mercier (John Travers) is eventually beaten to death and Brother Mac (Marc Warren) continues to abuse Patrick Delaney (Chris Newman). If this synopsis hardly suggests closure, the film's reliance on a sentimental, *Dead Poets Society* (Peter Weir, 1989) structure allows it to borrow from the codes of the redemptive melodrama. Thus, the boys learn Yeats and the poetry of romantic loss, and when it seems that Franklin will leave, Delaney steps forward and recites Eva Gore-Booth's 'Comrades' (1916), persuading him to stay. Critiquing this ending and the film's elision of the Spanish Civil War and Irish Catholicism under one undifferentiated regime of terror, Emile Pine (2011: 33) has argued that Mercier's death 'is represented as a sacrifice that ensures change and mercy for the other boys'.

If closure is one consequence of adherence to the structure of the melodrama, another quite different effect is the vicarious trauma of the sequences of physical and sexual abuse. Both *The Magdalene Sisters* and *Song for a Raggy Boy* include a number of scenes where the children are brutally punished. These include head-shearing (in both films), and, in the former, a brief cameo by the director, Peter Mullan, as the father who takes a strap to his daughter. Analysing *The Magdalene Sisters*, Martin McLoone has drawn attention to the sequence where the priest, Fr Fitzroy (Daniel Costello) begins to itch madly and then strip off his clothing, running naked into the bushes after Margaret puts stinging nettles in the laundry to punish him for sexually abusing Crispina. The latter, of course, has also acquired a rash, which she exposes to the congregation gathered at the open-air mass, pulling up her dress to her thighs. She begins to scream after the priest, 'You're not a man of God' over and over again so that the scene becomes unbearable to witness. 'This scene as a whole', McLoone (2008: 123) writes, 'marks Irish cinema's most devastating attack on the priest and all that he represents, his humiliation achieved through a combination of earthy humour and heart-rending anguish'. One could also add that it questions the concept of bearing witness. As the camera turns to the onlookers, local people from the neighbouring village, their faces are blank and apparently unable or unwilling to register the events. In later years, if asked, will they admit that they knew what was going on?

Just as *The Magdalene Sisters* challenges the viewer to watch, so too does *Song for a Raggy Boy*. Auxiliadora Pérez-Vides and Rocío Carrasco-Carrasco (2015) have argued that in Walsh's film, the beatings and sexual abuse reflect a regime of corporeal control that can only be broken by verbal expression, that is, through poetry and through the knowledge imparted in the end credits that Delaney becomes a journalist in later life. Thus, 'the subjects' renegotiation of the discourse of painful corporeality leads to a renewed version of their individuality' (2015: 20). These scenes of 'painful corporeality' punctuate *Song for a Raggy Boy* arguably to greater effect than the somewhat saccharine melodramatic narrative, leading one to question whether there is an alternative reading of the film that ignores the redemptive conclusion in favour of its affective visuals. In other words, the scenes of abuse are more memorable than the 'happy' ending.

· Abuse narratives and the white male redeemer

The casting of Aidan Quinn, the only major star in the film, in the role of Franklin inevitably places him at the centre of *Song for a Raggy Boy* and it is through him that the narrative is focalised. Indeed, it is hard to avoid the conclusion that the film is as much about his redemption as it is about the history of abuse. This trope is even more pronounced in Stephen Frears's *Philomena*. Scripted by Steve Coogan and Jeff Pope from Martin Sixsmith's (2009) *The Lost Child of Philomena Lee*, the film makes major changes to the original account of Sixsmith's project to help Lee (played in the film as a teenager by Sophie Kennedy Clark and then by Judi Dench) find her birth son. The real-life Lee became pregnant in her teens and was placed in the charge of the nuns at the Sean Ross Abbey in Roscrea. There she gave birth to a son, Anthony, and, under duress, signed a consent form for his adoption. Abandoned by her family, she was forced to stay on in the Abbey's laundries to pay back the £100 deemed appropriate recompense by the nuns for her 'care'. The most significant divergence from Sixsmith's book is the introduction of Sixsmith himself as a character. The book is written in the third person, reconstructing moments from Philomena and Hess's lives, with only the occasional authorial intervention explaining his research. In the film, Steve Coogan's Sixsmith vies with Dench for narrative centrality, so that the film is as much about his quest and his personal redemption in fulfilling it. Arguably too, making *Philomena* enabled Coogan, better known for his comedy persona, Alan Partridge, to reposition himself as a 'serious' actor.

In the film, then, Philomena reveals the story to her daughter, Jane (Anna Maxwell Martin) on Anthony's fiftieth birthday and Jane persuades Sixsmith (Coogan), who has recently lost his job, to undertake finding her brother. Despising his assignment on this 'human interest story', Sixsmith sets off to Washington with Lee. There they will find that Anthony, now renamed Michael Hess, worked under the Bush administration, rising to become chief legal counsel to George Bush Sr. The film's warmth is derived from its structure as a mismatched couple comedy, with Sixsmith's cynicism and his cultural snobbery being played off against Lee's earthiness. Some of that comedy makes for uneasy viewing, such as the sequence in the Irish countryside where Lee confesses to Sixsmith that she enjoyed the sex that made her pregnant and that, 'Well,

I didn't even know I had a clitoris, Martin.' There is just a little too much reliance here on the old trope of simple Irish charm versus sophisticated Anglo-Saxon reserve (as well as the 'shock' of an older person using the word clitoris) and that trope ghosts the film. So too does the suggestion that Sixsmith somehow substitutes for Philomena's lost son/lover. More successfully, *Philomena* explores how its titular character could still hold on to her faith after her experiences with the Catholic Church. As will be discussed further in Chapter 7, contemporary popular culture is infused with anti-authoritarianism, a sentiment that accelerated in the wake of the financial crisis. The old authority figures, notably the priest, repeatedly appear as emblematic of a power structure that has failed its constituency. Yet, alongside that anger at authority lies a sense of loss, which this film addresses, arguing for the power of forgiveness and tolerance.

Ken Loach, imperialism and pastoralism

Certainly the most controversial history film of the opening decade of the twenty-first century was Ken Loach's *The Wind That Shakes the Barley* (hereafter *The Wind*). His first Irish-set film since *Hidden Agenda* (1990), it was followed in 2014 by *Jimmy's Hall*. The common thread running through the first two films is Loach's understanding of Ireland as the test-case for British imperialism, while both the latter films explore the failure of socialism under the Catholic state. *The Wind* was widely viewed as the corrective to Neil Jordan's *Michael Collins* (1996). In the place of Jordan's eulogy to Michael Collins and the politics of peaceful compromise, Loach adjudges the Treaty to be an imperialist conspiracy to divide the Irish against each other. Another marked difference between the two films is Loach's focus on ordinary people and his setting in the Irish countryside (identifiably County Cork).

The Wind won the Palme d'Or at the 2006 Cannes Film Festival and drew the ire of the British tabloids, conservative press, and certain members of the Conservative party, notably Michael Gove. Columnist Simon Heffer (2006) expressed a commonly held right-wing view of 'red Ken' when he wrote in the *Daily Telegraph* of Loach as follows: 'He hates this country, yet leeches off it, using public funds to make his repulsive films. And no, I haven't seen it [*The Wind*], any more than I need to read Mein Kampf to know what a louse Hitler was.'

In Ireland, just as had been the case with *Michael Collins*, the media became the willing host to a spate of often ill-tempered disputes over certain of Loach's historical statements.[2] Historian Roy Foster (2006) published a critique of the film in The *Dublin Review*, arguing that Loach gave, 'a completely misleading idea of the historical situation in Ireland

Figure 11 Cillian Murphy in *The Wind That Shakes the Barley*

at the time' (2006: 46). The two crucial errors in *The Wind*, according to Foster, were the impression that IRA resistance was created in response to the Black and Tan reign of terror, and that those who opposed the Treaty did so for reasons of socialism, 'democracy' and anti-partitionism (2006: 46). Partially in response to Foster, and to other critics of the film's historical accuracy, Loach's historical advisor, Donal Ó Drisceoil, subsequently published an article in *Radical History Review*, defending the film as inspired by stories such as that of Ernie O'Malley, 'whose memoirs provided the inspiration for the character of the young medical doctor, Damien' (2009: 7), and Tom Barry, 'the famed West Cork guerrilla leader and British army veteran who led the legendary Kilmichael ambush and whose memoirs inform [Paul] Laverty's screenplay' (2009: 9). Meanwhile, Loach and Laverty have said in interview that they intended their film to be read as a comment on British imperialism in the context of the Iraq War (Laverty in Archibald, 2007: 30).

Despite Loach's intentions, few commentators on *The Wind* viewed it in the light of current British imperialism but, just as the debate over *Michael Collins* sparked huge public interest in the period (Barton, 2004: 142–4), so too did Loach's film, particularly given its potential to be interpreted as anti-peace process (Loach evidently sees the continuation of partition as unfinished business). In common with the director's oeuvre as a whole, *The Wind* relies on the codes of melodrama to convey its message and it was certainly its immersive melodramatic techniques that were in part responsible for its success with Irish audiences even as they drew the ire of the film's detractors. As John Hill (2011a: 220) has noted in his analysis of *The Wind* in the wider context of Loach's work, the director's 'mixing of "fact" and "fiction", the stark dramatic oppositions and melodramatic turns – are often the very elements that arouse such strong responses'. In particular, the divisions between Damien (Cillian Murphy) and Teddy (Padraic Delaney), two brothers who find themselves on either side of the Treaty debate, intensify the film's emotional impact, particularly at its ending when Teddy is forced to execute Damien. The latter is the classic reluctant hero, the doctor who is about to leave for England when a series of incidents caused by Black and Tan brutality convinces him to join the fight for independence. Damien is also the film's conscience, articulated most cogently in the sequence in which he executes the young man who was forced to inform: 'I studied anatomy for five years', he tells the socialist, Dan (Liam Cunningham). 'And now I'm going to shoot this man in the head. I've known Chris Reilly since he was a child. I hope this Ireland we're fighting for is worth it.'

Again, in keeping with the melodrama, and the Loachian oeuvre, the villains are one-dimensional and without the kind of family ties and backstory attributed to the heroes. No one would dispute the terror wreaked by the Black and Tans, themselves demobbed World War One veterans, and by the RIC (Royal Irish Constabulary). However, the associations created at the end of *The Wind* between the Black and Tans and the Free State troops are more difficult to justify. Loach's extended first section is devoted to the conflict between local and invader. The emotional high-point of this engagement is the sequence of Teddy being tortured by having his finger nails extracted (another instance of melodrama's capacity to traumatise vicariously). Having established the terror of the occupying forces, Loach then includes towards the shorter end section of his film a less than subtle edit that sees the defeated Black and Tans march out of the village and Teddy's Free Staters march in.

A consistent Loachian motif, particularly evident in the Irish films, is his investment in pastoralism to evince a natural order threatened by capitalist modernity. *The Wind* opens in a field where a game of hurling is being played, and much of the film's action takes place on heathery bogs and green fields. This is the habitus of the film's Irish protagonists, whose identities are determined by their open-air environment, whereas their enemies are associated with the darkened indoors of barracks and cells, or in the case of Sir John Hamilton, the anglicised big house. Ó Drisceoil (2009: 8) commends Loach for his engagement with issues of gender, particularly during the scene in the Republican court, in which the woman magistrate, Lily (Fiona Lawton) rules against a local merchant for charging excessive interest on a loan. Teddy's usurping of the magistrate's decision, he argues, 'hints at the postrevolutionary diminution of women's public role in Irish life'. Another key figure is Sinéad (Orla Fitzgerald), who may be Damien's love interest but equally holds strong political views that she is unafraid to act on. The strength of her depiction is, however, somewhat undermined by Loach's gendering of space and history and his fondness for pastoral settings. She is introduced to the narrative when the Black and Tans raid her family farm and kill her brother, Micheail (Laurence Barry), for refusing to identify himself in English. Yet, despite her active participation in the struggle, she is consistently identified with the home and the natural world. She lives with her grandmother, Peggy (Mary O'Riordan), a character whom Loach almost replicates in *Jimmy's Hall* in the person of Alice (Aileen Henry). Peggy (and Alice) are the classic emblems of Mother Ireland, the older woman who stands for a tradition of suffering and resistance. The most intimate scene between Sinéad and Damien takes place in an idyllic wooded grove; and in another moment of intense violence, her head is shorn in the yard outside her home. This space, as Pilar Villar-Argáiz (2007: 197) notes, literally stands in-between the political and the domestic and 'allegorizes, on the one hand, tradition, heritage and roots; and, on the other, an indomitable determination to fight back, to change the past for a better future'.

As these examples illustrate, Loach's radicalism is rooted in a reverence for tradition and an older way of life. His revolution is an agrarian one, fed by hundreds of years of injustice. Hill (2011b) has argued that Loach's Irish characters, when they appear in British-set films, function as a 'lumpenproleteriat'. But in Ireland, they are idealists and romantics. This theme is further developed in *Jimmy's Hall*, the factually based story of another doomed idealist, James Gralton, who returned to Ireland from the United States with the dream of establishing a socialist utopia in the form of a dance hall, where jazz might be played. I have analysed *Jimmy's Hall* in detail elsewhere (Barton, 2016), but, while the film enjoyed little of the critical and commercial success of *The Wind*, it remains closely related to the earlier film through its rural setting and melodramatic structure. In fact, it is easy to consider it as a successor to the earlier film, the inevitable working through of the triumph of a priest-ridden bourgeois Catholic state over the ideals of socialism.

Stephen Legg (2004: 103) has written as follows:

> Trauma and nostalgia are theoretically and practically linked. While nostalgia denotes a positive attachment to a past real or imaginary home, trauma denotes the negative inability to deal effectively with a past event. While both conditions represent problematic engagements with the past, nostalgia often focuses on a time and place before or beyond a traumatic incident.

This explains much of the appeal of Ireland as a site for the exploration of traumatic narratives. Over and again in the films discussed here, pastoral settings represent an older, innocent country. The 'stinging nettle' scene in *The Magdalene Sisters* is set in sun-drenched fields outside a quaint small village; a repeated shot of a field where the boys gather to harvest punctuates *Song for a Raggy Boy*, creating a space of solace outside the reform school. Philomena opens up to Martin on a walk through unspoilt rural Ireland. Loach, as we have just seen, offsets traditionalism, often configured through a strong matriarchal figure, against bourgeois modernity. Nostalgia and trauma are thus interwoven in these films, which rely on an appreciation of the spaces of this older rural Ireland, both by local and overseas viewers, to intensify their narratives of traumatic despoilment.

The Appendix demonstrates just how massive a popular success *The Wind* was in Ireland, as was *The Magdalene Sisters*. For certain sectors of the viewing population, particularly for *The Magdalene Sisters*, these films had a directly therapeutic effect and Mullan's film was welcomed as a vindication of their own repressed narratives. 'Maybe now Irish people will begin to believe', one commented after seeing a preview of *The Magdalene Sisters* (in McGarry, 2000). For another commentator, however, the response was different:

> The stories told in The Magdalene Sisters were horrific. Thankfully, it is all in the past. And let's hope that religious [sic] are never, ever, again allowed to abuse their positions, as was the case in these awful places in the past. But if you go to see this joyless film, remember that, just like priests, not all nuns are bad. (Donohue, 2002)

The relief contained within 'Thankfully, it is all in the past' reflects comments made by David Lloyd (2008: 32) in the context of the memorialisation of the Famine:

> If the function of therapeutic modernity is to have us lose our loss in order to become good subjects, then the very process of mourning the dead is at once their condemnation, their devaluation – perhaps not explicitly but

effectively a judgement of their inadequacy as subjects and the inadequacy of their cultural formations to modernity.

We might assume then that for many Irish viewers, these films became a way of expressing the pastness of their material; in other words, they functioned to allow local audiences to distance themselves from their own past, to 'other' that past. By becoming consumers of their own past, they were able to express their control over it.

Emigration as trauma narrative

The historical films discussed above revisit key Irish historical events, couching them most commonly in the language of trauma and melodrama. Another key traumatic narrative of Irish life, both in the past and present, is that of emigration. This forms the subject of several of the films from this period, notably *In America*, *Kings* and *Brooklyn*. Key to all three films is a concern with re-situating 'home', with the first two formally constructed around memory, or to be more accurate memories. *Brooklyn* is the most conventional of the three and comes closest to older understandings of melodrama (as the woman's film), rather than simply as a pervasive cinematic narrative mode (Williams, 1998). In this, it bears certain similarities to another, much less successful historical film, Jim Sheridan's *The Secret Scripture* (2017). Both productions share an investment in retelling Irish historical events from the perspective of a female protagonist (if less Mother Ireland than her cast-off daughters). Sheridan's film suffered critically from his evisceration of Sebastian Barry's highly regarded novel (from which the film is adapted) and his decision to render what remained as an old-fashioned period drama. Even this was hampered by plot inconsistencies as well as an unconvincing central love affair between Rose (Rooney Mara) and Michael (Jack Reynor). I will return to *Brooklyn* shortly, but for now, I will consider how Sheridan's earlier, much more successful *In America* and Collins's *Kings* rely on specific cinematic techniques in their attempts to render in an affective manner the construction of memory.

Kaplan (2001: 204) discusses how film reproduces the processes of traumatic memory by refusing 'the ordered sequence we associate with narratives. Images are repeated but without meaning; they do not have a clear beginning, middle and end. Rather they erupt into cinematic space, unheralded in the story as in an individual's consciousness'. Of particular relevance to a discussion of these films, particularly *In America* and *Kings*, is the use of the flashback to indicate acts of memory, and the use of degraded home-movie footage to support this.

Adapted from Jimmy Murphy's play *The Kings of the Kilburn High Road* (first performed in 2001) and set in the present day, *Kings* is the story of a group of middle-aged men in London's Cricklewood who come together for the funeral of one of their fellow Connemara emigrants. The narrative unfolds in a disjointed manner as the men variously recall their time together in Ireland as young men, and in particular an incident during a Galway hooker race when the dead man, Jackie (Seán Ó Tarpaigh) rescued Joe (Colm Meaney) from drowning. Joe is the only one of the group who has enjoyed any notable success in England, and this is the cause of some resentment, particularly given that he refused Jackie work on his sites. The remaining friends communicate together in Irish and through a shared and destructive relationship with alcohol, which it emerges is the reason for Joe turning down Jackie. Joe himself has developed an upmarket cocaine habit. As the men drink, so Jackie appears like a ghost on screen in a series of shots filmed in greyish washed-out colours. His is a disturbing memory, as much for the revelation of the manner of his death (by suicide) as for the loss it represents to his friends. By contrast, the flashbacks to the boat race are shot in intensified colour and processed to look like home-movie footage. In her analysis of the production of memory in *Kings*, in particular, the scene where Máirtín 'witnesses' Jackie's death (an event at which he was not actually present), Jennie Carlsten (2015: 159) writes that the flashback 'functions here in ways commonly associated with art cinema – to cast doubt on a version of events, to present the possibility of unreliable narration and as a subjective marker'.

Even life in the present day is presented in fragments, with glimpses of Máirtín's (Barry Barnes) failing marriage, and half-references to his abusive relationship with his wife, Maggie (Gabrielle Reidy) interwoven into the unfolding action. The men's lives, the film suggests, are as fragmented in the present day as are their memories. The dialogue refers constantly to the problematic definition of 'home'. This is at once Connemara, to where two of the men dream of returning to set up a business, and London. Yet, they are reminded, often by Jackie's father, Micil (Peader O'Treasaigh), who has travelled to London for his son's funeral, that there is no place for them in the new Ireland of the Celtic Tiger. In the pub, where they wake Jackie, the landlady hustles them into a side bar, rightly anticipating that they will disrupt her new, multicultural clientele with their drinking and rebel songs. With their 'private' language, and anachronistic performance of braggadocio alternating with self-pity, they are equally not part of modern, cosmopolitan London.

In America shares with *Kings* the use of home-movie footage as a device for conveying memory, although the two productions have little else in common other than emigration as a theme. Here, the flashback functions differently, less as traumatic shock and more as consoling memory. Written with his daughters, Naomi and Kirsten, Sheridan's film is a loose retelling of his family's arrival in America as illegal immigrants in the 1980s. With his daughters now renamed Christy (Sarah Bolger) and Ariel (Emma Bolger), the story adds in the death of their younger brother, Frankie, from a brain tumour, an inclusion based on the real-life death of Jim Sheridan's own brother, Frankie, as a child. In the film, their mother, Sarah (Samantha Morton) hopes for another child even though she has been warned this could be fatal for her. Their father, Johnny (Paddy Considine), is a struggling actor, who, most of all the family, has cut himself off from his emotions in an attempt to blank out his loss.

Throughout the film, Christy captures moments from the family's gradual adjustment to US life on her home-movie camera, on which she also has stored images from Frankie's childhood. Punctuating the diegesis with this remediated (faux) footage enhances the film's engagement with memory. Yet as one particular sequence – where her parents record Christy singing 'Desperado' at a school concert, which the film intercuts with Ariel and Christy watching old footage of the family playing together in the back garden in Dublin – suggests, home movies capture and store moments of shared happiness. In this manner, too, the film produces multiple layers of temporality, though the time of its own setting remains obscure. References to *E.T. the Extra-Terrestrial* (Steven Spielberg, 1982) locate *In America* in the early 1980s. However, as Sheridan has admitted:

> I didn't want everybody from the art department running around changing the license plates on cars in New York … So I gave (Christy) a camcorder and shifted it into the '90s, but I kept the tone of the '80s, so I made it the recent past, like a mythological past. (in Nuckols, 2003)

Whatever the motivation was, the effect of these temporal layers is to heighten the sense of the immigrant family living in two times, past (Irish) time and the present time of American modernity. Another temporal shift occurs with the inclusion in the narrative of African American Matteo (Djimon Hounsou) as a kind of spirit father to the Sullivan family. The associations between blackness and primitivism in the film have been widely critiqued (Vejvoda, 2009), and Matteo, just as E.T., serves as a magical bridge between the worlds of the living and the dead. Very certainly, too, the inclusion of the initially threatening and then benevolent Matteo, was designed to speak to new discourses on immigration in Ireland during the Celtic Tiger years.[3]

In *Kings,* the past can never be fully confronted but must always remain haunting and fragmentary. In *In America* by contrast, the family becomes reconciled to the loss of Frankie and the journey to America through recourse to popular culture, notably the invocation of E.T. as at once the exemplary immigrant and the lost child. Home as the film understands it, is less a physical entity than a feeling of belonging. The Sullivans learn to belong in America through creating networks of identification – with school and work, in the hospital where the baby is born – and through their friendship with Matteo. Rather as Eilis (Saoirse Ronan) will in *Brooklyn* (below) so the Sullivans will reconcile themselves to the processes of emigration and in doing so put Ireland behind them. This underlines the contrast with *Kings* (and other London immigrant narratives such as *I Could Read the Sky* (Nichola Bruce, 1999)) where the Irish are rendered as isolated, from home and host culture.

This questioning of belonging is also central to *Brooklyn.* Nick Hornby's adaptation is largely faithful to Colm Tóibín's (2010) novel and much critical praise went with justification to Saoirse Ronan for her interpretation of the central character, Eilis Lacey, who in the early 1950s emigrates to Brooklyn to work. On the death of her sister, she returns home to Enniscorthy to comfort her mother. Before leaving Brooklyn, on his insistence, she secretly marries her boyfriend, Tony (Emory Cohen) as an assurance that she will return. Back in Ireland, she is drawn to another young man, Jim Farrell (Domhnall Gleeson), and finds herself in the classic predicament of the melodrama, torn between two (decent in this case) men, and the bearer of a secret that will change everything.

The novel (and film's) strength is in couching its narrative in the mode of the day, the female melodrama, but stripping it of that mode's reliance on hyperbolic emotional language. Ronan is particularly effective in conveying how Eilis is changed by her time in Brooklyn, so that on her return to Enniscorthy she has gained enough self-awareness to position herself differently vis-à-vis its rigid social order. This movement towards a more developed sense of self is further indicated by the ever-stronger colours of Eilis's dresses, their assertive cut, and her confident application of make-up. Rather than holding her within the frame, the camera now steps back and watches as she marches firmly into her own future. Only towards the conclusion does the adaptation betray the tone of the novel; in the film, when Miss Kelly (Brid Brennan) confronts Eilis with the fact of her marriage, she retorts sharply, 'I'd forgotten … I'd forgotten what this town is like.' With this, the viewer is assured that she will be making the correct choice to leave small-minded Irish society, a message reinforced by the closing shot of her happy reunion with Tony. Not only that, the film includes a new scene: on the ship back to the United States, the newly confident Eilis repeats the advice she herself was given on her first voyage to a young woman that might be her – to lock the toilet door on the inside, to smarten up, to look confident on arrival – suggesting a cycle of successful female emigration. By contrast, the novel ends musing on memory and how it softens with the passing of time.

In this way, the film dispenses with the central theme of Tóibín's original, that over time Eilis will adapt to her circumstances, and replaces it with the instant gratification of a decision well made. The universality of the film's ending also places it at variance with the moving sequence at the Christmas dinner for the old Irish emigrants in Brooklyn, where the priest, Father Flood (Jim Broadbent) explains to Eilis that these men cannot return to Ireland. Perhaps, it is Eilis's embrace of modernity that allows her the freedom of choice denied the older generation, or the upward mobility she earns through gaining bookkeeping qualifications at night, or a greater flexibility afforded to her on gender grounds. The conclusive ending of the film, however, discourages the viewer from musing on these alternatives.

These differences aside, *Brooklyn* is a thoughtful reworking of the heritage film and of the emigrant narrative. It offers the conventional visual pleasures of the costume drama, and the strong female presence of the 1950s cycle of women's films without their punitive moralising. Eilis has not stepped straight out of a Douglas Sirk melodrama, rather she recalibrates it to suggest that emigration may be a financial imperative but that its trauma is not life defining. In common with so many of the Irish historical trauma narratives, *Brooklyn* points forward to a better future – the viewer's present. It also suggests that 'home' may be 'homes', that the emigrant individual can be at home abroad while still retaining an emotional link to their originating home.

As its box office performance overseas attests, it spoke to a much wider audience than just that of Ireland and one may guess that many of those who sought it out in cinemas found in Crowley's film validation of their own migrant histories. *In America* enjoyed similar critical and commercial success, particularly in the United States, where, on its release in the wake of 9/11, it was widely welcomed for its theme of coming to terms with grief (Crosson, 2008). Others, such as *Kings, The Wind* and *Jimmy's Hall*, testify to the losses inherent in the construction of modernity. All are mainstream releases and act as a reminder of the shift in film culture that has witnessed the erasure of the politically engaged, formally innovative cinema of the earlier generation of Irish filmmakers by proponents of conventional storytelling and, particularly, the language of melodrama.

Notes

1 Galvin's original memoir, which details the physical abuse at St. Conleth's reformatory school in Daingean, County Offaly, did not include sexual abuse. He has since said that it was there in the background but that his story was about redemption through education (Wallace, 2009). The sexual abuse strand in the film seems to be less well integrated into the plot, presumably because it wasn't in the memoir or Galvin's original screenplay.

2 For more on this, see Barton (2007).

3 For more on this mode of addressing issues of diaspora, see Moynihan (2013).

References

Archibald, D. 2007. Correcting Historical Lies: An Interview with Ken Loach and Paul Laverty. *Cineaste,* 23, 26–30.

Barton, R. 2004. *Irish National Cinema,* London and New York: Routledge.

Barton, R. 2007. The Wind That Shakes the Barley. *Estudios Irlandeses,* 2, 262–3.

Barton, R. 2016. Jimmy's Hall, Irish Cinema and the Telling of History. *Review of Irish Studies in Europe,* 1, 93–106.

Brown, D. 2003. *The Da Vinci Code: A Novel,* London and New York: Bantam Press.

Carlsten, J. 2015. Not Thinking Clearly: History and Emotion in the Recent Irish Cinema. *In:* Carlsten, J. and McGarry, F. (eds.) *Film, History and Memory.* London: Palgrave Macmillan.

Crosson, S. 2008. "They can't wipe us out, they can't lick us. We'll go on forever pa, 'cause we're the people": Misrepresenting Death in Jim Sheridan's *In America* (2003). *Estudios Irlandeses,* 3, 65–71.

Donohue, M. 2002. Not All the Religious Were Bad. The Irish Times, 1 November, p. 18.

Foster, R. 2006. The Red and the Green. *The Dublin Review,* Autumn, 43–51.

Heffer, S. 2006. *Bribe Your Own Voters First, Young George* [Online]. Available: www.telegraph.co.uk/comment/personal-view/3625404/Bribe-your-own-voters-first-young-George.html [Accessed 24 October 2017].

Hill, J. 2011a. *Ken Loach: The Politics of Film and Television,* London: BFI.

Hill, J. 2011b. Routes Irish: 'Irishness', 'Authenticity' and the Working Class in the Films of Ken Loach. *Irish Studies Review,* 19, 99–109.

James, N. 2003. Keeping It Clean. *Sight and Sound,* 13, 16–17.

Kaplan, E. A. 2001. Melodrama, Cinema and Trauma. *Screen,* 42, 201–5.

Legg, S. 2004. Memory and Nostalgia. *Cultural Geographies,* 11, 99–107.

Lloyd, D. 2008. Irish Times: Temporalities of Modernity, Dublin: University of Notre Dame/Field Day.

McGarry, P. 2002. Revisiting the Nightmare. *The Irish Times,* 5 October, p. B2.

McIntyre, A. 2016. Moone Boy: Nostalgia, Region and the Elision of Celtic Tiger Aspirationalism. *In:* Coulouma, F. (ed.) *New Perspectives on Irish TV Series: Identity and Nostalgia on the Small Screen.* Oxford and Bern: Peter Lang.

McLoone, M. 2008. *Film, Media and Popular Culture in Ireland: Cityscapes, Landscapes, Soundscapes,* Dublin: Irish Academic Press.

Moynihan, S. 2013. *"Other People's Diasporas": Negotiating Race in Contemporary Irish and Irish American Culture,* Syracuse, NY: Syracuse University Press.

Nuckols, B. 2003. Sheridan's film is a personal story. *Today* [Online]. Available: www.today.com/popculture/sheridan-s-film-personal-story-wbna3606802 [Accessed 16 October 2017].

Ó Drisceoil, D. 2009. Framing the Irish Revolution: Ken Loach's *The Wind That Shakes the Barley. Radical History Review,* Spring, 5–15.

Pérez-Vides, A. and Carrasco-Carrasco, R. 2015. Painful Embodiment in Aisling Walsh's *Song for a Raggy Boy* and Pedro Almodóvar's *Bad Education. Journal of Film and Video,* 67, 14–29.

Pine, E. 2011. *The Politics of Irish Memory: Performing Remembrance in Contemporary Irish culture,* Basingstoke: Palgrave Macmillan.

Sixsmith, M. 2009. *The Lost Child of Philomena Lee: Aa Mother, Her Son and a Fifty-Year Search,* London: Macmillan.

Smith, J. M. 2007. *Ireland's Magdalen Laundries and the Nation's Architecture of Containment,* Notre Dame, IN.: University of Notre Dame Press.

Sztompka, P. 2000. Cultural Trauma: The Other Face of Social Change. *European Journal of Social Theory,* 3, 449–66.

Tóibín, C. 2010. *Brooklyn,* London: Viking.

Vejvoda, K. 2009. The Blood of an Irishwoman: Race and Gender in *The Nephew* and *In America. In:* Barton, R. (ed.) *Screening Irish-America.* Dublin and Portland, OR.: Irish Academic Press.

Villar-Argáiz, P. 2007. Latter-day Mother Irelands: The Role of Women in *Michael Collins* and *The Wind that Shakes the Barley. Estudios Irlandeses,* 2, 183–204.

Wallace, A. 2009. Reprise for a Raggy Boy. *Irish Times,* 31 July, p. 14.

Williams, L. 1998. Melodrama Revisited. *In:* Browne, N. (ed.) *Refiguring American Film Genres: History and Theory.* Berkeley: University of California Press.

Short film
The Shore (Terry George, 2011)

Terry George's Academy Award-winning short film, *The Shore,* was a home-coming in more ways than one. For George, who is now based in the United States, it was his first Northern Ireland-set film since his trio as writer: *In the Name of the Father* (Jim Sheridan, 1993), *Some Mother's Son* (as writer/director, 1996), and *The Boxer* (Jim Sheridan, 1997). Following these, he gained inter-national recognition with *Hotel Rwanda* (2004) which he also directed. By his own admission, he struggled to repeat the success of the latter film, and so went back to Northern Ireland to film a story, or version of it, he had heard in his childhood. The reworked narrative concerns the return to Northern Ireland after many years in America of Jim (Ciarán Hinds), now travelling with his daughter, Pat, played by Irish-born Kerry Condon. She persuades him to reconcile with his 'blood brother', Pat (Conleth Hill), who has married Jim's childhood sweetheart, Mary (Maggie Cronin).

Shot on the County Down coast, close by where George grew up, *The Shore* opens with a twilit scene of men gathering mussels. Cued by an elegiac score, the *mise-en-scène* suggests a place before and outside of the Troubles. This remains the overall tenor of the film, which seems determined to function as a corrective to the screen history of Northern Ireland. Although it was the Troubles that tore the friends apart, there is little to suggest that Jim's return is conditional on the re-establishment of peace. Instead, it fits better into the therapeutic journey home subgenre more familiar from films set in the Republic. This impression is reinforced by George's borrowings from older modes of Irish cinematic story-telling: on their way to Pat's small cottage, Jim and his daughter ask directions of a gravedigger, who furnishes them with such complicated instructions they end up more bemused than enlightened. Once at the cottage, they holler out to Pat who is out with his mates collecting mussels again. The men mistake them for dole agents and attempt a runner. The confusion is ultimately smoothed over and the film ends with the two extended families sharing a meal of shellfish and singing songs together into the night. This comedic trope of the work-shy Irishman and his undermining of authority are redolent of British images of the Celtic Other from *Oh Mr Porter!* (Marcel Varnel, 1937) and *Whisky Galore!* (Alexander Mackendrick, 1949) and equally from their Hollywood equivalents, most notably *The Quiet Man*

(John Ford, 1952). Mary's role in the film is as nurturing housewife and inspirational matriarch, a lesson perhaps to the young Pat in essential femininity.

With its images of a peaceful, sun-drenched rural North and its conservative gendering, *The Shore* is more heritage film than historical deconstruction and a reminder of the difficulty of re-imaging post-Troubles Northern Ireland.

6

Filming Northern Ireland

Production background

One production has dominated the Northern audiovisual sector since 2009 when shooting began and that is *Game of Thrones* (HBO, 2011–). Filmed on locations including the Giant's Causeway, the eighteenth-century cobbled-stone alleyways of central Belfast, and at the Paint Hall Studios (part of the Titanic Studios in the Titanic Quarter), by the end of Series Seven the production had been credited with bringing a total expenditure of £166m on goods and services into the Northern Ireland economy (Northern Ireland Screen, 2016: 10).[1] The filming led directly to the building of two new sound stages at the Titanic Studios, and the development of Belfast Harbour Studios. It also resulted in Northern Ireland landing another fantasy series, *The Frankenstein Chronicles* (ITV Encore, 2015–), which shares the same executive producer and many of the crew of *Game of Thrones*. Tourism has been another major beneficiary of the *Game of Thrones* effect (Stone, 2016). Other film and television productions from the period include: *The Fall* (BBC, 2013–16); *The Journey* (Nick Hamm, 2016); *Miss Julie* (Liv Ullman, 2015); *Line of Duty* (BBC, 2012–); *The Lost City of Z* (James Gray, 2016); *Millie Inbetween* (BBC, 2014–); *Morgan* (Luke Scott, 2016); *My Mother and Other Strangers* (BBC, 2016); *A Patch of Fog* (Michael Lennox, 2015); *The Secret* (ITV, 2016); *Shooting for Socrates* (James Erskine, 2015); *The Survivalist* (Stephen Fingleton, 2016); *The Truth Commissioner* (Declan Recks, 2016); *We're Doomed! The Dad's Army Story* (Stephen Bendelack, 2015). The most notable documentary is *I am Belfast* (Mark Cousins, 2015).

Although this is not an exhaustive list of all audiovisual productions supported by Northern Ireland Screen, it is representative of the nature of the work being undertaken in the region. Thus, it includes, as well as *Game of Thrones,* six television (mini-)series; three feature films with no local narrative content (*The Lost City of Z*; *Morgan*; *The Survivalist*); one television film with no local narrative content (*We're Doomed! The Dad's Army Story*); and three feature films with local content: *Miss Julie,*

The Journey and *A Patch of Fog*.[2] Even the latter statement needs to be qualified, as *Miss Julie* is more akin to a runaway production than a film rooted in Ulster history. Ullman relocated her adaptation of August Strindberg's play to Ireland, where it takes place, like the original, over the course of a midsummer's night (in 1890). Shot in Castle Coole, County Fermanagh, with exteriors at Florence Court, the film's titles simply state that it is set in Ireland. However, Colin Farrell, who plays the valet, John, adopts an Ulster accent, as does Samantha Morton as the cook/housekeeper, Kathleen, thus locating it, for those who recognise their accents, in a specific geographic region. Yet, nothing else in *Miss Julie* has been adapted to this setting or this potent Irish political era. John and Kathleen are, by all indications, Protestant workers, but when the former challenges Miss Julie (Jessica Chastain), by saying 'My people, we don't carry on like you do. We don't hate and destroy each other, we make love for fun. Yes, it is a game and we play it when we get time off from work', it is hard to reconcile his attitude to sex with any kind of Northern Irish Protestant identity. Given the film's themes, of a landlord/worker relationship, its virtuoso acting performances, and strong female characters, this seems like an opportunity wasted.

Northern Screen also supports short films and has seen results from a funding strand called 'Shorts to Features': Stephen Fingleton's short *The Magpie* (2014) was the origin of *The Survivalist*, and Michael Lennox's *Boogaloo and Graham* (2014), which was nominated for Best Short Film (Live Action) at the Academy Awards in 2015, gave him the reputation to move on to *A Patch of Fog*. The organisation supports animation, including the work of Dog Ears, who co-produce *Puffin Rock* with Cartoon Saloon, and development work in gaming and multimedia.

This snapshot of four years of production (2014–18) very closely mirrors the situation in the Republic, discussed in Chapter 1. So too does the argument that subsidies for film production are justified by the amount of additional revenue these productions bring to the economy. As an industry, the Northern Ireland audiovisual sector is primarily engaged in creating content for runaway productions. Overall, these enjoy a much higher profile than locally themed feature films, many of which attract low audience figures and earnings.

Obtaining accurate figures for films screened in Northern Ireland is even more difficult than it is for films screened in the Republic. Table 1 draws on figures from the British Film Institute's site 'Weekend Box Office Figures', which collates box office figures for all British film releases (British Film Institute). The data covers the UK and Ireland. Given that it is taken after the weekend, it does not cover the final days of a film's release. Detailed figures commence in January 2007; thus the

Table 1 Box office returns: Northern Ireland-set film releases

Film title	Total no. of weeks	Total box office returns
'71	12	£1,022,970
Cherrybomb	5	£16,546
Fifty Dead Men Walking	12	£388,554
Good Vibrations	14	£308,294
Hunger	16	£801,600
The Journey	7	£78,175
Miss Julie	9	£29,540
Shadow Dancer	8	£782,033
Shooting for Socrates	8	£8,578
The Survivalist	3	£21,575

Source: British Film Institute, 'Weekend Box Office Figures'
www.bfi.org.uk/education-research/film-industry-statistics-research/
weekend-box-office-figures

table covers films from that period onwards. Not all films were supported by Northern Ireland Screen.

The Truth Commissioner was released in Belfast and Dublin only. *Anton* (Graham Cantwell, 2008), *Battle of the Bone* (George Clarke, 2008) and *A Patch of Fog* and *Peacefire* (Macdara Vallely, 2008) received festival screenings only.

Writing on the financing and infrastructure for Northern Irish film-making in the late 1990s and early 2000s, John Hill (2006: 185) noted that few of the productions made a return on investment. The chart above indicates that, once one excludes thrillers and the occasional successful art film, notably *Hunger*, little has changed in this respect, although, evidently, it does not take into account television sales and sales to viewing platforms. One of the most commercially, if not critically, successful films to come out of Northern Ireland, had no local funding; *Man About Dog*, a crime-caper movie about a witless trio of friends from West Belfast who happen upon a winning greyhound and go on the run to Clonmel from a corrupt bookie, J. P. McCallion (Sean McGinley), and a Traveller gang, became on release the highest-performing film funded by the IFB. With little to tie it to either place or politics, the film traded in highly gendered humour – 'Balls on them guys like Bengali tigers, what?', as Traveller Fergie (Pat Shortt) comments admiringly of the lads – that included sex romps with lustful Eastern European women and unremitting masturbation jokes. *Man About Dog*'s refusal to comment on politics laid down a marker of sorts, and what anchored it within Irish cinema generally was as much its two fingers to political correctness as its local accents, locations and casting.[3]

Game of Thrones has fundamentally altered the Northern Irish industry. As well as the volume of services required when the series is shooting, it has also increased the profile of the actors involved and provided considerable skills training. It is now common for a review of a Northern Ireland-set film to prompt readers to associate specific actors with their roles in *Game of Thrones*. Higher profile actors can, in turn, mean the difference between a low-budget feature film attracting funding or not. On the other hand, the fact that technicians are fully employed in large-budget productions means that independent filmmakers struggle to compete for these technicians' time, and to meet their wage expectations, a situation that is also mirrored in the Republic.

The challenge will be to maintain the sector when filming on the production ends. The newly developed filmmaking infrastructure and Belfast's proximity to London will certainly help, as will the fall in the value of sterling, which makes shooting in the UK cheaper for overseas companies. Compared with London, the cost of living in Belfast is substantially lower, adding to its attraction for runaway productions. Northern Ireland Screen funds script development, project development and slate development (for companies with two or more projects). They can invest a maximum of £800,000 for feature film and television production funding up to a ceiling of 25 per cent of the overall project budget. They advocate for 'productions which contribute to building a sustainable screen industry in Northern Ireland and which can show a direct economic benefit to the region. Projects must be commercially viable and able to demonstrate clear possibilities for commercial exploitation' (Northern Ireland Screen, 2017).

At the time of writing, it is also difficult to predict how Brexit will affect filmmaking in Northern Ireland. One certainty is that they will lose access to funding from Creative Europe, an EU programme with an annual budget of almost €1.5 billion.

Post-Troubles cinema

'We need a happy ending, son', O (Robert Carlyle) tells young Donal (Tyrone McKenna) in *The Mighty Celt* (Pearse Elliott, 2005). 'Not all stories can be bad ones.' Carlyle's words might have come from a manual on cinema after the Troubles, as indeed might his character. A reformed IRA gunman, he has returned to Belfast a new man. Taking a glance around his foul rental apartment, he wastes no time in purchasing a pair of novelty tiger slippers and pink rubber gloves before setting to work cleaning and redecorating the apartment to the sounds of Mud's 'Tiger Feet'. Following this, he finds himself a job as a supermarket security man. Soon the film will bring him face to face with the bad IRA man, Good Joe (Ken Stott) in a tussle for influence over the young boy who is at the heart of the film, Donal (Tyrone McKenna). Good Joe despises the peace process, while O refuses to consort with his old IRA friends, and instead takes up with his former partner, Kate (Gillian Anderson), opting for a night in front of the TV over a return to war. *The Mighty Celt* offers a stronger than usual role to Donal's mother and is helped by the casting of Anderson in the part. Yet, she remains defined by the home, by her life as sister and partner of gunmen, and by parenthood. Donal, on the other hand, is a child of nature, at his happiest in the outdoors training his greyhound, the eponymous Mighty Celt, and thus also outside the urban spaces that remain demarcated by sectarianism. Despite its charms as a sub-*Kes* (Ken Loach, 1969) coming-of-age narrative, Elliott, who also wrote the screenplay for *Man About Dog,* struggles with the film's discursive heritage, ending rather bizarrely with the reassertion of the rule of law under the guise of the Ulster Animal Protection Society. A more promising companion piece is another child-centred narrative, *Mickybo and Me* (Terry Loane, 2005), about two young boys from either side of the sectarian divide in 1970s Belfast who model themselves on Butch Cassidy and the Sundance Kid after a viewing of George Roy Hill's 1969 film of the same name. Thematically, *Mickybo and Me* shares much with *Into the West*, not least its borrowings from the Western for alternative models of male behaviour in a society of failed fathers. In *Mickybo and Me,* the Troubles form the political backdrop (and supply moments of black humour) to the two boys' adventures on the run together, but do not define them. Instead, the film explores the limits of imaginative escape in a society that remains constrained by historical violence.[4]

As a number of writers on post-Troubles cinema (Baker and McLaughlin, 2015; Ging, 2013; Hill, 2006; Lehner, 2011) have noted, the dominant narrative model of this period focuses on the foregrounding of a new type of masculinity. New Northern Irish narratives see the man of violence overcome his past, embrace romance, obtain employment in the service economy, and retreat into the private sphere of the domestic. The transition period of the peace process (the late 1990s) witnessed the beginning of this cycle with the production of a series of comedies and romances, including: *Divorcing Jack* (David Caffrey, 1998); *With or Without You* (Michael Winterbottom, 1998); *The Most Fertile Man in Ireland* (Dudi Appleton, 1999); *An Everlasting Piece* (Barry Levinson, 2000). Another comedy from the period, *Wild About Harry* (Declan Lowney, 2000) revolves around a celebrity chef and notorious womaniser, Harry McGee (Brendan Gleeson), who falls into a coma after an assault. When he recovers, his identity is transformed and he believes himself to be a new man. His loss of memory encompasses forgetting the Troubles, so that he, alongside Northern Ireland, can start afresh.

On the other hand, the signing of the Good Friday Agreement opened up a space for filmmakers to look back at the Troubles as a historical period. It also raised further questions of the purpose of such an activity – as a means of giving testimony, for instance, or of achieving closure. The failure to achieve consensus among the various groupings of the Troubles, encapsulated in the considerable hostility to many of the recommendations of the Consultative Group on the Past, whose 2009 report proposed, amongst other details, that £12,000 be paid to all families of victims of violence, including paramilitaries, and that there be an annual day of reconciliation and a public memorial (BBC News, 2010), is evidence of the continued ideological divisions surrounding memorialisation.

Testimony, history and healing: the docudrama

The new political landscape offers filmmakers the opportunity to divest the Troubles of their previous discursive history as irrational tribal violence. It also suggests that the Loyalist perspective might be treated with greater complexity than has previously been the case.[5] There is now a possibility that filmmakers may feel free to discuss other issues that concerned the inhabitants of Northern Ireland in the years of the Troubles, such as class divisions or LGBTQ identities. Yet, narrating this recent history remains fraught with contention. One medium favoured by a number of filmmakers is the docudrama with its promise of factuality. Films such as *H3* (Les Blair, 2001), *Bloody Sunday*; *Omagh* (Pete Travis, 2004); *Hunger* (Steve McQueen, 2008); *Five Minutes of Heaven* (Oliver Hirschbiegel, 2009); *The Journey* (Nick Hamm, 2016) all draw on real events and people and most share a desire to set the historical record straight. *Bloody Sunday* and *Omagh* are campaigning films, aimed at drawing public attention to miscarriages of justice – respectively, the Widgery Tribunal report into the Bloody Sunday shootings, and the failure to prosecute the Omagh bombers, following the car bomb attack in August 1998 that killed twenty-nine people, including a woman who was pregnant with twins, and injured over 200 more. At the other end of the spectrum lies *Hunger,* the work of a visual artist that charts the process of a man starving himself to death for a cause. Despite, however, their claims for being read as 'fact-based', it is interesting to see just how reliant these productions, like those discussed in the previous chapter, are on the codes of melodrama and on conventional gendering of space for effect.

Bloody Sunday and *Omagh* function as companion pieces linked by the involvement of British director, Paul Greengrass, who co-wrote *Omagh*, but handed over direction to Travis and both take the form of docudramas. I have previously discussed (Barton, 2004: 172–4) *Bloody Sunday*'s awareness of the imperative to present a balanced perspective on the actual events of January 1972 when the British army fired on unarmed civilians engaged in a peaceful march against internment. Yet, as Hill (2006: 1) has documented, the film incensed both Conservative politicians in Britain and Unionists in Northern Ireland for its alleged 'pro-Republican' bias. Local actor, James Nesbitt, who plays the community leader, Cooper, a Protestant leading a march for rights for Catholics, was attacked for claiming that Protestants in Northern Ireland 'felt a degree of "collective guilt" over the killings.' The controversy, as Hill (2006: 1) comments reveals 'how difficult it is for any film concerning Northern Ireland to transcend political divisions'.

According to Travis (in Grey, 2007: A6):

the families of Omagh watched 'Bloody Sunday' and were so inspired by the truthfulness of it that they approached Paul [Greengrass] to make 'Omagh' ... I think that says a lot about a filmmaker when ordinary people who have been through a terrible crisis say, 'We want you to tell our story.'

Greengrass himself (in Grey, 2007: A5–A6) has pointed to the reconciliation process in Northern Ireland as a possible model for the ending of other conflicts:

Early on I always felt that Northern Ireland, far from being this defigured [*sic*], violent abscess on the body politic, was in fact the most interesting dynamic melting pot in which much of today's, even tomorrow's politics, first took shape ... The solutions to the problems in Northern Ireland have given inspiration to solving conflicts in many parts of the world because they mirror most modern conflicts: namely two tribes, two traditions, two nationalisms wanting to occupy the same piece of land.

Both films share similar shooting styles – fast zooms; swift editing; fragmented sound tracks interspersed with almost complete silence; the use of natural lighting, and a reliance on a single camera to give an impression of news coverage. Both reproduce the killings and their immediate aftermath with visceral urgency, emphasising the state of confusion that followed each event as relatives frantically sought to establish whether their loved ones had been killed, and paramedics tried to deal with the wounded. *Omagh* also shares with *Bloody Sunday* a focus on a conflicted, faulty man, thrust into a leadership role that will challenge his humanism. *Bloody Sunday* plays out in almost real time, leaving little opportunity to develop back stories for those involved on the various sides. Even still, part of its trajectory is to counterpoint the sanctuary of the domestic with the threat of the politically contested public space. By the end, however, the boundaries between the two are dissolved as IRA volunteers queue on the stairwell to a housing block to sign up. *Omagh* builds towards a more conventional melodramatic conclusion. Bereaved father, Michael Gallagher (Gerard McSorley) in *Omagh* is faced with two conflicts, the public world of politics and the increasing damage his pursuit of the truth is causing to his marriage. In one extended set-piece, Gallagher, who has had a second telephone installed in his home, deals with calls from the media on one line as his wife, Patsy (Michèle Forbes), fields similar requests on the other. Cuts to her face indicate the strain she is experiencing. Eventually Michael realises this and comforts her, but it will take a dramatic showdown with his daughters to convince him to abandon his campaigning and pay attention to his wife and family's needs. Throughout *Omagh*, Patsy is associated with the domestic space and is repeatedly shown folding clothes, ironing, and caring for her family. She is also almost completely silent and often expressionless. While her blankness may well reflect her own inability to grieve, it also leaves the articulation of loss to Michael. Here *Omagh* is enormously aided by (local actor) McSorley's expressive range. Yet, it still requires an additional sequence when, after he has abandoned the campaign leadership, Michael returns to the workshop where he and his son Aidan (Paul Kelly) had worked together as mechanics. Patsy appears at the door, and stands silently as Michael says the following to her:

> He wasn't just my son, you know. He was my workmate. Everything. He was everything to me. And when I'm in the house and the three of you [Patsy and their daughters] are talking together, still doing all the things you've always done, and I tell myself it's unfair, I tell myself it's not true. Inside I feel he meant more to me, and I know that's awful to feel like that. Because I know how much you loved him. But I can't feel the way you feel, only the way I feel.

The film's conclusion, the press conference where Police Ombudsman, Nuala O'Loan (Brenda Fricker) announces that the informer who warned that an attack was imminent should have been trusted, and that a full enquiry into the attack did not take place, is filmed as the moment of reconciliation between Michael and Patsy. As Michael sits listening to O'Loan, Patsy hastily checks her appearance, calls her daughters, and drives to the conference, pushing her way through the reporters to her husband, who in turn, cuts through the press to his wife. Reconciliation is thus configured not as the coming together of the two tribes, but as the reinstatement of the family unit.

Joseph Moser (2013) has argued for a reading of *Bloody Sunday* as a 'dramatic reconstruction' of the events of the day, while McIlroy (2007) has termed *Omagh* a 'monumentary'. As both terms remind us, this kind of cinema of testament is determined by an awareness of its responsibility to tell the 'truth' of the past even as it demonstrates that truth is always relative and its narration subject to dramatic conventions. The same could be said for *Five Minutes of Heaven*, a 'what if' narrative of a reconciliation meeting, filmed for television, between the former UVF (Ulster Volunteer Force) killer, Alistair Little, and Joe Griffin, the brother of his victim, Jim Griffin. In real life, the men never met, but otherwise scriptwriter, Guy Hibbert, who also co-wrote *Omagh*, draws on factual background, such as Little's lifelong engagement, following his release from prison, in global reconciliation processes. With Little played by Liam Neeson and Griffin by James Nesbitt, this was also an acknowledgement of the stardom of two of Northern Ireland's best-known actors. In a nod to the redundancy of religious tags, Neeson, a Catholic, plays a Protestant, and Nesbitt, a Protestant, plays a Catholic. *Five Minutes of Heaven*'s meta-narrative, the filming of the meeting between the two men, points up the exploitative nature of such television. Yet, once Griffin refuses to walk into the room unless the cameras are turned off (so that he can kill Little), and the event falls apart, the film itself is forced into its own melodramatic resolution, with Little and Griffin squaring off in the latter's abandoned childhood home in a configuration that Stefanie Lehner (2011: 71) has described as 'strangely homoerotic emasculation'.

Lehner (2011: 71) has also usefully noted the problematic location of Griffin's trauma in the home, with his mother blaming him for not having saved his brother. He is thus emasculated equally by his mother, his bereavement and by his social standing, which is evidently less than Little's. This deployment of melodramatic conventions demands narrative closure, which *Five Minutes of Heaven* duly provides. Yet, as another man whose family was killed in a bombing described it, facing up to the perpetrator can be little like the television depiction. 'It had been suggested to me that this encounter could provide me with my own "five minutes of Heaven" just like Jimmy Nesbitt's character confronting Liam Neeson's loyalist killer character in the film of the same name', John McGurk (2012) wrote of facing up to Robert James Campbell, the only man convicted of killing several members of the McGurk family and twelve others in the McGurk Bar bombing of 1971. 'But what ensued for me was 15 minutes of limbo – as I witnessed an old man apologise to me over and over again but refuse to say more about what happened.'[6]

Figure 12 Liam Neeson and James Nesbitt in *Five Minutes of Heaven*

Filmmaking of this kind allows for the articulation of popular cultural understandings that trauma can (and should) be resolved. Recreating past traumatic events, in this formulation, enables those involved to re-live them but now with the anticipation of closure. That this has a basis in fact does need to be recognised, particularly when such films offer the real people behind the stories public recognition of their suffering. The *Irish Times* (Meredith, 2004) reported one family member saying after a private screening of *Omagh*:

A lot of people are just glad it's over, glad to get on with their own lives. I hope that the film will open the eyes of millions of people to the pain we're still going through … We're hurting with pain, day in, day out. When I go home tomorrow it's back to pain, pain, pain. Everybody else goes out, goes to work. I can't do that.

Omagh and *Five Minutes of Heaven* were made as television films, though both also had limited theatrical releases. One might guess that watching such films on television, in the home, might be a more salutary experience than seeing them in the comfortless public space of the cinema. They share with the other 'real-life' docudramas, an emphasis on the ordinariness of the people who became part of the history of the Troubles, an 'it could have been you' appeal to audiences. At the same time, their stories are told almost exclusively from the Catholic and Republican perspectives.

The hunger strikes on film

The same goes for the hunger strikes subgenre of films. The 1981 hunger strikes in which ten men died in protest against the British Government's insistence that they be treated as criminals instead of political prisoners are one of the most significant 'lieux de mémoires', to borrow from Pierre Nora (1989), of Republican history. Terry George's *Some Mother's Son* of 1996 established the narrative pattern of much of what was to come in the genre, gaining authenticity, as did *H3*, from the involvement of former prisoners in making the film (George was imprisoned in Long Kesh in the 1970s and *H3* was co-written by Laurence McKeown, a former hunger striker). As ideological foundation stones, the hunger strikes are visually familiar from wall murals and other public memorials with the men (notably Bobby Sands, who was the first to die) conventionally depicted as Christ-like martyrs.

The exception is Maeve Murphy's *Silent Grace* (2001), a fictionalised version of the incarceration of four women in Armagh jail in 1980–1 and their participation in the 'dirty protest', during which prisoners, who were demanding political status, smeared excrement on their cell walls. Murphy's film is distinctive because it is the only film made in this period with female protagonists and one of the few fictions even to acknowledge the part played by female Republican prisoners in the protest, a situation mirrored in Republican discourse at the time of the hunger strikes and since. In fact, three women went on hunger strike, but were told to desist by IRA command on the grounds that they would deflect attention from the male participants. In Murphy's version, the story opens with a young joyrider, Aine (Cathleen Brady), who, apparently on a whim, announces at her trial that she is a member of the IRA and is thus put in a cell block with three IRA prisoners.

The three women are initially hostile but soon friendships are formed, and the leader, Eileen (Orla Brady), who will go on hunger strike, becomes a kind of surrogate mother figure to Aine. The film is based on two stage plays by Murphy and retains much of the feel of the stage in its visual style and presentation; it is also evidently an extremely low-budget production. The other significant figure is the prison governor, Cunningham (Conor Mullen), who alternates between sadistic treatment of the women and empathy, and by the end, it seems that he as much as Aine has undergone a personal journey of self-betterment through coming to know Eileen. As Aileen Blaney (2008) has argued of the film, its analysis of the politics of the day is diluted by its focus on the sublimated love triangle between Aine, Eileen and Cunningham. In its favour, the film celebrates the bonds of friendships that form between women and is unafraid of celebrating femininity itself through small details such as Aine's sharing of her lipstick. Given the representational void into which she stepped with this debut feature, Murphy was careful to develop a visual iconography to complement her theme, particularly with her brief flash to an image of the Virgin Mary at a moment of emotional intensity. In this way, *Silent Grace* speaks to a very specific female experience of incarceration that previously only Pat Murphy had explored in her *Anne Devlin* (1984). Maeve Murphy herself (2017) has likened the silencing of her film, which received only a minimal release, to the silencing of women in history. In the same piece, she describes how *Silent Grace* had a second chance, when after due pressure, TV3 screened it in June 2017. Her message – that under improved circumstances silenced voices can be heard and suffering redeemed – is thus very much in tune with the tenor of post-Troubles, post-trauma discourse.

As the above discussion indicates, melodrama remains the dominant narrative framework even of the docudrama. *Hunger* – an auteur film by a black-British Turner Prize-winning artist – in many ways represents a different type of production. Co-written by playwright, Enda Walsh with McQueen, *Hunger* is a dramatisation of the incarceration and death of Bobby Sands. Michael Fassbender, who plays Sands, lost enough weight during the shoot to allow McQueen to film his body in its increasing emaciation without recourse to special effects. In this way, what starts as a prison story ends up as a study in bodily endurance. It is very different to, say *H3,* which was fundamentally an exploration of male comradery under oppression, and seemed to struggle with how to frame the strikers' martyrdom – as necessity or an excessive demand on the individual (perhaps not surprisingly given that co-writer McKeown was taken off hunger strike by his family).

Figure 13 Orla Brady in *Silent Grace*

Hunger is structured as a triptych, with the 'crucifixion' witnessed by Sands's mother in the final 'panel' rather the central frame. The centre-piece, instead, is a 20-minute staging, much of it shot in one take, of a debate between the priest, Father Dominic Moran (Liam Cunningham) and Sands over the morality of his decision to go on hunger strike. The opening segment is more crowded, with vignettes of prison life from the perspective of the guards and two other 'blanketmen', Davey Gillen (Brian Milligan) and Gerry Campbell (Liam McMahon). Thus, the film goes from multiple narrative strands, to two people, to focus on Sands alone. Its widescreen compositions underline its positioning as an art-work, as an object of contemplation rather than offering the intimacy of identification. As numerous critics have argued, the film's weakness is its refusal to engage in any detail with the politics of Northern Ireland, specifically the relationship between the hunger strikers and the IRA command outside the prison, and its erasure of the fact that while on hunger strike Sands was elected as a Member of Parliament. Emilie Pine, for instance, criticises *Hunger* for elevating Sands's martyrdom over all else, so that the viewer is left with only one possible conclusion, that he is 'an innocent victim of an oppressive system' (2014: 167).

Although the opening segment nominally offers a balanced perspective by suggesting that the guards are as much prisoners of the system as are the actual prisoners, the movement towards a focus on Sands, the extended sequences of physical brutality towards the prisoners, and small details, such as the UDA guard's refusal to help the emaciated Sands out of the bath, all endorse his martyrdom. Even the assassination of the prison guard, Lohan (Stuart Graham), when visiting his mother in the nursing home is filmed provocatively. The sequence closes with Lohan lying dead, in Pietà pose, in the lap of his senile mother, her face splattered with his blood. For a Protestant to be posed in such a Catholic image borders on the profane.

In the central segment, Sands explains his motivation for going on hunger strike to Fr Moran via a story from his childhood: when on a school outing he went against the instructions of his teachers and did what the other boys could not bring themselves to do, which was to put a dying foal out of its misery by holding its head under water until it drowned. Although this may explain his personality, it certainly does not offer any insights into the politics of the strike, rendering it instead the narrative of one man's principled stand against authority. It is also a very writerly, staged piece, reflecting Walsh's presence in the film. That the higher authority is Margaret Thatcher, a prime minister reviled by, among others, the artistic community, and present here only as a voice without a body (in audio excerpts from her speeches), is further designed to increase sympathy for the Republicans.

By largely depoliticising the narrative, McQueen relocates the film's emphasis on to the suffering body. Fassbender's performance of starvation becomes a compelling visual focal point, but even before that, *Hunger* has offered up multiple images of male hurt. Lohan, who is the first character introduced in the film, plunges his bleeding knuckles into a basin of water; the camera draws attention to the gash on Davey Gillen's head after his initial strip search; the riot squad line up, beating their shields with truncheons in a primordial rhythm to induce terror in the prisoners even before they brutally drive them down the corridor, and Lohan roughly shears Sands's head, leaving him bruised and bleeding. These sequences resonated with critics, who likened them to similar contemporary reports of torture from the Iraq War and from the Guantanamo detention centre. They also serve to emphasise the male body as the last boundary between civilisation and the breakdown of order. As Sands's final ecstatic look suggests, he has overcome his incarceration through the exercise of the ultimate expression of agency, his own self-willed death.

Another notable artistic strategy in *Hunger* is the near-absence of dialogue, and its replacement by sound effects, often of bodily activities, interspersed with a minimalist musical score.[7] The prison is often viewed as a series of empty, brightly lit corridors. In the opening sequences where Gillen joins Cain in the cell, and the two are later joined by Sands, one would have expected the men to banter amongst themselves as the prisoners do, for instance, in *H3*, where they shout messages in Irish (Gaolic) to each other and sing rebel songs. Instead, Gillen and Cain barely talk, communicating their resistance through their bodily fluids and orifices, smearing the walls with faeces, dumping their urine on the corridors, and concealing messages in their anuses. As Dario Llinares (2015: 224–5) has written of these scenes:

> These are extremely powerful acts because they take what is ostensibly self-harm, self-humiliation and emasculation and turn them into means of violent resistance … The acts of dissent represented in *Hunger* actually appropriate abjection as the ultimate means of attack against a system whose intent is to assert docility.

Hunger is a film whose effectiveness depends on the alternation between extremes of silence and sound, on its foregrounding of the hurt male body, and on its final movement towards ecstasy. McQueen has said the following in an interview (Corless, 2008: 27): 'The images only go so far, they never go all the way, it's impossible. What has to happen is you trigger something in people's imaginations or in their psyche that completes the picture.' Its flaws are not only its disinterest in the specifics of the political situation, but appear elsewhere, namely in the sentimentalised narrative of Sands's past and his visions of his childhood self when he is near death. At the same time, it is an undeniably powerful film that needs to be seen as one component in the memorialisation of the Troubles, rather than demanding of it that it speak for an entire historical period.

A strange coda to these post-Troubles historical films came with the release of Brian Kirk's *Middletown* (2006). Were Kirk not a Northern Ireland native, it would have been easy to write off his film as a misjudged attempt to exploit the region's reputation for hardline religious adherence and atavistic tribal violence. Set in an unspecified time (possibly the 1960s), the Middletown of the film's title is rent asunder by the return of its prodigal son, fundamentalist preacher, Gabriel Hunter (Matthew Macfadyen), whose imposition of a totalitarian form of morality soon sets him on a collision course with his brother, Jim (Daniel Mays) and Jim's pregnant wife, Caroline (Eva Birthistle). All comes to a head in a scene of fire and brimstone that echoes the film's Gothic look and biblical referencing. What *Middletown* proves is the difficulty filmmakers face in imagining the space of Northern Ireland, either rural, small town, or urban, as other than one of violence.

The enduring attraction of the thriller

As the box office figures (above) confirm, the thriller remains the primary medium through which audiences engage with Northern Irish narratives. Not only did *Fifty Dead Men Walking* (Kari Skogland, 2009), *Shadow Dancer* and *'71* (Yann Demange, 2014) do well at the local box office, *'71* took $1,270,847 on its US release, though *Shadow Dancer* performed poorly and *Fifty Dead Men Walking* went straight to DVD (Box Office Mojo, 2015).

It is tempting to see Marsh and Skogland's thrillers as companion pieces. Both revolve around the recruitment of informers by MI5 and both depend for their suspense on whether they will be caught by the IRA (and tortured and killed), and who is setting up their MI5 minder to cover up nefarious dealings in high places. Both films have period settings and both suggest that unduly strong bonds form between handler and 'tout'. In addition, both are based on books: Marsh's on a novel (by Tom Bradby, the former Northern Irish correspondent for ITN) and Skogland's by the real-life informer, Martin McGartland (written with Nicholas Davies). In the case of the latter, McGartland threatened legal action against the film on its completion, claiming that he was shown to have been participating in bomb attacks and torture, which he denies. The film's end credits now state that the screenplay was 'not written or approved by Martin McGartland or Nicholas Davies', but that 'at least 50 men who were targeted by the IRA are alive today because of the heroic work of Martin'. Bradby, by contrast, wrote the screenplay of *Shadow Dancer* and has declared himself fully supportive of the changes made to his original novel.[8]

Where the two films diverge is in the identities of their central characters. Martin McGartland (the film retains his name) is played by Jim Sturgess as an edgy, likeable minor criminal whose motivations for informing are never fully clear. *Shadow Dancer* opens with the killing of young Collette Mc Veigh's (Maria Laird as a child; Andrea Riseborough as an adult) brother Sean (Ben Smyth) in an exchange of fire on the street. Collette had bribed him to run to the shops for cigarettes in her place and will thus suffer from guilt into adulthood. The film then moves to 1993, when against the background of peace process negotiations, Collette, now a single mother, carries out activities for the IRA, as do her brothers Gerry (Aidan Gillen) and Connor (Domhnall Gleeson). All siblings still live at home with their mother (Brid Brennan) and Collette's child, Mark (Cathal Maguire). Collette is pressurised into becoming an informer by MI5 agent, Mac (Clive Owen), so that she won't go to jail and leave Mark without a mother.

Figure 14 *Shadow Dancer*

Fifty Dead Men Walking may be a version of the novel of the same name, but its introduction to McGartland, which sees him being chased full-tilt through Belfast's narrow alleyways by the police and the British army to the upbeat sound of 'Hit the Ground Running' (by Northern Irish band Phoenix 23), is a visual and aural lift from the opening of Jim Sheridan's *In the Name of the Father* (1993). Having explained the historical background to the film via a voice-over from McGartland's handler, Fergus (Ben Kingsley), *Fifty Dead Men Walking* swiftly abandons any effort at political engagement, instead depicting the Troubles as a thrilling real-life opportunity for the proving of masculinity and male friendships. *Shadow Dancer* too borrows from well-tested conventions of Troubles cinema, in its case from the lineage of British films about the conflict: the female terrorist whose activities are motivated by (misplaced?) motherly love; a subplot of IRA activism led by an irrational commander with a destructive blood lust (here Kevin Mulville (David Wilmot)), and a seduction and betrayal subplot. James Marsh's Belfast is a rundown city of small housing estates and scrubby patches of open grass, with, since the film was shot in Dublin, no recognisable landmarks. The McVeigh household seems little altered in the thirty years that separate the opening from the present-day sequences. The official buildings where Mac works, by contrast, are modern but at the same time furnished like a corporate boardroom. Perhaps because of its period setting and the need to deflect attention away from the borrowed location, browns predominate; however, it seems more that this is designed to suggest teleological murkiness. The moral colour-coding extends to Collette's unlikely vivid red raincoat, the marker of the scarlet woman, and is visually counterpointed by the muted business attire of her true nemesis, MI5 boss, Kate Fletcher (Gillian Anderson). *Fifty Dead Men Walking* has its own femme fatale, Grace, played by Rose McGowan (whose statement that she would have joined the IRA if she had lived in Belfast during the Troubles made headlines at the Toronto Film Festival of 2008). Grace's Mata Hari activities are contrasted in Skogland's film with McGartland's mother and his partner who are closely associated with nurturing motherhood and the domestic space.

Collette's reasons for taking part in the Troubles are traceable to the kind of tribalism that Hill critiqued in his original writing on the conflict (Rockett, Gibbons and Hill, 1987: 147–93). The only major alteration to this tradition is the film's ending, where it seems that murder will be rewarded. Thus, the 'good' family – Collette and her brother, Conor – drive off into the distance with her child, having dispatched Mac. *Shadow Dancer* is also careful to distance itself from earlier US versions of the Troubles thriller, chiefly through casting, and its measured, even slow pace and minimalist dialogue. The director, Marsh, is highly regarded for his documentary work, specifically *Man on Wire* (2008) and *Project Nim* (2011). His natural medium is the art film, and this is evident in the look and pace of *Shadow Dancer*, leaving it as a curious hybrid of international thriller and moody arthouse release. *Fifty Dead Men Walking* too is deeply uneven. This is nowhere more evident than in the choice of songs for the soundtrack, which opens with Stiff Little Fingers's punk anthem, 'Alternative Ulster', and closes with a maudlin ballad, 'We Will Have Won' (written by Kari Skogland and Ben Mink and performed by Paul Hyde), where a son comforts his father for having taken part in the conflict with lines such as, 'Father it's time your war is done; we'll be free, we will have won.' Playing over images from the film, it feels like a hymn to doomed masculinity, and a far cry from the energy that opened Skogland's film.[9] Even less convincing was Declan Recks's *The Truth Commissioner*, another tale of shadowy MI5 operatives and seductive honey-traps that struggled to map the international thriller formula onto a peace process narrative.

As the box office figures show, the most successful of the Troubles thrillers was *'71*. Essentially the account of one night of terror in Belfast, the film follows a new British army recruit, Gary Hook (Jack O'Connell), who finds himself separated from his unit after a street riot that ended in the death of one of his fellow soldiers. With two gunmen and a shadowy mix of IRA and Loyalists (some in league with British undercover officers) in pursuit, he is helped by a succession of local people, each of whom places their lives at risk by being with him.

In interview, Delange, for whom this was a first theatrical feature, spoke of wanting to create something 'more mythical and impression-istic' than realist (in Nayman, 2014). At the same time, however, he shot the daytime scenes on 16 mm to create a more authentic period feel. He also explained:

> I didn't see it as an issue movie or a message movie, but as something about human beings trapped in these situations. So I thought of *Army of Shadows* [Jean-Pierre Melville, 1969] or *The Battle of Algiers* [Gillo Pontecorvo, 1966], yes, but also *The Warriors* [Walter Hill, 1979] or the movies of John Carpenter.

The borrowings from apocalyptic and horror films alongside classic political cinema are evident in the film's visuals, in particular a sequence following a botched bombing, which results in the explosion of the pub, to which Hook has been brought by a loyalist child (Corey McKinley), just as he has stumbled out of it. His hearing temporarily impaired, Hook staggers through an orange mist of debris. At first, he seems alone in this post-apocalypse, but gradually others creep out of the gloom like zombie survivors. Eventually a woman takes the child's body from him and he moves on.

Hook's odyssey through Belfast recalls one of the most influential films set in Northern Ireland, Carol Reed's *Odd Man Out* (1947). Just as its wounded central character, Johnny McQueen (James Mason), lurches from one hiding place to another in the falling snow, so too does Hook, the snow replaced by gloom. At one point, McQueen is rescued by a child, at another he is taken in by reluctant helpers, who patch up his wounds. A key setting in the earlier film is a snug in the Crown bar.[10] In both films, the central character is almost entirely unspeaking, the obvious distinction being that in *Odd Man Out*, Johnny is a terrorist who has killed a man, while in *'71*, Hook is a British soldier. Like *Odd Man Out* too, *'71* was shot not in Belfast but on location in England; in the case of the latter film, in Liverpool, Blackburn and Sheffield.

Just as Reed's film deployed its unnamed (but easily identified as Belfast) Northern Irish city as a setting for a narrative concerned with universal themes of the suffering caused by acts of violence, so too does Demange create out of Belfast a nightmare of, as one of the officers reminds the trainees at the film's opening, a place that is at once in the UK but unrecognisable. Indeed, these opening sequences could just as easily have come at the beginning of a Vietnam film, and another reference point is surely

Apocalypse Now (Francis Ford Coppola, 1979). The film's analysis of the military, spoken by the doctor who is stitching Hook's wound without anaesthetic, also echoes the Vietnam war film: 'posh cunts telling thick cunts to kill poor cunts. That's the army for you. It's all a lie. They don't care about you. You're just a piece of meat to them.'

Odd Man Out was made in the immediate aftermath of World War Two, while *'71* appeared at a time when global terrorism was increasingly affecting ordinary citizens. Hook stands for the confused, decent British squaddie sent in to conflict zones of which he has no understanding. Just before the bar is blown up, a shot of him standing rigid in front of a pint that he hasn't ordered, terrified of being identified, heightens the sense of the exceptionalism of the normal. Equally, David Holmes's percussive score intensifies this sense of estrangement.

What distinguishes the three films that are discussed here from the earlier US-produced thrillers is their shared assertion of collusion between the British secret service and Loyalist paramilitaries and the use of IRA informers against their own communities. Northern Ireland in this configuration becomes the model for the state of exception. As Giorgio Agamben (2005) influentially argued, the suspension of legal norms is now embedded in Western 'democracy' and justified by the threat of terror activities.[11] Thus 'emergency becomes the rule and the very distinction between peace and war … becomes impossible' (2005: 22). While none of the productions makes any great effort to link the past of British imperialism (in Northern Ireland) to its present (the Iraq war, for instance), all three films feed into strong feelings of a secretive state, shady dealings in high places and the corruption of justice. In this sense, they are more the inheritors of Ken Loach's *Hidden Agenda* than, say, *The Devil's Own* (Alan J. Pakula, 1997). For all its widely praised production values, *'71* is little different from the other thrillers in foregrounding personal conflict over political analysis. Their endings agree that there is no political way out of the long history of the conflict other than withdrawal into personal space, most notably illustrated in the final shot of *'71*, where Hook is seen heading off, now in civilian clothing, over the Derbyshire moors of his childhood with his younger brother, whom he has removed from institutional care.

Other histories

Telling stories set in Northern Ireland during the Troubles that are not focused on paramilitary activities remains surprisingly challenging. *Good Vibrations* and *Shooting for Socrates* (James Erskine, 2014) both recreate significant moments from the past. The former tells the story of legendary music shop owner, Terri Hooley and his part in the punk movement, specifically in releasing The Undertones's 'Teenage Kicks'; the latter concerns Northern Ireland's Mexico '86 World Cup soccer campaign. Both are formally conventional, and both emphasise the potential for reconciliation that, on the one hand music, and the other sport, offer. It is interesting to note that both end in failure (Dooley's business collapses and the team are beaten), which reflects the reality of the events depicted, but equally allows for the acknowledgement of the values of stoicism in the face of adversity. Both also conclude with the celebration of community, *Good Vibrations* closing with a magnificent punk gig that is a testimony to youth, alternative music cultures, and shared passions while *Shooting for Socrates* accompanies the football fans after the final game as they link arms and walk singing through the Belfast streets. Hooley's final line: 'When it comes to punk, New York has the haircuts, London has the trousers, but Belfast has the reason!' retrospectively recreates punk as a utopian moment in Belfast's history.[12] Even more, the shop, Good Vibrations, is a utopian space within the sectarian city. This can, however, only be created at the expense of the home and home life – Hooley has, without telling his wife, Ruth (Jodie Whittaker), put up his house as collateral against the venture and she leaves him when she discovers this. Indeed, the punk movement in Belfast is also celebrated as a moment of freewheeling male companionship, a subtext that the film does nothing to refute. Both too share the casting of Richard Dormer (from *Game of Thrones*), as Terri Hooley, and as a working-class Protestant parent, Arthur, who is attempting to keep his football-mad young son from embracing sectarianism. The comparisons end there; *Good Vibrations* has an energy and forward momentum that eludes *Shooting for Socrates* which suffers from a failure to communicate any convincing dramatic tension. While the Troubles remain little integrated into the latter, they keep pace with *Good Vibrations*. Hooley's drug-dealing friend, Eric (David Wilmot) is chased out of Belfast by the paramilitaries and Hooley is beaten up for refusing to pay protection money. D'Sa and Leyburn manage to convey the threatening atmosphere that Hooley operated under with conviction, just as they give a real sense of how subversive punk was during that time.

Anyplace Ulster

In a review of *A Patch of Fog*, a critic from the *Guardian* wrote:

> Lennox's preoccupation appears to be to create what you might call a post-Troubles film: apart from the occasional shot of a relic of the conflict – such as a fortified police station – it is conspicuous by its absence.

Figure 15 Richard Dormer and Michael Colgan in *Good Vibrations*

> Instead, this is a thriller that could in fact happen pretty much anywhere, allowing its central metaphor, the fog of the title, to take centre stage. (Pulver, 2016)

The common thread that binds a number of recent Belfast-set films is their insistence on the 'anyplace-ness' of the city. Visually, this involves, as McLoone (2008) has discussed in relation to *With or Without You* and *Wild About Harry*, presenting an image of Belfast as a modern city that has left its past behind it. In *A Patch of Fog*, significant visual landmarks include the broadcasting building where local celebrity author, Sandy Duffy (Conleth Hill) is a regular on an arts review programme, hosted by his new lover, Lucy (Lara Pulver); the various stores where Duffy routinely shoplifts, until he is caught by obsessive store guard and stalker, Robert (Stephen Graham); and Duffy's own luxury modernist home, built on the proceeds from his major thriller and only publication, *A Patch of Fog*. In *Cherrybomb* (Glenn Leyburn, Lisa Barros D'Sa), the equivalent settings are the Titanic Leisure Centre and the different houses where the central characters live.

Cherrybomb is a determinedly ordinary story of teenage love rivalry set in Belfast. Its main interest for audiences was the casting of Rupert Grint as one of the leads, Malachy McKinney. Grint was by then trying to break free of the child star mantle that years of appearing in the

Harry Potter films had bestowed on him, and must have welcomed the opportunity to play a sixteen-year-old from Belfast who falls for his boss's daughter, Michelle (Kimberley Nixon) when she returns from London where she was living with her mother. A sequence of the pair attempting sex (before being disrupted by Michelle's father) was to become an internet talking point amongst Grint fans. The third member of the triangle is troubled boy Luke (Robert Sheehan), whose father is a drunk and whose brother is an upmarket property developer and drug dealer. Further actorly weight came with the casting of James Nesbitt as Dave, Michelle's father, and manager of the Titanic Leisure Centre where the two boys have casual work. For a youth film, *Cherrybomb* is more assured stylistically, with a pulsating sound track and swift editing, than narratively, and the storyline appears conservative for the genre. As a result, presumably, it initially failed to gain distribution, and its producers (ICM and The Little Film Company) resorted to urging Grint fans to petition online for a cinema release. Fans were encouraged to sign national petitions, post on social networking sites and internet message boards, as well as to print fliers and place advertisements in local newspapers. The strategy worked and the film enjoyed a short run (see the chart above). In many ways, *Cherrybomb* could have been a more interesting film, not least in its potential to discuss class in Northern Ireland. It is evident that Michelle's family is comfortably middle class and this seems to be partly what motivates her father's hostility to Malachy and Luke, the latter in particular. Class is an issue that so far has been invisible in Northern Irish-set cinema, rendered so by the dominance of the sectarian narrative. To refuse even to identify the teenagers by religion underlines the filmmakers' determination to avoid the old tropes of Belfast films, but lessens its dramatic potential. *A Patch of Fog* is also a very routine thriller, with more of the feel of an episode of a well-made television series than a big-screen theatrical release. The strategy of emphasising the modernity of the locations seems deliberate, a denial of the history embedded in the city's iconic historic buildings and in the inner-city working-class areas that either by proxy, or through actual location shooting, are so identified with Troubles cinema.

Conclusion

Northern Ireland cinema has thrown up some oddities, including *Battle of the Bone* (George Clarke, 2009), a cheaply made horror film set on 12 July that imagines Protestants and Catholics coming together to defeat marauding zombies and the offensive 9 *Dead Gay*

Guys (Lab Ky Mo', 2002), an equally cheap production about a young man from Northern Ireland and his visiting friend who become rent boys in London. (The latter caused walk-outs and outrage when screened at the Cannes Film Festival in 2002.) Overall, however, most of the productions of the post-Troubles period engage in some way or another with the legacy of violence. In saying this, it is important to recognise just how one-sided these narratives are. Just as the Troubles-era films concerned themselves above all with Republicanism, usually with some sympathy, and either ignored or pathologised Loyalism, so the post-Troubles films have signally failed to engage with the Loyalist position. Few examine the British role in the Troubles. Because of the structures of storytelling, the focus of most of these narratives is on the single emblematic hero. That individual trauma can stand in for collective trauma is already a dubious proposition and it is too much to expect of any one film to represent the multiplicity of experiences of those affected by the Troubles. But an approach that embraced diversity in terms of topics and settings could at least go some way towards this. Even considering that the single emblematic hero could be female would be a help. It seems to make little difference as to whether funding for these productions comes from Northern Ireland Screen or the Irish Film Board. Many were jointly funded by these and other public bodies, such as the BBC. As long as these various bodies foreground their role as generating income for the wider economy, then there is apparently little pressure on them to set the agenda in terms of who makes films and whom they represent. *Game of Thrones* has ensured that Northern Ireland has a robust screen economy; the opportunity is now at hand to develop an alternative indigenous production sector that tells the stories of the diversity of people who live there. To end on a note of optimism, the critical success of Lisa McGee's television sitcom *Derry Girls* (Channel 4, 2018–) suggests that there is an audience for sharply written, extremely local, female-centred narratives of the late-Troubles era and one hopes that others will follow her breakthrough production.

Notes

1 Northern Ireland Screen was established on 28 April 1997, taking over from the Northern Ireland Film Council. It also took over film funding from the Northern Ireland Arts Council.

2 *The Lost City of Z* opens in County Cork, which is the film's only Irish setting. *Line of Duty* moved to Northern Ireland for its second season and has remained there since.

3 For a discussion of *Man About Dog*'s place within national cinema and its commercial success, see O'Connell (2006).

4 For more on *Mickybo and Me* as adaptation, see Bastiat (2015).

5 On the under-representation and misrepresentation of the loyalist perspective, see McIlroy (2001).

6 As an alternative strategy, Cahal McLaughlin (2010) has usefully discussed his own approach to making testimony-based films, notably in his work with prisoners and others from Long Kesh/the Maze.

7 For an analysis of the use of sound and music in *Hunger*, see Melvin (2011).

8 For a detailed comparison of the book and film, see O'Donoghue (2013).

9 Another outcome of comparing Skogland's work with Marsh's is to note that the female-centred film is directed by a male, and the anthem to doomed masculinity by a female.

10 For more on the use of the studio in recreating the Crown bar and other settings, see McLoone (2008: 53–4).

11 Jessica Scarlata (2014) has usefully applied Agamben's theories to analyse the spaces of (primarily) female incarceration in Irish cinema, including in her monograph a number of films discussed in mine: *H3*; *Silent Grace*, *The Magdalene Sisters* and *Hunger*.

12 For more on the musical and utopianism, see Chapter 8. *Good Vibrations* is not the first film about Belfast's punk scene. John T. Davis's documentary, *Shellshock Rock* (1979) covers the period in detail and includes interviews with Hooley.

References

Agamben, G. 2005. *State of Exception,* Chicago, IL and London: University of Chicago Press.

Baker, S. and McLaughlin, G. 2015. From Belfast to Bamako: Cinema in the Era of Capitalist Realism. *In:* Monahan, B. (ed.) *Ireland and Cinema, Culture and Contexts.* Basingstoke and New York: Macmillan.

Barton, R. 2004. *Irish National Cinema,* London and New York, Routledge.

Bastiat, B. 2015. Mickybo and Me: A Cinematographic Adaptation for an International Audience. *In:* Monahan, B. (ed.) *Ireland and Cinema, Culture and Contexts.* Basingstoke and New York: Macmillan.

BBC News. 2010. *NI Troubles legacy plan gets frosty response* [Online]. Available: www.bbc.com/news/uk-northern-ireland-10677957 [Accessed 3 November 2017].

Blaney, A. 2008. All's Fair in Love and War? Representations of Prison Life in *Silent Grace. European Journal of Women's Studies,* 15, 393–409.

Box Office Mojo. 2015. '71 [Online]. Available: www.boxofficemojo.com/movies/?id=71.htm [Accessed 21 October 2017].

British Film Institute. *Weekend box office figures* [Online]. British Film Institute. Available: www.bfi.org.uk/education-research/film-industry-statistics-research/weekend-box-office-figures [Accessed 18 October 2017].

Corless, K. 2008. Hunger Interviews. *Sight and Sound*, 18, 26–7.

Ging, D. 2013. *Men and Masculinities in Irish Cinema*, Basingstoke: Palgrave Macmillan.

Grey, T. 2007. N. Ireland Pics Inform Future Work. *Variety*, 15–21 October, pp. A5–A6.

Hill, J. 2006. *Cinema and Northern Ireland: Film, Culture and Politics*, London: BFI.

Lehner, S. 2011. Post-Conflict Masculinities: *Filiative* Reconciliation in *Five Minutes of Heaven* and David Park's *The Truth Commissioner*. *In*: Magennis, C. and Mullen, R. (eds.) *Irish Masculinities Reflections on Literature and Culture*. Dublin and Portland, OR: Irish Academic Press.

Llinares, D. 2015. Punishing Bodies: British Prison Film and the Spectacle of Masculinity. *Journal of British Film and Television*, 12, 207–28.

McGurk, J. 2012. Meeting the Man of my Nightmares. *Belfast Telegraph*, 27 May, p. 2.

McIlroy, B. 2001. *Shooting to Kill: Filmmaking and the "Troubles" in Northern Ireland*, Richmond, BC: Steveston Press.

McIlroy, B. 2007. Memory Work: *Omagh* and the Northern Irish Monumentary. *In*: McIlroy, B. (ed.) *Genre and Cinema, Ireland and Transnationalism*. New York and Abingdon: Routledge.

McLaughlin, C. 2010. *Recording Memories from Political Violence: A Film-Maker's Journey*, Bristol, UK and Chicago, IL: Intellect.

McLoone, M. 2008. *Film, Media and Popular Culture in Ireland: Cityscapes, Landscapes, Soundscapes*, Dublin: Irish Academic Press.

Melvin, A. 2011. Sonic Motifs, Structure and Identity in Steve McQueen's *Hunger*. *The Soundtrack*, 4, 23–32.

Meredith, F. 2004. A film made so people won't forget; tomorrow RTÉ is showing a docudrama that re-creates the horror of the omagh bombing and its aftermath. For some survivors of the atrocity, watching it is unbearable. *Irish Times*, 21 May, p. 7.

Moser, J. P. 2013. *Irish Masculinity on Screen: The Pugilists and Peacemakers of John Ford, Jim Sheridan and Paul Greengrass*, Jefferson, NC and London: McFarland.

Murphy, M. 2017. *Silent Grace and Silenced Women's Voices* [Online]. Available: www.irishtimes.com/culture/tv-radio-web/silent-grace-and-silenced-women-s-voices-1.3130844ß [Accessed 17 November 2017].

Nayman, A. 2014. Interview (with Yann Demange). *Sight and Sound*, 24, 10.

Nora, P. 1989. Between Memory and History: Les Lieux De Mémoire *Representations*, 26, 7–24.

Northern Ireland Screen. 2016. Adding Value, vol. 2. Northern Ireland Screen.

Northern Ireland Screen. 2017. Funding. [Online]. www.northernirelandscreen. co.uk/funding/ [Accessed 20 October 2017].

O'Connell, D. 2006. Man About Dog. *Estudios Irlandeses,* 1, 180–2.

O'Donoghue, D. 2013. Shadow Dancer. *Cineaste,* Summer, 50–2.

Pine, E. 2014. Body of Evidence: Performing *Hunger. In:* Holohan, C. and Tracy, T. (eds.) *Masculinity and Irish Popular Culture: Tiger's Tales.* Basingstoke and New York: Palgrave Macmillan.

Pulver, A. 2016. A Patch of Fog Review – Belfast Thriller Treads a Well-Worn but Nicely Acted Path. *The Guardian* [Online]. Available: www.theguardian. com/film/2016/jun/22/a-patch-of-fog-review-belfast-thriller-treads-a-well-worn-but-nicely-acted-path [Accessed 25 October 2017].

Rockett, K., Gibbons, L. and Hill, J. 1987. *Cinema and Ireland,* London: Croom Helm.

Scarlata, J. 2014. *Rethinking Occupied Ireland: Gender and Incarceration in Contemporary Irish Film,* Syracuse, NY: Syracuse University Press.

Stone, R. 2016. Cinematic Pilgrimages: Postmodern Heritage Cinema. *In:* Cooke, P. and Stone, R. (eds.) *Screening European Heritage: Creating and Consuming History on Film.* Basingstoke: Palgrave Macmillan.

Short film
Six Shooter (Martin McDonagh, 2004)

Martin McDonagh's entry into filmmaking with *Six Shooter* proved that he could transfer his iconoclastic, scatological writing style from one medium, the stage play, to the other, without losing his creative edge. Recognisably a McDonagh production (and as much as they may distinguish themselves one from the other, brothers Martin and John Michael share actors, themes, settings, and models of dialogue across their films), *Six Shooter* is at once recognisably Irish in theme and setting, and also globally legible.

At the heart of the film is Brendan Gleeson's Donnelly, a mountain of a man, his face sagging with grief at the loss of his wife that morning in hospital. Announcing the death, the doctor tells him that he is looking after two women who have experienced cot deaths and a woman whose son had blown her head off with a gun. Taking the train west, Donnelly finds himself seated across Kid (Rúaidhrí Conroy), a foul-mouthed youngster whose own mother has died in the night, and just up from one of the couples that lost their baby.

Most of the action takes place on the train, with Kid taunting the mother (Aisling O'Sullivan) that she must have killed the baby herself because he was so ugly. Other encounters are between Donnelly and a cheeky trolley attendant, played by Gleeson's own son, Domhnall, and ultimately between the passengers and the police, called when the mother throws herself off the train. They have their own reasons to catch Kid. *Six Shooter* abounds with cinephile references, not least to John Ford's 1939 *Stagecoach* and its series of encounters between the law and ideas of respectability. Instead of John Wayne's Ringo Kid, however, we just have Kid, a psychopath child in an emerald green shirt. The conceit of eliding the west of Ireland with the American West is a familiar motif in Irish cinema, notably in *Into the West* (in which Conroy appeared as a child) and opens up possibilities for depicting, even celebrating lawlessness. At the same time, it also allows for an acknowledgement of the transnational exchanges between Ireland and America, not just of people, but of culture. Kid's clothing ought to alert us to one of the most iconic, and most frequently referenced, artefacts of this cultural sharing, and that is to John Ford's *The Quiet Man* which, as we explore further in the next chapter, continues to inform so many contemporary cultural representations. However, where the short film departs from its cultural reference points is that the train is apparently going nowhere much. The journey to the countryside, normally a recuperative possibility in films made in and about Ireland, has little relevance to the characters, who barely look out the window. They might as well have passed the time in a café.

The extreme, but comic violence, particularly during the sequence in which Kid relates his childhood experience of seeing a cow explode, but also the various deaths at the heart of *Six Shooter*, tie it in to an Irish trope of morbid humour, but again points the film outwards to the influences of Quentin Tarantino, and before him Sam Peckinpah, the doyens of American screen violence. As much as it is an auteur work, then, *Six Shooter* productively references transnational models of filmmaking to move it outside of a narrow Irish framework.

7

Rural and small-town Ireland on screen

The shift in emphasis from the country to the city as the preeminent site for exploring identity politics in the Celtic Tiger years and later has opened up interesting new opportunities for the depiction of Irish rural and small-town life. The material reasons for the city displacing the countryside as the locus of Irish cinematic narratives are to do in the first place with technology. Just as the new digital technologies of the 1990s were unsuited to the production of historical films, so their grainy images were equally inappropriate for pastoral photography. Mobile hand-held cameras bred their own aesthetic of swiping, zooming and swift cutting that seemed more in keeping with the fast pace of city life than of the countryside. Only the horror film, as we saw in Chapter 3, has consistently deployed low-budget contemporary filmmaking techniques to desanctify the rural.

As has been widely discussed, Irish romantic nationalism traditionally drew its foundational myths from Celtic mythology and from an idealisation of rural Ireland as the real Ireland, untrammelled by the corrupting modernity of the colonial capital of Dublin. The seminal productions of the 1970s to mid-1990s, such as Bob Quinn's *Poitín* (1978), Pat O'Connor's *The Ballroom of Romance* (1982), Jim Sheridan's *The Field* (1990), Cathal Black's *Korea* (1996) and Neil Jordan's *The Butcher Boy* (1997), constructed an alternative vision of rural Ireland and the West as constricted, patriarchal and often brutal (McLoone, 2000; Pettitt, 2000; Barton, 2004; Holohan, 2010; Ging, 2013).

For the generation of filmmakers who debuted in the Celtic Tiger period, the interrogation of the myth of romantic Ireland was an ageing trope (Barton, 2004: 110–12). Identity politics moved centre-stage alongside a new focus on individualism, consumerism, lifestyle and leisure activities fuelled by the Celtic Tiger economy. This then left something of a hiatus in the representation of rural Ireland on screen in these years. As this chapter will discuss, recent films have knowingly taken older archetypes of rural life and reconstructed them to answer to present-day concerns. On television, the Irish-language channel TG4 has consistently challenged perceptions of rural and small-town Ireland as bucolic backwaters in soaps and mini-series such as *Ros na Rún* (1996–) and *An Bronntanas* (2014). On TV3, *Red Rock* (2015–), which revolves around two feuding families in a small seaside town on the outskirts of Dublin, may notionally adhere to the soap opera format, but is a harder, darker series than the conventions of that genre usually allow. RTÉ's *Pure Mule* (2004–5) was also credited with introducing a range of contemporary issues to its depiction of Midlands Ireland. Only the tourist films, specifically *P.S. I Love You* and *Leap Year*, with their globalised production histories and address, insisted on retaining a vision of the Irish countryside as the site of old-fashioned values and charms.

There is nothing to suggest that rural dwellers in the Celtic Tiger years or during the recession were immune to consumerism or to concerns around opportunity. In the boom, rural depopulation accelerated and subsequently, as the recession took hold, rural dwellers, many of them young people, emigrated in vast numbers, heightening a phenomenon often seen as epitomised by the fall in those available to play traditional rural Irish sports, particularly Gaelic football and hurling. It is equally the case that poor rural broadband services, the closure of rural post offices and emergency departments in local hospitals, changes in planning regulations to limit one-off rural housing, and the failure to attract multinational businesses to relocate to the countryside have exacerbated an already existing sense that the metropolitan centre cared little about the concerns of those outside its borders.

Those Irish filmmakers who have taken as their settings rural and small-town Ireland do not comprise a homogenous movement, yet most share the same bleak vision of the countryside. Some provide a sense of continuity (usually with the depiction of rural and small-town Ireland as dystopian) with the older Irish rural dramas whereas others tear into such narrative conventions to force the viewer to reconceptualise the space of the rural. Where realism fails, then other modes, notably of utopianism, reflect on that failure. Only a few filmmakers focus on the rural as a space for middle-class consumption and play, or as offering redemptive possibilities. In the same vein, familiar archetypes come up for re-examination, inviting comparisons between previously dominant structures of power, notably those embodied by the guard and the priest, and the current crisis of authority. The film to which rural Irish dramas are held in thrall remains John Ford's *The Quiet Man* (1952) and whether it is a train arriving in a rural station (*Calvary*) or an encounter on a stone bridge (*Garage*), or the reworking and re-gendering of a love affair between an American visitor and an Irish native (*P.S. I Love You* and *Leap Year*), or a barely heard melody (*Breakfast on Pluto*), all roads seem to lead back to Ford's opus.

The frailty of rural masculinity

Lenny Abrahamson's *Adam & Paul*, *Garage* and *What Richard Did* form a loose trilogy of films that explore the intersection between place and identity.[1] The second film in the trilogy, *Garage*, relocates Abrahamson's central male character from Dublin to rural Ireland of the Celtic Tiger to provide a merciless deconstruction of the idealisation of country life. The film's 'hero' is Josie, played in a bravura casting decision by Pat Shortt, who until then had been best known as a stage and television comedian. His series, *Killinaskully* (RTÉ, 2004–8), a compilation of skits on rural life, enjoyed enormous popular success locally, although it was derided by the critics. As the *Irish Times* reviewer surmised of its almost 500,000 a week audience:

> I don't know how those figures break down, but I'd guess that most of these viewers already live in their own version of Killinaskully. They're less likely to be Dubliners and more likely to represent, to borrow a phrase, the people who have their dinner in the middle of the day. The urban/rural divide is still very much in evidence in the success of Killinaskully – a programme that is said to quieten some rural pubs quicker than the sound of an approaching Garda car at 2am. (Hegarty, 2008)

In overseas territories, therefore, Shortt's performance history was meaningless as *Killinaskully* did not export, but it carried interesting local resonances specifically to urban, metropolitan viewers for whom his humour was alien. Hegarty's analysis also serves as a reminder that most narratives of Irish rural life on screen are constructed from the metropolitan centre and reflect that centre's taste and concerns. Shortt's Josie reworks the old stereotype of the village idiot, elevating him to the core rather than the margins of the narrative. Despite his lumbering gait and social awkwardness, he appears confident in his running of the eponymous garage, a filling station on the outskirts of an unnamed small town in the Irish Midlands. When the garage owner, Mr Gallagher (John Keogh), lands an unasked-for teenage assistant, David (Conor Ryan) on Josie, he and the boy gradually build up a friendship. On one of his regular visits to the village pub, Josie misinterprets the kindness (mixed with neediness) of a young woman, Carmel (Anne-Marie Duff), touching her on the back when they dance, and is sharp enough to realise that he is condemned to life as a single man. On top of this, in his

Figure 16 Pat Shortt and Conor Ryan in *Garage*

incomprehension of normative behaviour, he shows David a porn video and when word of this emerges, everything falls apart.

Garage was scripted by Mark O'Halloran who has frequently spoken in interview of his own upbringing in rural Ireland and how (in Crosson and Schreiber, 2011: 136–7):

> I think that the countryside has been represented a hell of a lot in Irish cinema, but it's always been represented wrongly as far as I am concerned. It used to treat the countryside as being one big long joke, and I lived in that 'joke' for seventeen years and it wasn't very funny.

As in *Adam & Paul*, characters communicate by alternating between Beckettian non sequiturs, fragmented sentences and silences. Edits often create unexpected juxtapositions, and Josie in particular may be moved from the garage, to the outdoors, to the pub without any warning, reflecting the fact that he, just as Adam and Paul, is unable to gain mastery over space. This fragmentation of space and subjectivity is central to *Garage* and in this context, Abrahamson has explained: 'I'm interested in the spaces between the significant moments in life, the parts that are usually discarded in memory and also – almost as a matter of principle – in conventional cinematic storytelling' (in Wood, 2008). Even still, neither script nor direction completely jettisons formal narrative conventions so that Josie's gradual slide into desperation is signposted through a series of encounters with other characters. These encounters serve a double function. Structurally, they allow the audience to gain insights into Josie's character that he himself could not articulate. At the same time, they allow for an exploration of the dysfunctionality of rural life. The doyens of the pub openly mock Josie in a one-sided exchange of banter that in another film would be marked as homosocial bonding but here suggests cruelty layered on top of loneliness. 'Town looks after its own', Josie tells David, whom he knows to be a 'blow-in' and out-sider like himself. And, in certain ways it does, with the local guard, Michael (Denis Conway) displaying particular empathy towards Josie when he questions him about showing Conor the porn video and giving him alcohol.

While the new opportunities for property development are in part the cause of the disruption – Mr. Gallagher wants to build apartments in the place of the garage, and as he says, 'houses are flying up around the lake' – the film also refuses to sentimentalise the older ways of the coun-tryside. Thus, in one encounter, Josie meets Sully (Andrew Bennett) on a picturesque stone bridge over the river. Birds sing in the background, and the sound competes with the whimpering of a litter of puppies Sully is carrying in a sack. These, he explains to Josie, are the unwanted off-spring of the family dog and Tierney's collie, 'five of them, pure awk-ward'. He slings the sack into the river and even as he commiserates with Sully, Josie's expression shows a flicker of empathy. This is, he understands, where the countryside disposes of its unwanted inhabitants and at the end of the film he too will follow the puppies.

Complementing the silences is Abrahamson's decision to restrict the score (by Stephen Rennicks) to the opening and closing credits. This aural minimalism finds its counterpart in punctuating shots of the empty spaces of the Irish Midlands. The credit sequence, which is accompanied by Rennicks's eerie, plangent score finds Josie traversing the lonely bogscape near a little-used narrow-gauge railway of the kind employed by Bord na Móna (the Irish Turf Development Board) to transport fuel. Only at the very end of the film does Abrahamson provide the shot of a still, early morning river, which one might expect of a film set in the Irish countryside, but then this moment of pastoralism is ruptured, first with two shots of flies on its surface, and then with the intrusion of death.

This is not the Bog Gothic of horror cinema, which is just the kind of representational convention that *Garage* passes over in its search for a truthful story or as Abrahamson has said (in Crosson and Schreiber, 2011: 139): 'The key is, *not* to represent, if you can, as a filmmaker, and try, at least in these kinds of films, to go against whatever the dominant motifs are in the audience's head. And yet the audience then always recognises it as truer, in the end.'

The audience did recognise a truth in *Garage*, which was the second-highest-grossing Irish film (after *Becoming Jane*) of 2007, with a local box office take of €305,952 (Sheehy, 2008). In this it repeated the achievement of *Adam & Paul*, which made its budget back at the local box office (Lavery, 2005).

Slow cinema and rural cinema

Slow cinema is conventionally associated with auteur, arthouse cinema. In the Irish context, arguably Abrahamson's films fit the category, although there are other, less well-known, but more defined examples of the movement in local filmmaking. Globally, auteurs such as Carlos Reygadas, Alexander Sokurov, Béla Tarr and Apichatpong Weerasethakul have followed in the tradition of Chantal Akerman, Theo Angelopoulos, Andrei Tarkovsky and others in favouring long takes and long shots, slow camera movement, minimal editing, sparse dialogue and the rejection of melodramatic narrative structures. In his discussion of slow cinema, Ira Jaffe (2014) identifies these features as consistent with the movement, or arthouse genre, as well as the following: flat, 'affectless' characters; locations off the beaten track; plot and dialogue that 'gravitate towards stillness and death and tend, in any case, to be minimal, indeterminate and unresolved' (2014: 3). Although such techniques might seem to describe Abrahamson's cinema, his films, including the non-Irish-set films, notably *Room*, demand an intense engagement with his characters that counters the concerns with 'affect' that accompany much of twenty-first-century cinema.[2] On the other hand, Collins's *Silence* lends itself easily to such an analysis, as does another film with strong documentary overtones, Gerard Barrett's *Pilgrim Hill* (2013).

Pilgrim Hill opens as a mock documentary, with farmer Jimmy Walshe (Joe Mullins) sitting in his kitchen recounting his life to date to camera. We soon learn that he is in his forties, a bachelor small farmer caring for his invalided father. Jimmy's mother committed suicide when he was a child, his father was abusive and Jimmy is resigned to a life of loneliness. Matters will get worse when his cattle are diagnosed with TB and the film ends with them being removed for slaughter. Running to just eighty-five minutes, *Pilgrim Hill* unfolds in a series of vignettes, the 'to-camera' sections interspersed with conventional dramatic encounters, and plays out at a dolorous, elegiac pace with infinite attention to small detail, such as the purchase of four slices of ham in the shop and the echo of the ticking clock. Even the conclusion (when Jimmy finally cracks up and attempts to bar the men from removing his cattle) is shot with minimal melodrama, no dialogue, the camera unusually far from its central character and to the accompaniment of a score that is now heard for the first time. The interiors of the farmhouse are shot in gloomy natural light and the landscape is glimpsed through windscreen wipers in the rain, or as a narrow, constricted space of bogland and water-logged fields.

Made on a budget of €4,500 with completion financing from the Irish Film Board, *Pilgrim Hill* was funded and cast locally in Kerry, with the lead taken by a farmer with some experience in amateur dramatics (Clarke, 2013; Guerin, 2013). To many people's surprise, *Pilgrim Hill* performed well (for a low-budget, 'difficult' Irish film) at the local box office, taking around €70,000 (Brady, 2013).[3]

The only character with any significant screen time other than Jimmy is his friend, Tommy (Muiris Crowley), who is, he says, 'still unemployed, riding the dole train'. Jimmy recognises that life is passing him by, spelling it out in his final 'interview': 'My future is thirty acres on the side of a hill out in the back end of nowhere, no prospects, maybe a life in the pub and grow old, like so many people I've seen. Nobody. So many people who've given up and just exist.' Tommy too may dream of emigrating (to Dubai or Canada), but for all his pursuit of the pleasures of consumerism – gleaming white trainers and an evening out at the local night club – he is as stuck as Jimmy in this emotionally and economically impoverished backwater. The pub is even less welcoming than its counterpart in *Garage*, with Jimmy seen sipping a lone pint, for which he will be breathalysed on his return home by an officious young guard who is new to the parish. This depiction of rural Ireland is familiar from the films of the 1980s and early 1990s, although it is one that Irish cinemagoers largely lost sight of during the Celtic Tiger years. With its absorption in despairing masculinity, *Pilgrim Hill* is less innovative thematically than technically, and it is notable that the only female speaking part goes to Jimmy's father's carer, Margaret (Corina Gough). Still, Barrett's recuperation of these older themes is in itself a reminder that the Celtic Tiger did not so much erase the concerns of the past as mute them. *Pilgrim Hill* is probably too short to satisfy the category of slow cinema fully, but it shares many of its features.

Rescue fantasies and rural settings

The slow-paced rural drama reinforces the old dichotomies between fast/ urban and slow/rural. While this may still bear some reflection of reality, it has been challenged by other filmmakers determined to upend these (and other) conventions. One such film is Tom Hall's *Sensation* (2010).

Hall is a long-time Irish independent filmmaker. With John Carney as a writer/director duo, his work includes: *November Afternoon* (1996), *Park* (1999) and the television series *Bachelors Walk*. Hall's first solo film as director, *Wide Open Spaces* (2009), was a little-seen comedy starring Ardal O'Hanlon and Ewen Bremner and revolved around two out-of-work friends who decide to set up a Famine theme park. To situate *Sensation* within Hall's CV, one needs to return to the earlier films, particularly *Park*, with its very problematic rape narrative. Whereas Carney (who wrote the music for *Sensation*) has moved between mainstream and independent, Hall has remained more closely associated with provocative, non-generic filmmaking. The opening pre-credit sequence of *Sensation* radically undermines the aesthetics of Irish pastoralism and announces the film's intentions. In it, the central character Donal (Domhnall Gleeson) is seen herding a flock of sheep through a gate. Birds are singing, the sun is shining and a dog barks in the distance. An unsteady hand-held camera follows him into the field and to a hedge where he unpacks a porn magazine and proceeds to masturbate vigorously. After this, he goes into a dirty farmhouse kitchen with kittens climbing over unwashed dishes, and as retro 1970s-style pink titles begin to emerge on the screen, he calls his father. When he finds him dead in his stair-lift, he blankly presses the remote control and the chair continues its journey down the stairs, with the dead man slumped in it.

If this opening sequence is challenging, the film becomes even more difficult as it progresses, very particularly with its foregrounding of the rescue fantasy as its central theme. Sigmund Freud (1966) theorised that the rescue fantasy arose out of the boy's realisation that his mother had sex with his father and was therefore not a saint but a whore. His need to 'rescue' her is transferred to the prostitute whom he now fantasises about rescuing and restoring to a state of purity. In *Sensation*, Donal orders a sex worker, Kim (Luanne Gordon) from the nearest city, Limerick, and they embark on a relationship. Kim, who is a New Zealander, borrows money from Donal for a breast augmentation procedure in London and the two go into business together, running a brothel populated by overseas sex workers. Donal, who is depicted as sexually and socially immature, also attempts a relationship with a local shop assistant, Melanie (Kelly Campbell). In the end, the guards raid the brothel and arrest Donal. His solicitor advises him to blame Kim, with whom he already has a masochistic, punitive relationship. In the courtroom, he experiences a change of heart, and in an ending that closely mirrors that of another rescue fantasy, *The Crying Game* (Neil Jordan, 1992), Kim visits him in prison and the film suggests that they may have a future when he is released.

Figure 17 Patrick Ryan and Domhnall Gleeson in *Sensation*

Set against the backdrop of the financial crisis, *Sensation*'s ideological position is murky. On the one hand, it establishes sex work as a capitalist enterprise that may substitute for regular employment. Kim, inevitably for such narratives, is a smart woman who unfortunately has 'fallen', but treats sex work with dispassion, as just another industry. Beneath this businesslike exterior, however, she is emotionally (and physically) damaged and thus ripe for 'rescue'. Aware of its own clichés, the film has her demand of Donal and his equally emotionally limited friend, Karl (Patrick Ryan), 'Where do you guys get this rescue fantasy? … It's not *Pretty Woman*.' Canning and Ging (2012) have trenchantly and very reasonably critiqued Hall's film for its gender politics and specifically its positioning of women. And yet, the intentions behind *Sensation*, one may assume, were not to replicate the old paradigms but to challenge the established imagery of rural Ireland and with it to illustrate the consequences of a national history of rural sexual repression. By displacing sex work onto women from outside Ireland, Hall undermines his own project (as he does too often with this difficult narrative). Melanie's worry that she may have been infected by sex with Donal suggests the pollution of the pure Irish woman at a remove by the impure foreigner. At the same time, Hall also reinforces the recurring narrative trope of having the non-native woman liberate the local Irish male from his inadequacies, here specifically by positioning Kim as mother/lover, in the unexplained absence of Donal's own mother.

Queering rural and small-town Ireland: *Breakfast on Pluto*

The tensions evident in *Sensation* between rendering rural Ireland familiar enough to be artistically legible and disrupting the paradigms that facilitate this are shared by many of the productions discussed in this chapter. If *Garage* remains the most complete exploration of the layering of present on past in contemporary rural Ireland, it is also distinctive for its queering of the rural space. Fintan Walsh (2013: 217) has usefully argued of *Adam & Paul* and *Garage* that 'although the queer is only subtly implied in these works – in the odd couplings, frustrated desires and complex intimacies – in a timely fashion the films go some way to register the excluded place and space of queerness in Irish film and culture'. Thus, the heteronormative family is consistently shown up as a sham, with the central characters of each film in (usually futile) search of alternative relationships. Another work that foregrounds its queering of small-town Ireland is Neil Jordan's *Breakfast on Pluto*. Functioning as a compendium of Jordan's filmic tropes, from the rescue fantasy, to gender-bending, to the Troubles, one of its touchstones is inevitably *The Butcher Boy*. This should not be surprising given that this is Jordan's second Patrick McCabe adaptation after *The Butcher Boy*, if one with a radically reworked ending. Both films foreground a young adult who does not fit into the parochial conformity of their environment. The Otherness to the community is articulated via, amongst other narrative devices, the acerbic comments of local middle-aged women/gossips gathered in village shops. Jordan's cinema opens itself easily to critique when it trades on this kind of gender stereotyping, but it remains, at its best, formally playful and deconstructive in a way that few other contemporary filmmakers have achieved. The village of Tyreelin on the Cavan border with Northern Ireland is a liminal space not just geographically, but in terms of its production of identity. Walsh (2013: 216) is dismissive of Jordan's characters as too bounded by 'rigid narrative and extensive allegory.' However, his identification of 'queer' as accounting for 'non-normative identities and relationships which, although not expressly homosexual, are queerly unfixed and unsettling,' (Walsh, 2013: 216) maps with ease on to *Breakfast on Pluto*. Here, the young Kitten Brady (Conor McEvoy, then Cillian Murphy) grows up in the late 1960s with a Down syndrome boy, Lawrence (Seamus Reilly), a mixed-race girl, Charlie (Bianca O'Connor, then Ruth Negga), and a future IRA man, Irwin (Emmet Lawlor McHugh, then Laurence Kinlan), as her friends, while developing into her own identity as a transgender woman. As they enter their teens, divisions occur, particularly once Irwin joins the IRA, which is here depicted as the breeding ground of hegemonic masculinity.

The film is narrated by Kitten, whose whimsicality informs it both visually and at the level of plot. Her identity as an unreliable narrator is signalled in an early schoolroom scene, where she composes a classroom essay imagining her moment of conception in a quasi-rape scene (another problematic Jordan motif) between Father Liam (Liam Neeson) and Ely Bergin (Eva Birthistle), whom Kitten consistently imagines as the performer Mitzi Gaynor (b. 1931). Kitten's multiple encounters, from the showband led by Billy Hatchett (Gavin Friday) through working as a Womble with John Joe Kenny (Brendan Gleeson), as a magician's assistant to Bertie (Stephen Rea), to being mistaken for an IRA bomber in London, are bathed in hyperreal colours and accompanied by a soundtrack of hits of the period from Bobby Goldsboro, Kris Kristofferson, T Rex, and others. As the film progresses, Kitten's dress becomes increasingly stylised and with her glammed-up hairstyle and immaculate lipstick, she eventually most closely resembles Mitzi Gaynor. Thus, the child decides ultimately against rescuing her mother, but instead makes herself over to become her fantasised Other.

In a major change from the original novel, Jordan's film ends with Kitten (Pussy in the McCabe original) reconciling with her father, the priest, rather than fantasising about burning down his church and with it committing parricide. Instead, the locals burn the church and Kitten and Father Liam move to London with Charlie and her baby. As Anne Mulhall (2013: 235) writes: 'This new queer multicultural family is Jordan's version of the utopian re-engendering of herself and the community of the excluded that Pussy fantasises at the end of the novel.' Thus, in *Breakfast on Pluto*'s ending, small-town Ireland's potential to exist as a queer space is shown to be as contingent as it will be in the later *Garage*. One of the film's most affective scenes is the moment when Lawrence spots the bomb disposal robot and runs towards it, mistaking it for one of his much-loved Daleks, and is blown up. Where so much of *Breakfast on Pluto*'s emotion is defrayed through Kitten's refusal to engage seriously with life, this scene is played 'straight' as tragedy. Charlie's mixed-race identity is never discussed, and ostensibly the town turns against her because she is a single mother. As we noted in Chapter 3, colour-blindness is a problematic strategy, ignoring as it does the real issues of race. Jordan draws attention to the positioning of Charlie as an 'out' character by insisting on her empathy with Kitten and Lawrence while refusing to discuss her racially marked identity.

The problem here, as it so often is with Jordan, is the refusal of ideology in favour of artistry. The queering of small-town Ireland is a trope rich in potential. Yet in *Breakfast on Pluto* it is played for entertainment value, even as a shock tactic. How incongruous and funny it is to take a Down syndrome boy, a mixed-race woman and a transgender woman and place them in an Irish border town! The same issues arise in one of *Breakfast on Pluto*'s plot detours when Kitten performs as Hiawatha alongside Billy Hatchett, who seems to be (Jordan never shows the pair making love) Kitten's first lover. Kitten's guileless performance and the relationship with Hatchett are consistently signalled as unnatural through the other band members' disapproving glances. Subsequently, across the border in Northern Ireland, the (regressive nationalist) crowd pelts them with missiles. That Kitten should not only be performing in drag but as a native American becomes another of the film's jokes, as if all transgressive behaviour is equal.

With its postmodern and authorial resistance to ideological positioning, Jordan's *Breakfast on Pluto* offers itself up to an alternative reading, where Kitten represents a future beyond gender binaries and in an alternative space of religious, gendered and racial tolerance. In this sense, then, it is reductive to test the narrative for plausibility, but rather to consider it more akin to John Carney's *Once* and *Sing Street* (2016) and the utopian musical (discussed further in the next chapter). As Carney does in *Sing Street*, so Jordan borrows from glam-rock to situate his characters in a global movement of freedom from older, gendered conventions (although in *Breakfast on Pluto* the references are more local with the casting of Gavin Friday, frontman of former Irish glam-rock band, The Virgin Prunes). The soundtrack propels and acts as a commentary on the narrative, no more so than when Kitten sets off to the accompaniment of Middle of the Road's 'Chirpy, Chirpy, Cheep, Cheep (Where's your mama gone?)' to find her mother. The soundtrack also references previous cinematic and gendered fantasies of Ireland, specifically in the sequence where Kitten imagines her moment of conception. For once, it is accompanied not by hit tunes of the day but by the theme music to *The Quiet Man*. Aurally, then, the space of *Breakfast on Pluto* functions as a chronotope through its invocation of a mix of anachronistic and current popular cultural markers. Visually, too, the film's vivid colour schemes reference the classic Hollywood musical, itself one of the queerest of genres. This reading thus allows for *Breakfast on Pluto* to reimagine Ireland through a queer lens. It does not absolve the film from the race, gender and other issues referenced above, but it does suggest how it offers affective pleasures over and beyond its political incoherence.

From *The Stag* to *Mad Mary*: new queer spaces

The work of John Butler – *The Stag* (2013), *Handsome Devil* (2016) – is particularly interesting in its reworking of popular cinematic subgenres, the stag weekend and the high-school/Dead Poet's Society male melodrama respectively.[4] Butler is also interesting in terms of his identification as a gay man and his casting in both films of openly gay actor Andrew Scott. Both films have predominantly rural settings, although this is more important to *The Stag* than to *Handsome Devil*. In the former, Ruth (Amy Huberman) persuades Davin (Andrew Scott) to take her fiancé Fionan (Hugh O'Connor) and their group of male buddies to the countryside on a stag weekend. Davin is not just Fionan's best friend, but also still entertains lingering feelings for Ruth. The weekend is thrown into chaos when Ruth insists that they also invite her super-macho brother, The Machine (Peter McDonald). *The Stag* very consciously draws on discourses around newer models of Irish masculinity as metrosexuality (Ging, 2013: 182–9); thus Fionan explains that, 'I don't enjoy being in all-male company', and, to reinforce an obvious point, the wedding organiser, Linda (Justine Mitchell), just prevents herself from using the obvious descriptor for Fionan in conversation with Ruth: 'He is so metro … politan.'

Scott's Davin in *The Stag* is written as a straight man, but his deep antipathy towards The Machine, and his performance generally are more suggestive of an underlying gay identity. The audience hardly needs The

Figure 18 Brian Gleeson, Andrew Scott, Peter McDonald, Hugh O'Conor, Michael Legge and Andrew Bennett in *The Stag*

Machine to complain 'This is very gay' when the other men insist that he practise apologising to his wife, Rachel (Amy de Bhrún) by substituting Davin for Rachel in a role-play exercise. Curiously, it is ultimately The Machine who is revealed to be the most empathetic member of the all-male group. It is he who persuades Simon (Brian Gleeson) to discuss his company's financial losses in the recession, comforting him that his own losses are substantially larger. Just as the film serves as a reminder of the use of the countryside as a space of commodified leisure for the Irish middle-classes, it also allies itself with The Machine's comment as he surveys the campfire gathering, 'you couldn't put a price on this'. Having taken the drug MDMA and lost their clothing while skinny-dipping in the dark, the men are reduced by the end of the film to cavemen attire; stripping off the accoutrements of civilisation, is, the film suggests, restorative. Thus, the countryside retains its older associations of spiritual rebirth.

In the closing sequences, The Machine makes the following speech at Ruth and Fionan's wedding, before singing U2's 'One':

> In recent times, we've taken a hell of a beating what with the economy and Europe tearing us a new one and the Church being total assholes about everything. But we've got to forgive ourselves, forgive each other and learn to love ourselves again. Because, the thing is, we're Ireland. And that, my friends, is deadly.

Discussing his positioning within the new Irish filmmaking landscape, Butler has said in interview (Mullally, 2017) that films such as *The Young Offenders, Sing Street* and *A Date for Mad Mary* are not 'so overtly about trying to figure out who we are … there is a confidence to work within subgenres and not necessarily towards the question of what is Irishness. I think that's all that matters.' Yet, it is this very desire to address the national situation that sits oddly within the light tone and generic expectations of *The Stag,* and which Butler dropped for *Handsome Devil.* That film is set in neither an identifiable time nor place, but rather somewhere in rural Ireland in the recent past, within an exclusive boys' boarding school. It also functions as an interesting companion piece to *What Richard Did.* Here Butler foregrounds gay themes in his story of the growing friendship between two schoolboys, Ned Roche (Fionn O'Shea) and Conor Masters (Nicholas Galitzine). The former is ruthlessly teased for his obviously gay identity; the latter is the star of the rugby team, but will also turn out to be gay. The charismatic English teacher, Dan Sherry (Andrew Scott), formulates the film's central message with his exhortation never to speak in a borrowed voice: 'You spend your whole life being somebody else', he admonishes the boys, 'Who's going to be you?' He too is a gay man and part of his own journey is to admit this and bring his partner with him to the final set-piece rugby match, where the team will be challenged to accept Conor as a gay rugby player. As this summary suggests, *Handsome Devil* is not without its own clichés, yet it is an important contribution to Irish cinema's very modest array of gay-themed films in that it positions itself within, only to queer, mainstream genre filmmaking and refuses the narrative tradition of the sad young gay man, associating the boys instead with cool music and strong friendship. (It is, however, very much in the tradition of Irish cinema in its refusal of explicit sex.)

A Date for Mad Mary might have as easily been set in a big city as in Drogheda and, as I discuss further in the next chapter, is consistent with a number of recent films with female protagonists in ignoring those connections between place and identity that define many of the male-centred narratives. This does not detract from Thornton's intense exploration of female friendships and outsiderdom. Instead, it emphasises the importance of the network to feelings of belonging. The film opens with Mary's (Seána Kerslake) release from Mountjoy Prison, where she has been serving a sentence for attacking another young woman. As she prepares to leave, so she rehearses aloud her speech for her best friend, Charlene's (Charleigh Bailey) imminent wedding. The speech emphasises the two friends' refusal to engage in normative behaviour at school; but,

Figure 19 Seána Kerslake in *A Date for Mad Mary*

when they reunite, Mary discovers that Charlene has changed and is anxious to put her wild days behind her. This means distancing herself from her friendship with Mary. She also announces that Mary may not bring a 'plus one' to the wedding. Much of the trajectory of the film is devoted to Mary's obstinate pursuit of a date and her growing attraction to the official photographer-cum-lead singer in a local band, Jess (Tara Lee).

It is not just Mary's attraction to Jess (and the suggestion that more may lie behind her old friendship with Charlene than either realises) that makes *Mad Mary* so queer, but rather the film's exploration of the consequences of her alienation from her family and peers. Certainly, it is easy to feel sympathy for her shock at her friend's 'bridezilla' moment, but a shot of the scar on the face of the young woman she attacked serves as a reminder that social conformity is not always regressive. Kerslake's performance invites the viewer to share her disdain for her peers' conformism, but suggests that outsiderdom is not the romantic option that the conventions of the teen movie suggest it to be.

New strangers

An old trope of Irish rural and small-town dramas is the arrival of a stranger into a small community – an event frequently characterised as the intrusion of modernity into tradition, and one with often-traumatic consequences. In film terms, one of the most traumatic of these is Jim Sheridan's *The Field* (1990), with a more comic version being the earlier *This Other Eden* (Muriel Box, 1959). Contemporary reworkings of this narrative include Jordan's *Ondine* and *Halal Daddy* (Conor McDermottroe, 2017), with the stranger now racially marked as Other. Neither film offers a particularly useful reworking of the old narrative formula; instead both reflect a surprising conservatism in terms of how they depict the Other. As I have discussed elsewhere (Barton, 2014) Jordan's *Ondine* can be squarely placed within the narrative tradition of the white Irish (male) being emotionally rescued by the immigrant Other. Here, Jordan draws on the Selkie myth that also informed the narrative of *Song of the Sea* for a film that produces an equally reductive representation of motherhood and gendered identities. In the film, fisherman Syracuse (Colin Farrell) hauls a young woman (Alicja Bachleda) in with his catch; she tells him her name is Ondine. He hides her at his 'gypsy' mother's old home in a secluded inlet on the coast where he lives, following his separation from his wife, Maura (Dervla Kirwin). The latter lives in the local small town with her new partner, Alex (Tony Curran) and her daughter with Syracuse, Annie (Alison Barry). Syracuse, known locally as Circus, is treated as the village clown, and we soon learn that his marriage ended when he gave up alcohol and Maura kept on drinking. As he explains to Ondine, 'This is Ireland. Men like me don't get custody.' Annie suffers from kidney disease and is partially wheelchair bound. A bookish, fanciful child, she becomes convinced that Ondine is a Selkie, although the film ends with a more prosaic explanation for her appearance – she is a Romanian drug mule.

As a number of writers have argued, water sites in Jordan's cinema function as romantic spaces for the exploration of desire (Chouinard, 2010; Rockett and Rockett, 2003) and Jordan's fascination with shape-shifting and folklore are central to his writings and filmmaking (Zucker, 2008). We saw above how Jordan tends to favour oblique, humanistic narratives over direct confrontations with Irish socio-political issues. The collision of the two – the mythic and the social – in the revelation that Ondine is in fact Johanna, a Romanian drug mule, involves an uncomfortable tonal shift that highlights *Ondine*'s reliance on unreconstructed gender positions. In other words, the shift into a form of social realism forces the film into placing Ondine and Maura as each other's opposites – the kindly Eastern European, who makes Annie feel at home and who falls in love with Syracuse, versus the drunken Irish mother, whose lover may, the film suggests, harbour paedophile yearnings towards the child. Ondine's depiction bears strong resemblances to that of the Girl in *Once* (which will be discussed in the next chapter), if here the union between the nurturing woman and the lonely man are realised. Meanwhile, the use of the term 'gypsy' over 'Traveller' to describe Syracuse's mother banishes the social problems of the present-day Traveller to the safety of a romanticised past.

Paul McGuirk (2016: 260) has written of *Ondine*'s present-day setting that this 'is a society that is fractured and disorientated. The old stories have proven inefficacious and it is necessary to generate new narratives in order to make sense of the changing circumstances.' Yet, it seems with *Ondine* that when Jordan sought out a new narrative for a new era, he only found old tropes – the fractured family, the damaged father/husband, the bad mother and the rural as a restorative site – adding in a new arrival in the shape of the foreign Other as a more desirable nurturer (of the damaged Irish male, the innocent Irish child). Just as he reworked the Selkie legend, so it fell apart, unable to accommodate the new narrative conditions.

Much the same occurred with *Halal Daddy,* McDermottroe's version of the encounter between the stranger and the small Irish community. Set in Sligo, the film, which was written by Mark O'Halloran, is specific about the effects of the recession in setting much of its narrative around the closure of a local meat factory and the consequent loss of jobs, notably that of its manager, Martin Logan (Colm Meaney). The other related plot line concerns Raghdan Aziz (Nikesh Patel), who has escaped Bradford and his controlling father, Amir's (Art Malik) plans for an arranged marriage, and come to live with his easy-going uncle, Jamal (Paul Tylak) and aunt, Doreen (Deirdre O'Kane). Raghdan has fallen for Maeve (Sarah Bolger), Martin's daughter, and enjoys hanging out with a group of their surfer friends. Amir's arrival puts paid to Raghdan's easy life, as the former plans to convert the old factory into a halal butchery with Martin as its new manager. The film plays out as a culture clash very much along the lines of *East Is East* (Damien O'Donnell, 1999), but without the latter's dark conclusion.

McDermottroe's characters are familiar from earlier iterations of Irish cinema: Meaney's Martin is a crusty paterfamilias with a soft heart; Doreen is plain-speaking and motherly even as she regrets her and Jamal's inability to have children. She and Jamal, in a pale reflection of her Noeleen in *Intermission,* enjoy slightly risqué sex, and the film goes to some pains to present their marriage as a coming together of soulmates with their racial difference an irrelevance. The one gay man, Jasper, is German. In the same vein, British Muslims, in the shape of Jamal, are industrious and open to any business opportunity while remaining socially conservative. Eventually, Jamal's encounter with the happy-go-lucky Irish will free him up to appreciate that there is more to life than ambition, and Raghdan and Maeve will save the day by setting up a hippy emporium (something like Dublin's Dandelion Market in the 1970s), that exploits surfer culture for its commercial possibilities.

Halal Daddy's pitch is to celebrate rural and small-town Ireland as a restorative, multicultural space. To do so, it has to view racial difference through the prism of the domestic rather than the socio-economic, rendering invisible the political framework within which its characters are operating. The Otherness of halal butchery, which became a brief talking point in radio phone-in shows following the film's release, is reduced to a few cutaway shots to flinching onlookers. Similarly, the film's opportunity to discuss the replacement of failed local industry with outside corporate start-ups is lost in its determination to gloss over all such contemporary issues. Despite a strong cast, and this utopian vision of a new multicultural Ireland, the film achieved only modest returns, taking approximately $11,662 (under €10,000) at the Irish box office (Box Office Mojo, 2017).[5]

Old journeys

The Irish countryside has long functioned as a restorative space for the jaded metropolitan, while in the horror films that same space represents atavistic horrors. *Intermission*'s (near) conclusion envisages the country-side in short order as escape and horror, with Lehiff leading Detective Jerry Lynch into the Dublin mountains where the former will accidentally meet his end. In keeping with that film's overall tone, the journey into the countryside is played out ironically, nodding to the associations between rural Ireland and Celtic spirituality and to the tradition of the chase film, while also reworking that trope. By contrast, Peter Foott's 2016 cult hit, *The Young Offenders*, has a jaunty pace that youth audiences find enjoyable. It intersperses mock philosophical musings with the story of two young men who plan to make their fortunes by purloining some of the cocaine that has washed ashore in west Cork. (*The Young Offenders* also resolves the space/time issue of shooting a chase film in a small country by having the boys ride bicycles.) It plays knowingly with the stereotypes of urban disadvantage (the boys' background) and rural iso-lation (the lonely farmer who takes them in). Under the humour, the film manages to explore both types with some empathy, dropping its comic mode in the sequences between Jock Murphy (Chris Walley) and his abusive, alcoholic father (Michael Sands) and in the encounter between the two young men and the elderly farmer (Pascal Scott), who, in recog-nition of his alchoholism, is tied to a chair by Jack, so that the whiskey is out of reach.

The success of *The Young Offenders* lay in part in its ability to revisit old archetypes with some empathy. Rural Ireland is in so many ways an overdetermined setting for narratives of emotional healing that it is a challenge for filmmakers to renegotiate the inherited cinematic tropes of those older stories. One can detect in, for instance, Steph Green's *Run and Jump* (2013), a determination to avoid the predictable signifiers of rural Irish life in her family drama set in Kerry. Here, the stranger to the community is Ted (Will Forte), an American doctor who had come to study Conor (Edward MacLiam), as he returns home after suffering a stroke. Conor's wife, Vanetia (Maxine Peake) is a force of nature and awakens Ted's repressed emotions even as she cares for her much-altered husband. *Run and Jump*'s achievement is to create an unconventional enough Irish mother to establish that Ted falls for Vanetia not because she typifies the 'wild Irish girl', but for her strength of character.

The only two films of the era to play the journey to rural Ireland as one of spiritual transformation with any sincerity, *P.S. I Love You* and *Leap Year*, are generally (and justifiably) greeted with no little derision by commentators.[6] The former is an adaptation of Cecilia Ahern's best-selling novel of the same name; the latter concerns the decision by its central character, Anna Brady (Amy Adams) to travel to Ireland where she believes it is a custom to propose to your boyfriend on 29 February.

Both films' narratives are driven by the quest of a single, female tourist, a trope that interestingly reworks the premise of *The Quiet Man*. Yet, the opportunity to frame the Irish countryside and its people from a female perspective is thrown away by both works' embrace of the romcom formula. In order for Holly (Hilary Swank) in *P.S. I Love You* to overcome her grief at the early death of her adored Irish husband, Gerry (Gerard Butler), she has to fall in love with an equally sensitive and charming local Irish replacement, William (Jeffrey Dean Morgan), who looks uncannily like the deceased. He will enable her return to the joy of living just as in *Leap Year*, Declan (Matthew Goode), will reorient Anna from her obsession with the contemporary world of consumer capitalism to the mystical world of Irish romance as he guides her around a ruined castle narrating the old myth of the lovers Diarmuid and Gráinne. Thus, only through male intervention can both women achieve full selfhood.

P.S. I Love You and *Leap Year* are easily dismissed as globalised product. The casting of the local Irish love interests, Gerard Butler and Matthew Goode, in an era where so many Irish male actors are comfortably playing romantic leads, is hard to explain and the storylines dust down a mantelpiece of old stereotypes that hardly needed retrieval. Yet, both (particularly *P.S. I Love You*) enjoyed considerable commercial success and remind us that, just as there are audiences aplenty for *Mrs Brown's Boys* or *Killinascully*, so too dreams of the universal Irish welcome still play out vividly in the wider cultural imagination.

Old stereotypes reworked: *The Guard* and *Calvary*

Two films by John Michael McDonagh, *The Guard* and *Calvary*, both set in the west of Ireland, take on the archetypes of Irish rural fictions, the guard and the priest, and rework them first of all as comedy and secondly as tragedy. Both star Brendan Gleeson and his casting is key to McDonagh's revisionist project. *The Guard* concerns a rural policeman, Gerry Boyle (Gleeson), whose scabrous take on metropolitan attitudes does nothing to endear him to his superiors or to his cop 'buddy', black American FBI agent, Wendell Everett (Don Cheadle). Generically a police procedural, the film wastes little time on suspense and the key plot points regarding the criminal activities of a group of drug smugglers are solved without fanfare. Indeed, *The Guard* is as much a Western as a police procedural, with Boyle the lone law enforcer whose willingness to step outside the acceptable limits of legality allows him to confront the criminals on their own terms. McDonagh's own penchant for controversy, notably his comments discussed in the introduction that *Calvary* was not an Irish film, is refracted back onto his characters, particularly onto Boyle, who needles Everett at a police briefing on the planned drug bust with remarks such as 'I thought only black lads were drug dealers … And Mexicans.' This kind of provocative performance of racist attitudes carries with it echoes of the work of the younger McDonagh, Martin. His *In Bruges*, another film starring Gleeson, is also structured around the male/buddy formula and also plays on Irishness as the antidote to conformist, metropolitan political correctness, while his Irish plays notoriously rewrite Synge and the revivalists with scatological irony. 'I'm Irish sure, racism is part of our culture', Boyle informs Everett in a line that could have equally described Colin Farrell's character, Ray, in *In Bruges*. John Michael McDonagh (in Johnston, 2011) has said of *The Guard*'s theme of country versus city:

> There's an anti-Dublin feeling in Connemara, which is reflected in the film as well. The whole attitude in Dublin is basically that they control the country, politically, financially and culturally. But where did it get them? They've brought the place to its knees – that's where it got them.

Just as Gleeson's somewhat similar comments (also cited in the introduction) on the social significance of *Calvary* seem to have been lost on its audience, so *The Guard* was not interpreted as a commentary on the economic crisis. The film was well reviewed in the media, mostly for its sharp, playful dialogue (even if, in the United States, the trade press recommended that subtitles should be provided to decode the accents) and, as we have seen, performed strongly at the home and overseas box offices. This success may be attributed to McDonagh's melding of a provocative Tarantino-esque idiom with a long tradition of representing rural Ireland as subversive of the centre's egregious bureaucracy. The centre is varyingly Dublin (as the source of sexually transmitted diseases, amongst other slurs) and England (an Irish-speaking family recommend to Everett, who is trying to question them, to 'go over to England if you want to speak English'). Local in-jokes include a poster for middle-of-the-road country singer Daniel O'Donnell, on otherwise musical sophisticate Boyle's wall and, inexplicably, the naming of one of the gangsters after Irish liberal nationalist, Francis Sheehy Skeffington (1878–1916). Dialogue not plot drives the film, with the referencing of Sheehy Skeffington as one of a plethora of empty signifiers. Characters seem often to appear on screen for little reason other than to furnish unpredictable exchanges, such as Sheehy Skeffington (Liam Cunningham) and the other gangsters who discuss Nietzsche, or the IRA man (Pat Shortt in a cowboy hat) who responds to Boyle's surprised question: 'There were gay lads in the IRA?' with the explanation that this was the only way they could infiltrate MI5.

At the same time as *The Guard* trades in transnational modes of subversive play, it delivers many of the conventional pleasures of films set in Connemara, notably elegantly composed shots of the landscape and the ocean. Its globally legible idiom further allows the cosmopolitan viewer to enjoy the undermining of centrist-meddling and to relish the visual imagery of the West just as that viewer's predecessors enjoyed the works of Synge and the revivalists, or John Ford and *The Quiet Man*. Where the revisionist filmmakers of an earlier time, Bob Quinn in *Poitín* for instance or Jim Sheridan with *The Field,* worked to destabilise that bucolic vision of the West through depicting its isolated communities as violent and morally void, here McDonagh celebrates the West as a counter to the homogenising reach of the centre.

His second film, *Calvary,* is a much more complex production, and one that has divided critics over its merits and, if it had one, its message. The film opens to a man's voice telling the priest (Gleeson) that he is the victim of clerical sexual abuse – 'Orally and anally, as they say in the court reports. This went on for five years.' His revenge will be to kill a good priest, 'There's no point in killing a bad priest, but killing a good one, that would be a shock.' He gives the priest, whom we later learn is Fr James, a week to put his house in order before he meets him on the beach and kills him. McDonagh has spoken in interview (Johnston, 2014) of his influences in making the film, specifically Robert Bresson's *Diary of a Country Priest* (1951) and Alfred Hitchcock's *I Confess* (1953). *Calvary* also shares with *The Guard* something of the structure of the Western, with all events leading to the final showdown, and of the police procedural as the audience is invited to guess the identity of the speaker.[7] An even greater panoply of minor characters appears, with their contribution to advancing the plot being less important than their performance of weirdness. The weirdness may be played for laughs but it adds up to the depiction of this small Sligo parish as morally and socially abandoned. Yet, its occupants are familiar from numerous Irish village films, and, of course, *The Quiet Man*. They are Brendan Lynch (Pat Shortt), the publican whose premises the banks are repossessing, the battered wife, Veronica Brennan (Orla O'Rourke), and the 'black fella', Simon (Isaach De Bankolé), who beats her up (or possibly someone else does). Michael Fitzgerald (Dylan Moran), financier turned squire tempts Fr James with drink (the priest is a recovering alcoholic) and money, and taunts him with empty talk of penance. This depiction of rural Ireland as marked by complete moral abandon is contextualised against the background of a loss of faith in all authority, of State and Church. The narrow outlook of the villagers is contrasted with widescreen compositions of the Yeatsian landscape and overhead shots of surfers in the Atlantic waves.

Figure 20 Brendan Gleeson in *Calvary*

Yet, when the boy Mícheál (Mícheál Og Lane) paints the view, two dark figures he cannot explain appear. They are ghosts, he thinks, from a story he has been reading.

Amidst all this Fr James is a towering figure, his characterisation enabled by Gleeson's tightly framed physique. Not only is he a father in the clerical sense, he joined the church late in life and has an adult daughter, Fiona (Kelly Reilly), a fragile figure, who arrives in the village with her wrists bandaged from a failed suicide attempt. In another angle on fatherhood, the most abject of the villagers, cannibal-psychopath Freddie Joyce, is played by Gleeson's son, Domhnall. It is to Fiona that Fr James explains that the most underrated aspect of religion is forgiveness, and who will, the film's conclusion suggests, forgive her father's killer. She and the newly widowed Frenchwoman, Teresa (Marie-Josée Croze) seem to be imagined as akin to angels, free floating above the community of grotesques. As this characterisation suggests, *Calvary* rests on a bedrock of familiar archetypes. Yet, there is a complexity to the characters too. Following the conventions of the melodrama, they are excessive; taken together they form a chorus that articulates terrible collective pain over and beyond each one's individual failings.

The director's statement (in Romney, 2014: 69) summarises *Calvary* thus: 'The mise en scène indebted to Andrew Wyeth. The philosophy to

189

Jean Améry. The transcendental style inspired by Robert Bresson.' The reference to Wyeth, the classical American realist painter does not quite do justice to some of *Calvary*'s more grotesque compositions, such as a close-up of the butcher, Jack Brennan's (Chris O'Dowd) side of meat, nor does Wyeth sit easily alongside Améry whose writing was dedicated to keeping alive the memory of the Holocaust, of which he was a survivor. Most interesting is the assumption of transcendentalism. The reference is most likely to Paul Schrader's 1972 publication, *Transcendental Style in Film: Ozu, Bresson, Dreyer*. Here Schrader argued that through certain commonalities in style, these three directors achieve the expression of transcendence or 'the Holy'. To what extent this analysis can be transferred to other works is debatable, as indeed is Schrader's thesis generally, given his own acknowledgement that the critic's job in detecting the transcendent in art could only lead to recognition of 'the ineffable, invisible and unknowable' and ultimately then to silence (Schrader, 1972: 8). Neither too does this fully account for the baroque style of *Calvary*, which is structured on layers of violence, with the violence of the Catholic Church at its heart. It is a much more Catholic style than the austerity that the Calvinist Schrader prized in Bresson. Yet the question remains as to whether the death of the priest and his daughter's forgiveness of the killer, if that is how the film ends, allow for some form of transcendence. Throughout *Calvary*, the villagers lash out against God but meet with His silence. Words, as they recognise, are clichéd, and dramatic narratives are, like Abbey plays, 'corny'. The majestic shots of Ben Bulben and the ocean suggest the possibility of immanence. Yet the villagers, with the exception of the child Mícheál, are immune to their environment. By the time it reaches its ending, *Calvary* has lost much of its cynicism, but the meaning of the montage, following the death of the priest, of the villagers going about their lives, is elusive. Finally, it is up to the audience to conclude whether the death of the good priest has changed anything.

Conclusion

Calvary is without doubt an Irish film, drawing on intense contemporary anxieties about the failure of authority, and anger about the legacy of the Catholic Church. Its Yeatsian backdrop suggests a history (a terrible beauty) that precedes man-made conflict, but no longer has the power to determine how people act. Here, as in the most compelling of the rural films, the loss of the old orthodoxies, so assured in works such as *The Quiet Man*, leads to an emotional void. The older generation of filmmakers could deconstruct the dreams of romantic nationalism, but for the current generation there is nothing left to deconstruct. Whether through a sense of moral emptiness (*Garage*, *Pilgrim Hill*) or shock (*Sensation*) or utopian alternatives (*Breakfast on Pluto*), the rural dramas discussed here dig beneath the old certainties of rural life to find, not so much horror, as nothing. At the same time, rural and small-town Ireland offer themselves up to new meanings, queering these spaces in often productive ways. Curiously, the voiding of this older landscape of its prior associations has left it more open to filmmakers to play with new identity formations. In this sense, many of the films that have emerged out of this setting challenge assumptions around Irish identities in more complex ways than those set within what have become, as the following chapter discusses, the narrower discursive borders of the city space.

Notes

1 Evidently, this is also the central preoccupation of *Room*. Here I focus on the main Irish-set films.

2 Fredric Jameson influentially argued that postmodern culture was marked by, amongst other symptoms, 'the waning of affect' or emotional depthlessness (1991: 10–16).

3 It is impossible to obtain exact figures for its box office take. The figure of €69,333 was reported towards the end of its theatrical run.

4 *The Stag* was released as *The Bachelor Weekend* in the United States, where the phrase 'stag weekend' is unfamiliar.

5 This is an estimate of the local box office, based on Box Office Mojo's figures for the UK, Malta and Ireland. Since the film was only released in Ireland, then it follows that this constitutes its local take.

6 For more on tourist films set in Ireland, see Barton 2016. For more on *P.S. I Love You*, see Dibeltulo (2015).

7 In fact, it is a cheat. The opening voice-over is not delivered by the actor who plays the killer.

References

Barton, R. 2004. *Irish National Cinema,* London and New York: Routledge.

Barton, R. 2014. From Symbol to Symptom – Changing Representations of Fatherhood in Recent Irish Cinema *In:* Holohan, C. and Tracy, T. (eds.) *Masculinity and Irish Popular Culture.* Basingstoke: Macmillan.

Barton, R. 2016. The Ironic Gaze: Roots Tourism and Irish Heritage Cinema. *In:* Cooke, P. and Stone, R. (eds.) *Screening European Heritage, Creating and Consuming History on Film.* London: Palgrave Macmillan.

Box Office Mojo. 2017. *Halal Daddy* [Online]. Box Office Mojo. Available: www.boxofficemojo.com/movies/intl/?page=andid=_fHALALDADDY01 [Accessed 20 September 2017].

Brady, T. 2013. Rotten Potatoes. *Irish Times*, 10 May, p. 28.

Canning, L. and Ging, D. 2012. From Rural Electrification to Rural Pornification: Sensation's Poetics of Dehumanisation. *Estudios Irlandeses*, 7, 209–12.

Chouinard, A. 2010. Water-sites in the Fiction and Cinema of Neil Jordan. *Wasafiri*, 25, 73–7.

Clarke, D. 2013. Alone on the Hill. *Irish Times*, 29 March, p. A10.

Crosson, S. and Schreiber, M. 2011. 'If Irish Cinema is going to be really great it has to stop worrying too much about being "Irish cinema"': QandA with Lenny Abrahamson and Mark O'Halloran. *In:* Huber, W. and Crosson, S. (eds.) *Contemporary Irish Film, New Perspectives on a National Cinema*. Vienna: Braumüller.

Dibeltulo, S. 2015. Old and New Irish Ethnics: Exploring Ethnic and Gender Representations in *P.S. I Love You*. *In:* Monahan, B. (ed.) *Ireland and Cinema, Culture and Contexts*. Basingstoke and New York: Palgrave Macmillan.

Freud, S. 1966. A Special Type of Choice of Object Made by Men. *In: The Standard Edition of the Complete Psychological Works of Sigmund Freud*. London: Hogarth Press.

Ging, D. 2013. *Men and Masculinities in Irish Cinema*, Basingstoke: Palgrave Macmillan.

Guerin, H. 2013. *Pilgrim Hill (review)* [Online]. RTÉ. Available: www.rte.ie/entertainment/movie-reviews/2013/0410/448347-pilgrimhill/ [Accessed 14 September 2017].

Hegarty, S. 2008. Shortt Shrift for the Critics. *Irish Times*, 5 January, p. B2.

Holohan, C. 2010. *Cinema on the Periphery: Contemporary Irish and Spanish Film*, Dublin: Irish Academic Press.

Jaffe, I. 2014. *Slow Movies: Countering the Cinema of Action*, London: Wallflower Press.

Jameson, F. 1991. *Postmodernism, Or, The Cultural Logic of Late Capitalism*, Durham, NC: Duke University Press.

Johnston, T. 2011. Director John Michael McDonagh Tells Trevor Johnston How He Gave the Police Procedural an Irish Spin in 'The Guard'. *Sight and Sound*, 21, 48.

Johnston, T. 2014. God's Lonely Man. *Sight and Sound*, 24, 30.

Lavery, B. 2005. Film: Light Look at Dublin's Dark Side. *The New York Times* [Online]. Available: www.nytimes.com/2005/06/17/arts/film-light-look-at-dublins-dark-side.html?mcubz=0 [Accessed 13 September 2017].

McGuirk, P. 2016. *Neil Jordan: A Quiet Man in Babylon, the Films*, Dalkey: Kalergo.

McLoone, M. 2000. *Irish Film: The Emergence of a Contemporary Cinema*, London: British Film Institute.

Mulhall, A. 2013. A Cure for Melancholia? Queer Sons, Dead Mothers, and the Fantasy of Multiculturalism in McCabe's and Jordan's *Breakfast on Pluto*(s). *In*: Giffney, N. and Shildrick, M. (eds.) *Theory on the Edge: Irish Studies and the Politics of Sexual Difference*. New York: Palgrave Macmillan.

Mullally, U. 2017. 'I was gay and I was into sport. I had such trouble resolving those two things as a kid': John Butler's films always echo his own life. So what happened when he went back to his teenage years at Blackrock College for 'Handsome Devil'? *The Irish Times*, 18 February.

Pettitt, L. 2000. *Screening Ireland: Film and Television Representation*, Manchester: Manchester University Press.

Rockett, E. and Rockett, K. 2003. *Neil Jordan: Exploring Boundaries*, Dublin: Liffey Press.

Romney, J. 2014. Calvary (review). *Sight and Sound*, 24, 69–70.

Schrader, P. 1972. *Transcendental Style in Film: Ozu, Bresson, Dreyer*, Berkeley and Los Angeles: University of California Press.

Sheehy, T. 2008. Reaching an Audience. *Film Ireland* [Online], September/October. Available: http://filmireland.net/2009/01/30/reaching-and-audience/ [Accessed 14 October 2017].

Walsh, F. 2013. Mourning Sex: The Aesthetics of Queer Relationality in Contemporary Film. *In*: Bracken, C. and Radley, E. (eds.) *Theorising the Visual: New Directions in Irish Cultural Studies*. Cork: Cork University Press.

Wood, J. 2008. Garage: QandA with Director Lenny Abrahamson. *The Guardian* [Online]. Available: www.theguardian.com/film/2008/jun/28/features.culture [Accessed 12 September 2017].

Zucker, C. 2008. *The Cinema of Neil Jordan: Dark Carnival*, London: Wallflower.

Short film
New Boy (Steph Green, 2007)

Adapted from a short story by Roddy Doyle, Steph Green's short film depicts the first day at primary school for African student, Joseph (Olutunji Ebun-Cole). Welcomed by his teacher (Norma Sheahan), he receives a mixed reception from the other students. One suggestion, that he sit beside Pamela (Sade Oyewole), another African student in the class, is quickly rejected by Pamela herself. Seated right behind Joseph is his chief tormentor, Christian (Simon O'Driscoll), who taunts him with references to Live Aid and will subsequently bully him in the playground. Meanwhile, the class goody-goody, Hazel (Sinead Maguire), informs on Christian to the teacher and signals her sympathy to Joseph. As the latter observes his new classroom environment in silence, he experiences flashbacks to his schooling in the unnamed country of his origin and witnessing the capture and murder of his teacher-father (Byron Kumbula) by insurgents.

New Boy ends with two of the boys, Christian and Seth (Fionn O'Shea), lined up against the wall with Joseph between them, all now in trouble following the playground fight. Refusing to snitch on each other, they watch Hazel remonstrating with the teacher. Joseph remembers his former classroom and begins to laugh. The two boys join him, and with mutual understanding established, their teacher forgives them. The conclusion speaks to a mode of soft multiculturalist orthodoxy that is familiar from other Roddy Doyle writings and whose message is that, fundamentally, people are people, regardless of origin or skin colour. One can imagine the film finding a place in the school curriculum where it will undoubtedly be welcomed by educators. As an example of a well-made short film, there is nothing to fault about *New Boy*. Steph Green, who followed this with *Run & Jump*, has a background in television and her direction is assured. The colour palette alternates between vibrant blues and yellows in the African scenes to a duller grey in Ireland. Small details of the children's interactions in the Irish school, and the undertone of unreconstructed sexist commentary, even from Hazel, that are directed at their teacher accumulate to construct an atmosphere that is tonally distinct from the African classroom. It is up to the viewer to spot that the latter caters only for boys, and has a male teacher, and to draw their own conclusions from this distinction. In the end, the film also suggests that male solidarity, achieved through conventionally gendered behaviour (fighting), will trump race differences.

This language of multiculturalism is not necessarily the most productive medium for discussing race in Irish fictions – in book or film form – particularly given its denial of difference. Nor is relying on white authors and filmmakers to speak for the racial Other guaranteed to convey the trauma of the refugee experience. Such comments are perhaps unfair to what is evidently a well-intentioned production, but we may guess that it was its unchallenging message that so recommended it to the Academy.

8
Images of the city

The focus in this chapter is on Dublin as the emblematic Irish city. Belfast, as we saw in Chapter 6, has accrued an iconography and narrative positioning of its own that is very specifically connected to Troubles history. Other Irish city films exist: Cork was the setting for Kirsten Sheridan's 2001 *Disco Pigs* and *Snap*, while *Angela's Ashes* and *Cowboys and Angels* (David Gleeson, 2004) take place in Limerick. *The Young Offenders* moves between the city (Cork) and the countryside. The reason for focusing on Dublin, however, is that as a setting it determines narrative and character in ways that only *Angela's Ashes*, with its insistence on the defining presence of Limerick, can match.

In the Introduction, we touched on Conn Holohan's account of Dublin as lacking a centre of power or any identifying features. In an earlier essay, Kevin Rockett made similar comments on Dublin's failure to establish a specific visual iconography. He also (2001: 223) argues that the cinematic adaptations of Roddy Doyle's Barrytown novels – *The Commitments* (Alan Parker, 1991), *The Snapper* (Stephen Frears, 1993) and *The Van* (Stephen Frears, 1996) – share 'an unremarkableness of place; his [Doyle's] suburbia is devoid of history or memory, and it displays the sameness and oneness with other nameless modern working-class estates anywhere else in Europe or, indeed, further afield'. Jenny Knell (2010: 218), on the other hand, has written of the Barrytown trilogy as establishing Dublin 'as a legitimate Irish film setting'.

All these critical approaches are valid in so far as Dublin on film, even as it has accrued a certain iconography – the commuter train line (the DART) that runs along the coastline and through the city; the Luas (tram) line; the Ha'penny Bridge (and more recently the James Joyce Bridge) that link the north and south sides of the Liffey, the Spire that replaced the old Nelson's Pillar in O'Connell Street – is a small-scale place where small-scale stories play out.

Without the conventional indices of urbanity that the city film relies on for narrative meaning – either the tourist attractions of, say, Paris or London, or the ethnic neighbourhoods and *noir*ish backstreets of New York or Los Angeles – the Irish city film struggles for legibility both domestically and in the international marketplace. The situation has been exacerbated by the relative weakness of Irish television drama. RTÉ makes its own long-running urban soap opera, *Fair City* (1989 – present), but, while it attracts respectable audiences, its characters have not achieved anything like the iconic status of their equivalents in *Coronation Street* (Granada Television, 1960 – present) or *EastEnders* (BBC, 1985 – present). Since the early 2000s, the only home-produced drama that made any national impact was *Love, Hate* (RTÉ, 2010–14). Running to five seasons, this gangster series achieved substantial viewership figures and extensive media coverage of its storylines. Its characters passed swiftly into the public domain, becoming shorthand for Dublin criminality. It also transferred successfully to UK television.[1] As discussed further below, its actors moved easily between television and film, creating syntactical connections between both media.

While exogenous filmmakers, particularly British filmmakers, have been regularly attracted to Irish historical films as topics, and the Irish tourist film is a globally inflected genre, the Dublin film has remained the preserve of local productions. There are exceptions – the Dublin sequences of the Bollywood production *Ek Tha Tiger* (Kabir Khan, 2012) are one example – but overall the city is most visible on film globally when it doubles for other locations, as in *Penny Dreadful* and numerous British runaway productions. The prime attraction of Dublin as a setting for local filmmakers is as a locus for the discussion of problematic modernity. These films are often crime narratives and common visual motifs include suburban disadvantage and an inner city of dark alleyways and rundown public housing. By contrast, Dublin's Celtic Tiger office buildings, along with its spaces of leisure and consumption – its cafés and shopping centres – reinvent the city as a site of globally interchangeable lifestyles, much as do the equivalent Belfast-set productions.

Martin McLoone (2008: 46) has described the cinematic city of the Celtic Tiger as characterised by:

> luxurious apartments and well-appointed offices, their beautifully decorated rooms looking out onto spectacular cityscapes; a city of conspicuous consumption conducted in contemporary art galleries, trendy restaurants, stylish coffee and wine bars, and modernist pubs. Above all, this is a Dublin of promiscuous sexual abandon, the new cinema's final affront to the values of the old Ireland.

Yet, curiously, as much as this description applies to the earlier films of the Celtic Tiger, particularly *About Adam* and *Goldfish Memory*, with their celebration of the ending of the inhibitions of old Catholic Ireland (Barton, 2004: 111–12), the subsequent city films were far more likely to see Dublin as proof of the failure of social progress. Whereas the early Roddy Doyle adaptations mentioned above had celebrated a 'poor but happy' ethos, in subsequent productions, including Doyle's own scripted television series *Family* (BBC/RTÉ, 1994), poverty leads to feelings of alienation, often expressed through the performance of compensatory hyper-masculinity.

In the place of a semiotic cityscape, Irish urban cinema, particularly those films set in Dublin, concentrate on intimacy – too much, not enough – and connectivity, negotiating the city's networks and their connections to the wider world. 'The spatial', Doreen Massey has argued (1994: 4):

> can be seen as constructed out of the multiplicity of social relations across all spatial scales, from the global reach of finance and telecommunications, through the geography of the tentacles of national political power, to the social relations within the town, the settlement, the household and the workplace.

These spatial dynamics play out differently in each film, but what distinguishes the Dublin-set films from other Irish city films is a much stronger sense of an urban identity and the boundedness of the city space. As I shall explore below, the individual's entitlement to move through the city constitutes one spatial challenge, but moving outside the city, if only as far as Dublin's coastal suburbs, is a journey into a contrasting social space, whose parameters are as much historically as geographically determined. In older Dublin narratives – *Into the West*, for example – the central characters escape the degradations of the urban space to the freedom of the countryside. Only in a very limited number of contemporary films, such as *The Young Offenders*, *The Stag* and, to an extent, *What Richard Did*, do the characters move between the urban and the rural, and it is notable that the two latter films are concerned with middle-class characters who enjoy particular privileges of mobility.

The most commercially successful Dublin film of the late Celtic Tiger period, however, shared nothing with the cinema of conspicuous consumption nor the crime cycle, other than a miniscule budget. With its celebration of bohemian anti-materialism, John Carney's *Once* of 2007 defined Dublin as a space of intimacy and connectivity. If this seems to place it at diametric odds to most of its contemporaries, the film constitutes an important intervention in the redrawing of the city space in post-modernity, and it is thus with an analysis of *Once* and the contemporary Dublin musical that this chapter starts.

Musical Dublin

Once tells a simple story of a Dublin busker, known only as the Guy (Glen Hansard) who meets a classically trained Czech immigrant musician, the Girl (Markéta Irglová) busking on Dublin's upmarket shopping area, Grafton Street. The two fall in love and start playing together and eventually record an album that includes 'Falling Slowly', a musical number that went on to enjoy considerable commercial success following its Academy Award win. The Guy is recovering from an unhappy relationship with a woman who has left Ireland for London. He discovers that the Girl has a child and a husband who is waiting to join her; she is torn between love and duty but ultimately both realise that their relationship is unsustainable and the Guy leaves for London. The film was shot in under two weeks on a budget of €100,000 under the Irish Film Board's micro-budget scheme (Carroll, 2007). Using DV (digital video) cameras allowed Carney to convey a sense of unrehearsed, almost guerrilla-style filmmaking, which was to become one of the film's selling points:

> it looks like it was made by amateurs, but that was actually intended in a way. It was all sleight of hand: how do you make something seem like it's not a musical; how do you put a different jacket on something to make it look like it's not just a sentimental, feel-good story between two people? Because that's what it is, essentially – but it doesn't feel like that. (John Carney in McDermott, 2014)

As both Neasa Hardiman (2011) and Nessa Johnston (2014) have argued, Carney's promotion of the film as a small indie production up against the big guns of Hollywood was crucial to its success. Both also agree that his shooting and recording styles, with little post-production, created associative links between the film and Ireland as a space of peripherality and authenticity. Discussing the poor quality of the DV camerawork, Hardiman (2011: 86–7) argues that the emotional locus of the film's affect is thus, unusually, not the image track but the soundtrack. The inclusion of street sounds on the music track in the busking sequences emphasises 'liveness' (Johnston, 2014) as does the decision to record the performances 'as live' (Hardiman, 2011: 87). A number of writers (Gallagher, 2012; Tracy, 2007) have pointed to the film's favouring of a 1980s Dublin feel, while Johnston (2014: 28) further notes the following about the film's characters:

> They exude poverty, albeit a vaguely bohemian, artistic one. The musicians in *Once* are all buskers or amateurs, performing their music in the street or in modest domestic spaces, at the fringes of the commercial sphere. In this

Figure 21 Markéta Irglová and Glen Hansard in *Once*

way, while the characters depicted might be part of Celtic Tiger Ireland, the prosperity and materialism of it seem to pass them by.

Central to any analysis of the film is its relationship to Dublin, which emerges as a place of creativity, of play and of communality. To navigate the film's spatial politics, it is important to remember that it is a musical and thus emerges out of a genre, which is marked, as Richard Dyer (2002) has influentially argued, by utopian yearnings. In the musical, characters conventionally escape from the 'real' world into a world of fantasy, often facilitated by the musical numbers. In *Once*, the Guy and the Girl occupy a Dublin that they refashion through song. To achieve this, they (and the film) must obliterate competing narratives of Dublin life. Thus, at the start, the character known only as 'heroin addict' emerges out of an alleyway, where he has urinated, to attempt to rob the busking Guy of his takings. This character never reappears, yet he stands in for the numerous, in Debbie Ging's (2013: 154–81) formulation, 'underclass, criminal and socially marginalised men', who occupy central positions in other Dublin films. This effect is enhanced by the casting of Darren Healy, who has conventionally played addicts and outsiders, notably in *Crush Proof* (Paul Tickell, 1999) and *Savage* (Brendan Muldowney, 2009) and who himself has attracted media coverage for a personal narrative of anti-social behaviour (Barton, 2011). In itself, the sequence plays no part in furthering the filmic narrative and *Once* could have as easily started with the encounter between the Girl and the Guy.

If *Once*'s opening points to a film that never was, the remainder provides an often dreamily utopian vision of Dublin, where the central characters move freely between private domestic spaces and the public spaces of streets and cafés and out to the city's wealthy seaside suburbs of Sandymount and Killiney. In one extended sequence, the Girl leaves the apartment she shares with her mother and daughter, 'borrowing' some change from the child's piggy bank, and pops in to a local shop to buy batteries so that she can listen to the Guy's songs on her portable CD player. Apparently listening to the music, she walks through Dublin's night-time streets with the occasional passer-by barely glancing at her. The soundtrack, however, plays future music, the songs as they will sound after she has booked a recording studio and they have strung together an ill-matched assortment ('oddballs' the technician initially calls them until he understands the quality of the music) of musicians, most of them also buskers. Dublin, the film insists over and again, is a city of dreamers, of musicians, of artists. Even the bank's small loans manager (played by musician, Sean Millar), in an unusually clichéd sequence, on hearing their music pulls out a guitar and jumps onto his desk singing.

Sitting behind Carney's film is another iconic Dublin musical, Alan Parker's 1991 adaptation of Roddy Doyle's novel, *The Commitments*. The obvious link is the shared casting of Glen Hansard, who played the minor character Outspan in the 1991 film, before his band, The Frames (with whom Carney played as bassist) took off. *The Commitments* remains one of the best-known Irish films internationally and its construction of Dublin is as constitutive of the city as John Ford's vision of the Irish countryside was in *The Quiet Man* of 1952.[2] The key difference between the two films is that, where in *The Commitments* Jimmy Rabbitte (Robert Arkins) struggles to open up Dubliners to the rhythms of R&B, in *Once*, music is organic to the city, arising easily out of its bohemian way of life, and crossing physical, ethnic and generational boundaries, the latter point underlined when older singers spontaneously perform traditional songs for the shared pleasure of the Guy and his friends at a basement party.

Interviews with Carney indicate that he was determined that this should be an insider's film:

> I think I used a lot of the techniques and knowledge I picked up on *Bachelor's Walk* [his television series about twenty-somethings in a shared house on Dublin's quays] about where the light is good on certain days in the city. Many film-makers doing a Dublin film will want one shot of Grafton Street, one shot of O'Connell Street with the Spire, and one shot of a Luas going by. I hate film-making like that. I prefer letting the city to be a secondary character. Dublin is not all SUVs and property. (in Carroll, 2007)

This explanation hints at the texture of the film that prompted the comments on its anachronistic qualities from Tracy and Gallagher. Yet it is also a reminder of something that was often forgotten in the sometimes hyperbolic responses to the boom – that Dublin was not simply divided into those who enjoyed fantastically wealthy lifestyles and those who were abandoned to poverty, but that the Celtic Tiger also opened up the city to a new liberalism that allowed for multiple ways of being. In another interview, Hansard suggested that 'There are probably some people who'd go, "Oh, we liked you better when you were poor and needed us," but I think the bubble has to burst a bit. I'd like to see an artistic backlash to all this bingeing, blowing money and living on credit' (in Courtney, 2007). It is possible, then, to see *Once*'s anachronistic vision of Dublin as an artistic strategy that roots itself in aestheticised Bohemianism. However, the film's very contemporary shooting style and its reliance on new digital technologies prevent it from sliding into heritage aesthetics. Instead, it works as an utopian revisioning of contemporary life in which old-fashioned values of communality and artistry are retrieved from the past to reimagine an alternative present outside of SUVs, property development and 'bingeing, blowing money'.

Carney followed up *Once* with two idiosyncratic small films, *Zonad* (2009) and *The Rafters* (2012) that made little impact locally and none on the international box office. He returned to the musical with the American-set *Begin Again* (2013). In 2016, he released *Sing Street*, a third musical that brought him back to Dublin as a location. Loosely autobiographical, the film opens in the 1985 recession with fifteen-year-old Conor, aka Cosmo (Ferdia Walsh-Peelo), learning that as a result of his parents' financial difficulties he will have to leave his fee-paying Jesuit school and downsize to Synge Street and the Christian Brothers. When Conor spots a teenage girl, Raphina (Lucy Boynton), across the road from the school entrance, he gambles on attracting her by inviting her to be filmed in his band's upcoming music video. She agrees and he is swiftly forced to form a band, which consumes the greater part of the film's narrative. Interspersed with developing the band and getting the girl are snapshots of Conor's family life. His parents, played by Aidan Gillen and Maria Doyle Kennedy, are at loggerheads and will announce their split. His older brother, Brendan (Jack Reynor) contributes to Conor's haphazard upbringing through a haze of dope and the prism of his own failure to make it musically. It is Brendan who admonishes Conor that he mustn't form a cover band, but compose his own numbers. Heavily influenced by Duran Duran and the New Romantics, Conor rolls up into school in make-up and coiffed hair, which draws the ire of the principal, Brother Baxter (Don Wycherly). The film concludes with the band's performance at the year-end concert and Conor and Raphina's departure in his grandfather's small boat for the UK and fame and fortune.

Sing Street evidently bears certain resemblances to *Once*, and like that earlier film, evokes *The Commitments*, particularly with the shared casting of Doyle Kennedy. Its temporal setting permits Carney to linger in the period (the 1980s) that ghosted *Once*. Perhaps to avoid heritage associations, *Sing Street* has a very strong feel of the present day, particularly in its 'can do' central character and its relatively unproblematic depiction of religious education in the 1980s. Like *Once,* other occluded narratives lurk behind the film's utopianism. In one sequence, Brother Baxter calls Conor into his office and demands that he remove his make-up. Enraged at the boy's smart response (that in the eighteenth century it was common for men to wear make-up), he orders Conor into his bathroom. Viewers watching this may have anticipated a scene of sexual abuse to follow; instead 'all' Brother Baxter does when Conor refuses is follow him down the corridor and plunge his head into a basin in the toilets.

Technically, *Sing Street* is a more sophisticated production than *Once,* with the music performed by sessional players and post-synched (though Walsh-Peelo, a former boy soprano, sings).[3] As Carney has discussed, funds were 'flowing in' from the Broadway production of *Once* and this allowed him to write the lyrics and try them out immediately with a five-piece band in a studio that he hired beside his office (Gant, 2016: 12). It is interesting to note that he told another interviewer that '*Sing Street* is a fantasy film about the American Dream, in a sense. It's just dressed up as an Irish film' (in Robinson, 2016). This seems to explain the film's soft approach to the recession of the 1980s, and its reluctance to invite comparisons with the Irish recession that dominated the period of its making. Irishness and Dublin, in strong contrast to *Once,* are almost incidental to *Sing Street*; so even is Raphina, whose appearance changes on each occasion that Conor sees her, and who even pretends to be her own younger sister after her first attempt to reach London fails. As much as the American high-school prom sequence is overtly signalled as a fantasy, so it seems is Raphina. Instead, the real relationship is between Conor and his alternative/better parent, that is, his brother, Brendan. Played with charisma by Reynor, Brendan is at once cool and vulnerable. He of all the children understands best the disappointment their mother feels in her marriage, yet he still responds to the news of the split with outrage and hurt. When Conor – in a plot point foreshadowed by one of the few time-specific comments on Irish society, a television news item commenting on the forced immigration of young people to the UK – resolves to go to London with Raphina, it is to Brendan that he turns, and the film closes with his brother jumping up and down on the quay-side, fist pumping with glee.

Both *Once* and *Sing Street* agree that making music in Dublin may be personally rewarding, but it is hardly the panacea to all of life's problems. In *Once*'s firmly neoliberal conclusion, the Guy must capitalise on his talent, record his songs, and travel to London, not just to lay them at the feet of his estranged lover, but also, as the Girl explains to the small loans manager, to 'secure a lucrative deal'. Ironically, this too was to be the fate of *Once*. The first hints of its success came when it won the World Cinema Audience Award at the Sundance Film Festival of 2007; then Steven Spielberg announced that: 'A little movie called *Once* gave me enough inspiration to last the rest of the year' (Breznican, 2007). Even before its Academy Award nomination, the film took a respect-able $6.5m from 140 theatres in the United States (2007). Yet, as noted in Chapter 1, in Ireland Carney's film received limited distribution and minimal box office takings. Carney needed, it seemed, overseas acclaim before achieving local recognition. By the time of the making of *Sing Street*, Carney had taken the advice of his own characters and secured a lucrative deal, in this case via the Weinstein Brothers who acted as co- executive producers and distributed the film in the United States. *Sing Street* took €1.05m at the Irish box office (Lynott, 2017). It took $3,237,118 at the US box office (Box Office Mojo, 2016).

Ethnicity, gender, spatiality

Both films serve as a reminder of the uneven dynamics of gendered and ethnic mobility. If the Guy's lyrics are ostensibly love songs to his absent girlfriend, the film more than suggests that his true love is the Girl. Nevertheless, even though she is soon revealed to be a classically trained pianist with considerable cultural capital (he fails to recognise the Mendelssohn that she plays), her narrative function is primarily to nurture the Guy's talent and facilitate his music making. Throughout the film she is defined by caring, through her love for her small daughter, and her relationship with her mother, who speaks little or no English. The film both recognises this disparity of gender roles and reinforces them in its final sequence (one that must have consumed a generous amount of its tiny budget), when a sweeping crane shot reveals the Girl sitting, framed tightly by the window, at the piano that the Guy has paid for. She looks out, towards the Guy perhaps, but there is no suggestion that she will follow him to London. In *Sing Street*, by contrast, the Irish woman is free to travel but only via male agency.

When they ride on the Guy's father's motorbike out to Killiney, the Girl answers the Guy's question about her relationship to her husband, 'Do you love him?' in Czech. Even to an untrained linguist, her reply evidently translates as 'I love you'. Why can't he abandon his lover and she her husband and set up as a new multicultural family in Dublin? Carney bookends his musical with two conflicting realities, that is, of Dublin as the locus of drug-taking and criminality, and of the secretive and unspoken. Even his ethnic relations bespeak a soft multiculturalism; how different would this film have been if the Girl were an African immigrant, not a white Eastern European with a background in playing classical piano music?

Dublin and the spaces of modernity

Once is a key Dublin film as much for its fantasy of the city space as its occluded realities. Repeatedly in Irish cinema to traverse the city is to experience its multiple temporal and spatial modalities. These journeys explore the contrasts between the old city streets and the new developments, its shopping malls and workspaces, or, as McLoone has discussed, its spaces of consumption and leisure. One such film, Lance Daly's *Kisses* (2008), focuses on two young people from disadvantaged backgrounds who escape from their suburban homes to the city centre and spend the night there together. Daly's Dublin is an immigrant city, where kindly Others watch over the runaways (Barton, 2009). Only the native white Dubliners threaten them, first in the home where Kylie (Kerry O'Neill) is sexually abused and Dylan (Shane O'Neill) is physically abused, and then in the city, where Kylie is kidnapped. The Dublin alleyway here, as in *Once* and *Adam & Paul* (discussed below) becomes a kind of faecal passageway, associated with the city's waste populace. In *Kisses*, Kylie and Dylan spend the night on flattened cardboard boxes only to wake up and find that she has been asleep on top of a dead body. By contrast, the two young people make the brightly lit shopping centre their own, spinning around it on Heelies. The anonymous mall, as was mentioned in the Introduction, may be a non-space in Marc Augé's

(1995) terms (a creation of supermodernity defined by consumption and exchange), yet here this is liberating – an escape from the rundown suburbs where people live too closely together, and from the old city's threatening streets.

These (non-)spaces of modernity recur throughout the city films, bearing varying semiotic value. The opening sequence of *Intermission* also takes place in a shopping mall, where Lehiff (Colin Farrell) introduces himself to a waitress (Kerry Condon), sweet talks her and then robs her till after smashing her in the face. There follows a chase through the mall with the guards in hot pursuit. This space is marked out as offering an illusory, liberating modernity (the same consumer opportunities that other citizens of the globalised western world enjoy) that is swiftly replaced by the rundown featureless outdoor spaces of a working-class suburb. Very particularly, the two friends John (Cillian Murphy) and Oscar (David Wilmot) are employed in a supermarket and warehouse whose spatial dynamics, illustrated through overhead shots of identical, symmetrical aisles, reflect soulless, repetitive work. The manager, Mr Henderson (Owen Roe), enforces his authority through recourse to Americanisms ('One more incident like this and I will TCB, as they say in the States, I will Take Care of Business') that simultaneously distances him from and endorses a non-indigenous labour model.

The criminal city

Like many Irish films of this period, *Intermission* is about criminal activity. As we have seen in Chapter 1, it played strongly at the local box office, but despite its narrative structure of fragmented but interconnected stories that borrowed from global cinema practices of the day, such as *Lock, Stock and Two Smoking Barrels* (Guy Ritchie, 1998) and the work of Quentin Tarantino, Crowley's film performed poorly overseas, specifically in the United States.[4] In common with the vast majority of Irish crime narratives, and the work of Richie and Tarantino, *Intermission* is a caper film or heist film. As Kristen Moana Thompson (2007: 4) has written, '[h]eist films afford a powerful screen identification with criminals breaking the law'. Thus, 'the pleasure of watching stories about illicit worlds and transgressive individuals' is essential to the genre.

Early twenty-first-century Irish cinema extended the fascination with charismatic criminality that John Boorman's *The General* had so successfully initiated to a proliferation of comedy thrillers. Boorman's film and *Ordinary Decent Criminal* (Thaddeus O'Sullivan, 2000), another biopic of the so-called 'General', Martin Cahill, found inspiration in the contrasts between an older Dublin of dark, threatening spaces and the new postmodern surfaces of Celtic Tiger commercial development (Pettitt, 2004). Boorman in particular, drew on the British social-realist tradition of linking criminality to social inequality. The obvious issue that arises out of this generic model is that such films will reinforce dominant associations between poverty and criminality, hence the necessity to include a performative element that signals a break with realism. At the same time, the performative violence so associated with this genre runs the risk that instead of denaturalising aggression, it offers it as titillating entertainment.

Ging (2013) has discussed the Irish crime film of the 1990s and 2000s in depth, noting in particular its construction of marginalised masculinity. She borrows from similar discourses around British 'underclass' films to identify the cycle as 'Irish Lad Wave', namely, films that consciously parody political correctness and are fuelled by a post-feminist discourse that is dismissive of gender-political activism. She also shares with Negra (2013) a reading of the flourishing (female-led) service economy of the Celtic Tiger as giving rise to a discourse of male marginalisation. Thus, the characters in films such as *Crush Proof*, *Last Days in Dublin*, *Intermission*, *The Halo Effect* (Lance Daly, 2004), *Man About Dog*, *In Bruges*, *Savage* and *Perrier's Bounty* (Ian Fitzgibbon, 2009):

> can be read as genuine protest masculinities that articulate the concerns of men who are socially excluded from the patriarchal dividend and who represent their powerlessness as a threat. However, they can also be understood as attempts to re-establish stable, hegemonic norms and practices in the face of changes that have little or nothing to do with class oppression. (Ging, 2013: 164)

The question mark that hangs over the ideological intent behind these releases, particularly their lack of engagement with the real-life concerns of local communities is, as Ging points out, highly problematic. Are they genuinely committed to exploring issues of exclusion or are they simply playing out the latest twist in the ongoing crisis of masculinity for entertainment purposes? It is easy too to see these films as attributing to these marginalised men a licence to behave badly that reflects their makers' and proposed audience's fantasies of a lifestyle free of middle-class inhibitions.

Since the publication of Ging's seminal study of representations of masculinity in Irish cinema, the production line of Irish crime films has shown little sign of slowing down. Thus, we could add to her list: *Between the Canals* (Mark O'Connor, 2010), *The Guard* and *Stalker* (Mark O'Connor, 2012); *The Young Offenders*, and *Cardboard*

Gangsters (Mark O'Connor, 2017). The recent dominance of this genre by O'Connor (*Cardboard Gangsters* was the top-grossing Irish film of 2017) invites reflection on his filmmaking practice, particularly given his frequent arthouse references (not least the appropriation of *Stalker* as a title for a story about street-level drug dealers).

Race, gender and the crime film

In March 2011, just in time for the St Patrick's weekend festival, O'Connor's *Between the Canals* opened at the Irish Film Institute in Dublin, where it played for one week. Filmed over the course of twelve days with a largely non-professional cast, *Between the Canals* was widely welcomed as a breath of fresh air in a cinematic landscape where crime narratives had become so common as to be widely ridiculed.

The film is dominated by a then-unknown Irish actor, Peter Coonan, who plays Dots, a hyperkinetic rising inner-city drug dealer with a missing front tooth and a tendency towards spontaneous violence. His mate, Liam (Dan Hyland) wants to go straight and provide for his partner, Gemma (Anne Marie Martin). Over the course of one day, St Patrick's Day, they hang out with a motley crew of users and criminals, overnighting with a Nigerian drug gang until a new day dawns. If this synopsis suggests a re-run of old clichés, the film's location shooting, soundtrack and performances test the argument. Making a virtue of necessity, *Between the Canals* features a number of photo-montages, with the first coming before the credits. Here a series of dissolves of old Dublin photographs depicts street views of the slums from the colonial era, through the Rising of 1916, to the north inner city of today, where the film was shot. The point may be obvious (nothing has changed) but it remains unusual for a film of this genre to provide a historical commentary on social neglect. The soundtrack intersperses traditional numbers such as The Dubliners' 'Johnny McGory' (a variation on 'Take Her Up to Monto', about Dublin's old red-light district, the 'Monto'), with compositions from the Pogues, Damien Dempsey and others. Dempsey provides the one recognisable face on the screen, taking the role of Chambers, the gang boss. The non-professional actors deliver their lines awkwardly, recalling more the documentary mode than fiction film, while Coonan produces the performance that holds the production together.

It was on the basis of his appearance in *Between the Canals* that Coonan was cast in *Love/Hate* as the psychopath, Fran. Another minor character in O'Connor's debut, the youth Aido, was played by Barry Keoghan, who also migrated to *Love/Hate*, playing Wayne. The latter actor in particular came to represent a certain Dublin 'type' in early twenty-first century cinema (although since then he has become a sig-nificant star and now has access to a much wider range of roles), at once society's victim and its threat, and appeared in walk-on parts in an extra-ordinary amount of the films discussed in this chapter. The circulation of types between cinema and *Love/Hate* reinforces a sense of Dublin as an enclosed space, with actors as much as narratives struggling to escape its discursive boundaries.

Between the Canals (a title that draws on Dublin's canal-bound top-ography) is particularly noteworthy in its contrasting treatment of two Irish cinematic tropes, one fundamental to the national imaginary, the other recent, namely the representation of women and of race. In a very conventional manner, its female characters are confined to the domestic sphere and to roles as mothers or grandmothers. Gemma angrily pushes a baby in a pram around the flats, demanding that Liam go straight for the sake of their baby. Her hectoring, scolding tone renders her the conventional castrating woman of popular cultural representations – a type ramped up to hysteria pitch in O'Connor's later *Stalker*. In this film, Dots's only respite in the day is to sit at his grandmother's (Bridget Fennel) table and be served the traditional Dublin dish, coddle, for lunch. Uncritical and adoring, her sole function (in a scene that was virtually replicated in O'Connor's subsequent *King of the Travellers* (2012)), is to reveal Dots's repressed emotional warmth.

It is interesting to note that these particular gender paradigms are presented as normative, whereas the equally problematic representa-tion of the ethnic Other is, in a conventionally postmodern manner, at once played straight and ironised. Analysing this encounter, Zélie Asava (2013: 142–50) is damning of its execution and ideological assumptions. In the film, Dots, Liam and Scratchcard/Scratcher (Stephen Jones) enter with some awe the upmarket apartment block occupied by the Nigerians. A party is being held to celebrate St. Patrick's Day and a camp young man, Shafi (James Akpotor), greets them and introduces them to his boss and occasional lover, Philip (Yomi Ogunyemi). The latter emerges from a bed covered in faux leopard skin brandishing a machete. The remainder of the encounter between the two parties is couched in relentless cliché:

Philip: You don't mind that, do you, me calling you Paddies? Because that's what you are. You can call me 'Blackie' or 'Chocolate'.
[...]
You Irish were taken as slaves just like we were. Irish and the Blacks have been together for hundreds of years. And you cannot change that.
Scratchcard: 'Respect man ... The Black Irish and all, isn't it?
Philip: 'You know what the problem is? You Irish are turning white.

Figure 22 Dan Hyland, Stephen Jones and Peter Coonan in *Between the Canals*

Shortly after this exchange, Philip will dance on the bed proclaiming, 'I'm a fucking black leprechaun.'

A positive interpretation of this scene would see it as foregrounding and problematising cultural clichés of identity construction, in particular the lengthy and contentious history of relations between African-Americans and Irish-Americans.[5] The accusation that the Irish are turning white reflects Negra's (2013: 25–6) analysis of popular cultural expressions, such as the campaign for Snickers ('Get Some Nuts') that featured Mr T exhorting 'so-called Irish men' to toughen up. This, she argued, aligned Irish recessional masculinity 'with a broader transnational dynamic in which the white man is consistently placed as the sign, symptom and victim of recession.' The film itself suggests that historic lack of opportunity, not just during the recession, is the cause of Dots's and his companions' criminality, so that in this case their hypermasculinity functions as compensation for low social expectations.

Asava's reading of the scene involving the Nigerians as loaded with racist assumptions is equally valid and as she herself notes (2013: 144): 'Whether the script intends to mock political correctness or parallel different racist terminologies is unclear, though the reduction of black masculinity to animalistic sexuality through costume, framing, language and movement is not paralleled in the Irish characters.' Herein lies the classic conundrum of postmodern critical analysis and one that the crime films covered here raise over and again. As *Between the Canals* suggests, a film can be at once committed to discussing the social realities of disadvantaged urban identities (consistently masculine in the Irish case) and deliver toxic race and gender messages (as does, for instance, another crime movie, *Headrush* (Shimmy Marcus, 2003)). By the time of the release of O'Connor's debut, the director was already distancing his work from that of his contemporaries and claiming a new authenticity and right to speak. The critics agreed, although audience feedback on the Internet Movie Database (IMDb, n.d.) suggested otherwise, with viewers complaining not just about their failure to understand the Dublin accents, but equally, O'Connor's clichéd vision of Irishness.

Between the Canals does not exist in a vacuum when it comes to problematic jokes about racial difference in Irish cinema (it also pops up with a veneer of innocence in *Sing Street*, when the band decides to recruit a black kid on the grounds that he must be musical and we have discussed its treatment in *The Guard*). At the same time, O'Connor's depiction of the Nigerians is highly problematic and, along with his regressive vision of female identities detracts from his aspirations to be taken seriously as arthouse auteur in the tradition of Tarkovsky.

Space, class and mobility

In a now fundamental consideration of how individuals occupy the city, Michel de Certeau (1984) followed Tuan (1977) in proposing that space and place are not fixed entities, but, in de Certeau's formulation, are transformed by the walker, who endows them with his [*sic*] own meaning. Tuan, as we saw in the Introduction, understood space as limitless and untrammelled and place as defined and ontologically controlled. Thus, the city is made and remade by those who traverse it, with individuals creating out of its space their own place. Two contrasting Dublin-set films illustrate this argument and its obverse (the failure to create space from place): the first is Lenny Abrahamson's debut, *Adam & Paul*; and the second is another debut, Donal Foreman's *Out of Here*.

Adam & Paul, like *Garage*, was scripted by Mark O'Halloran, who also takes the role of one of the (unnamed) junkies who constitute the central characters in the film. (The credits reveal O'Halloran to be Adam, with Tom Murphy playing Paul.) *Adam & Paul* is rooted in the Irish literary tradition, notably through its referencing of James Joyce's *Ulysses* (1922) and Samuel Beckett's *Waiting for Godot* (1953). Abrahamson's film is very certainly 'writerly'; yet as much as its central characters, two addicts who traverse the city in search of a fix, emerge out of these

Figure 23 Mark O'Halloran and Tom Murphy in *Adam & Paul*

iconic works, the film equally recalls silent cinema, notably the comedies of Buster Keaton, Charlie Chaplin, or Laurel and Hardy. Abrahamson and O'Halloran (in Crosson and Schreiber, 2011) have termed it 'vaude-villian', and its absurdist humour, jaunty score (by regular Abrahamson collaborator, Stephen Rennicks) and propensity for filming with a sta-tionary camera, so that characters move in and out of the framed space, lend the work a sense of (film) history that adds depth to its contem-porary narrative. There is also an innocent quality to the two addicts that reflects that early cinema comedic tradition.

Adam & Paul opens with its two central characters waking up on a rubbish tip in a suburban wasteland, follows their day as they cross the city looking for 'what's his name', who they trust will supply them with heroin, through to nightfall, when they fall asleep on Sandymount Strand, and on to the next morning, when the film ends. Holohan (2010) has pointed out that the two addicts are denied a 'homespace', and are condemned to live on the streets, where too they are Othered by those whom they encounter, whether it is their former friends, the shopkeepers, or the brother of a one-time girlfriend, whose apartment they enter, looking for items to rob. Adam and Paul may traverse Dublin, but this still doesn't enable them to turn space into place. They literally have no place in the city, for they (unlike, say, the Girl in *Once*) lack the agency to make it. More than that, they are prevented from doing so, not so much by the dominant order, in the manner that de Certeau (1984) envisaged in his writings, but by the city's other dwellers who police the boundaries of their own places. Mark O'Halloran (in Crosson and Schreiber, 2011: 130) said of writing the film that 'I felt there was almost two time systems working in Dublin, one which was sort of "junkie time", which was all in slow motion, and then there was this crazy dance going on in the middle of Dublin and everyone was just busy, busy, busy around their days.' Abrahamson's modulated pace of filming and the slightly hesitant, jerky walk of the two central characters as they move into and out of frame combine O'Halloran's 'junkie time' with a sense of out-of-placeness in Dublin's otherwise intimate, connected world. The viewer is positioned to feel both empathy and alienation (the latter very specifically after the men mug a Down Syndrome boy) vis-à-vis the addicts in a manner that is far more nuanced than that proposed by the crime films. Abrahamson and O'Halloran extended their interest in examining issues of social dispossession in Dublin in 2007 with their four-part television series, *Prosperity* (RTÉ), although in this instance favouring the aesthetics of social realism over the slightly surreal (junkie time) feel of *Adam & Paul*.[6]

Foreman's debut, by contrast, speaks for and to a constituency largely ignored by Irish filmmakers and writers, that is, young, middle-class urbanites. *Out of Here* was made on a miniscule production budget of €25,000 that was crowd-funded (Brady, 2014) and received completion funding from the Irish Film Board. It concerns art college dropout, Ciaran (Fionn Walton), who returns to Dublin after a year of travelling abroad. As he moves through the city, he encounters his old college friends, strikes up a relationship with Melissa (Aoife Duffin) and attempts to reconnect with former girlfriend, Jess (Annabell Rickerby). 'I didn't want it to be a big statement', Foreman said of his film, 'I wanted it to be a collaboration with the city and that moment and with the actors. Too many Irish film-makers say "I want to make a universal story, it could be set anywhere." That was something I didn't want to do' (in Brady, 2014). As a consequence, *Out of Here* is very much focused on themes of intimacy and connectivity. In common with *Once* and *Adam & Paul*, Foreman spends little time on Dublin's architecture or its tourist sights, and when, in an early scene, Ciaran stops and contemplates a public statue, it is one of Dublin's least known monuments, to nationalist William Smith O'Brien (1803–64) in O'Connell Street. Instead, the city often appears out of focus or fragmented. Ciaran himself is even less defined. Although he occupies nearly every frame of the film, his is a negative presence. The audience is invited to piece together his relationships with his friends and his family, and to guess at his state of mind. He is gradually revealed to be uncertain about the wisdom of returning, because, it seems, of his difficulty in reconnecting with his peer group. In one sequence, a group of activists in a gallery space are discussing the direction that the Dublin Occupy Movement ought to take. Ciaran drifts in and then wanders out again, but the camera remains with the activists as if it hadn't noticed that he had left. Only once, when he meets a group of performers on the street and is encouraged to join in, does he come to life, acting out a traumatic incident from his time abroad. Taking a proffered prop/hat, he grows increasingly animated, recounting how he met a young woman on his travels and his humiliation the next morning when he discovered that she had robbed him.

News items playing in the background remind the viewer that *Out of Here* is set in the recession; we discover too that Ciaran's father, Dermot (Arthur Riordan) has lost his job. Yet, this doesn't account for Ciaran's anomie. Nor is it clear that by the end of the film, anything much has been resolved.

Tracy (2014) has written of *Out of Here*:

> Its rejection of traditional narrative practices (particularly ill-fitting genres), its cosmopolitan tone, its sensitive and fresh portrayal of masculinity and relationships, and its use of locations that 're-map' cinematic Dublin, all contribute to a film less defined by a sense of national identity than a sense of place.

Although Tracy also identifies *Out of Here* as 'mumblecore', itself arguably a generic mini-category, Foreman's film is very much in the arthouse tradition of displaying minimal drive towards narrative resolution, avoiding conventional generic tropes, and foregrounding character types that had hitherto been poorly represented within the national cinema. What is particularly interesting about *Out of Here* is the focus on young, middle-class Dubliners – a character type that, perhaps surprisingly, has received minimal representation in Irish cinema. In Foreman's film, this entails removing his central character from the city spaces to Dublin's southside coastal suburbs – an area closely identified with middle-class privilege, and the one space where Ciaran seems to feel comfortable.

Out of Here ends with Ciaran swimming off the popular bathing spot at Seapoint, just in view of a row of middle-class Victorian villas that were the location for the therapist, Dr. King's (Andy Serkis) rooms in Ian Fitzgibbon's *Death of A Superhero* (2011). Just up in the coast is Killiney, where in *Once* the Girl tells the Guy in Czech that she loves him. Between the two is Dalkey, the location for Kirstin Sheridan's

Dollhouse (2012), filmed in her father, Jim Sheridan's, then-property, about a group of inner-city Dubliners 'invading' a middle-class home. The highly improbable ending of John Carney's *Sing Street* finds, as we have seen, the two young lovers setting off in a rowing boat from Dalkey's Coliemore Harbour bound for fame in England. Most of the action of *What Richard Did* is set on the Southside (as this coastal area is conventionally referred to), only moving out as far as Wicklow's coast, another location much favoured as a holiday and weekend destination by the Dublin middle classes.[7] In these films, the southside routinely connotes an escape from the anomie of the city. In *Death of A Superhero*, the story of a Dublin teenage cancer sufferer, Donald (Thomas Brodie-Sangster), the therapist provides a safe space for him to work through his anger at his impending death. King's book-lined, untidy office is marked as bohemian and intellectual – a space with a history unlike the modern house that Donald shares with his brother and parents.

The very stability of southside Dublin's Victorian and Georgian architecture can, however, as *What Richard Did* suggests, entrap its inhabitants. The eponymous Richard (Jack Reynor) in Abrahamson's third feature lives in a period house that would not look out of place in a British middle-class heritage film, with an elegant drawing room and French windows giving on to a slightly overgrown but generously sized garden. The film is loosely based on Kevin Power's (2008) *Bad Day in Blackrock,* which in turn draws on the real-life incident in 2000, when a fight involving a group of teenagers broke out outside the Club Anabel nightclub, which resulted in one of them, Brian Murphy, being killed. The ensuing coverage made much of his assailants' wealthy backgrounds and that they were alumni of the elite Blackrock College secondary school for boys. In Abrahamson's film, Richard, a charismatic school rugby player, causes the death of Conor (Sam Keeley) in a fight. If on the surface of things, the hostility between the two arises when Richard moves in on the latter's girlfriend, the film hints at other more complicated reasons for Richard's antipathy towards Conor, notably the latter's 'out-of-placeness' as someone with roots in the countryside. Conor can, for instance, sing traditional unaccompanied Irish songs, which seems to irk Richard unnecessarily. It seems as if, the film hints, Richard envies the other for his access to an 'authentic' Celtic identity, which his more acculturated suburban background has denied him. When Richard's father, Peter Karlsen (Mads Mikkelsen) learns of his son's crime, he instantly moves to protect him, warning him not to confess and promising that he knows 'people' who will ensure that he is not charged. Once the invisible threads of privilege are pulled, Richard is left with little choice, it seems. He may briefly consider the idea of doing

Figure 24 Jack Reynor in *What Richard Did*

time but, in the end, he stays silent and the film concludes with a view of Dublin's Georgian buildings that both celebrates their architectural heritage and leaves the viewer to consider that they are impregnable facades for middle-class power and privilege.

Conclusion: the gendered city

The *flâneur* is typically a male figure and even now, the old dichotomy of male/active, female/passive still holds remarkable sway. As theorists such as Massey (1994: 10) remind us, in classic representations: 'Woman stands as metaphor for Nature ... for what has been lost (left behind), and that place called home is frequently personified by, and partakes of the same characteristics as those assigned to Woman/Mother/lover.' Even if, in reality, as Massey also notes (1994: 6–10), the gendering of space in contemporary life has radically changed, in Irish cinematic fictions the public space is routinely signalled as a male domain and the domestic space as female. Ging's analysis of the Irish city crime film as the *locus classicus* for the examination of masculinity-in-crisis remains as relevant now as when she initially formulated it. Similarly, if less aggressively, the Dublin musicals and art films such as *Adam & Paul* foreground male subjectivities. This trend leaves little if no room for the representation of women in the city space other than as mothers, grandmothers, sisters and lovers. Even a production such as *Intermission* that seems determined to break with older gendered behavioural patterns resorts in its conclusion to the most conservative of messages, reasserting the desirability of love, marriage and long-term fidelity. This perspective is most clearly articulated in a conversation between Sally (Shirley Henderson) and her mother, Maura (Ger Ryan). Sally has just realised that her 'ronnie' (facial hair) is an embarrassment, which has launched a discussion about love and relationships. Sally asks her mother why she never remarried. Maura explains why not: 'Who could ever give me what he gave me anyway … his love for one thing, my home, the times we had … the children he gave me.' The scene ends with Sally confessing how lonely she has been (without a boyfriend) and Maura comforting her.

Those filmmakers that have attempted to rupture these entrenched, conservative assumptions have struggled to carve out a female space in the city. Lance Daly's *Life's a Breeze* (2013) illustrates just how challenging it is for filmmakers to reverse such tropes. The story of *Life's a Breeze* revolves around a Dublin grandmother, Nan (Fionnula Flanagan), whose hare-brained family, led by her stay-at-home adult son, Colm (Pat Shortt), gives her period terraced house a full make-over. In doing so, they throw out her old mattress where she has stashed her life savings. When challenged as to why she did not put her money in the bank, she responds with one of the film's many references to the banking crisis and consequent recession: 'Have you not been listening to the news? It was safe here.' The remainder of *Life's a Breeze* sees the family and, once they have gone public with their quest, the nation, attempt to find the mattress, which has been illegally dumped by the man hired to dispose of Nan's old belongings.

In common with Daly's previous Irish films (he also has made one non-Irish film, *The Good Doctor* (2011)), *Life's a Breeze* is episodic and character-centred. He again draws an empathetic performance from a young actor, here Kelly Thornton who plays the other main character, thirteen-year-old Emma. The film's great strength comes from the burgeoning relationship between Emma and Nan, and Daly's practice of interspersing the action with point-of-view shots of Emma's cool gaze at her irresponsible wider family. If the film had kept the grandmother/granddaughter relationship as its focus it would have provided a welcome corrective to the caper films and to the male-centred Dublin narratives. Instead, its depiction of the harum-scarum family, particularly their wearying mugging and posturing, destabilises its trajectory. *Life's a Breeze* has valid social points to make, particularly via Colm, the film's 'manboy', whose position as family joke is signalled as less comic than his siblings, even his mother, assume. Spatially, the film is confusing, with the area behind Nan's house apparently and implausibly a waste-ground occupied by Dublin inner-city youths building bonfires for Hallowe'en. This spatial indeterminacy may well be a consequence of co-production funding with Sweden, where some of the location shooting took place, but detracts from the strong sense of the local achieved by works such as Daly's earlier *Kisses* and by extension of Dublin as determining the tone of the narrative.

It is this relationship with Dublin's spaces that seems to have inhibited filmmakers from creating more persuasive female-driven narratives. A cluster of such films – *Glassland*, *Patrick's Day* (Terry McMahon, 2014), *Mammal* (Rebecca Daly, 2016) – all problematise in various ways women's relationships with the city and with the home. In *Glassland*, it falls to Dublin taxi driver, John (Jack Reynor) to care for his alcoholic, housebound mother, Jean (Toni Collette). After a number of drinking episodes, he manages to have her taken into a private sanatorium but finds himself caught up in criminal activities in order to pay for her care. In *Patrick's Day*, the eponymous Patrick (Moe Dunford), a young man with mental health issues, escapes the care of his controlling single mother, Maura (Kerry Fox), and his psychiatric institution when he falls in love with Karen (Catherine Walker), an alcoholic who becomes pregnant with their child. In *Mammal,* Margaret (Rachel Griffiths) consoles herself for the death of her son by entering into a relationship with a young man, Joe (Barry Keoghan) from a disadvantaged background, and becomes involved with his criminal activities.

As these brief plot synopses suggest, all three films share similar concerns with unstable family structures, disturbed mothers and suffering sons. Of the trio, the most problematic is *Mammal* with its quasi-incestuous central relationship and the suggestion that Margaret may find solace in a provocative sexual relationship with a young man defined by social disadvantage and criminality. It is an intensely alienating film, which propelled it to the far end of the arthouse spectrum without necessarily guaranteeing its feminist credentials. The other two releases enjoyed higher profiles and reviewed well. One particularly noticeable feature is the casting in the role of the mother of two Australian actors and one New Zealand actor (Fox). Nothing in the plot lines requires this and one can only speculate that the reasons for this coincidence lie in the scarcity of Irish screen actors of that generation who are guaranteed to attract funding, combined with a desire to distance these problematic mothers from actual Irish womanhood. In the end, both *Patrick's Day* and *Glassland* evince far more sympathy for the traumatised offspring of these inadequate mothers, with *Glassland* going so far as to cast the son as the mother's rescuer. Both also go to some lengths to disrupt the conventional associations of mother and homemaker. Yet, this does not mark a liberation for the mothers in question, as it doesn't in *Mammal*. Instead, they are left without a home space (unless one includes institutionalisation) or a sense of being at home in the public space. To compare this with *Brooklyn*, in Crowley's film, Eilis is associated as much with public spaces of leisure (the beach and the dance hall) and professional work (as a shop assistant and later as a bookkeeper), as with the home – a far more progressive envisioning of women's place in space in what is ostensibly a more conservative genre (the history film).

Another intensely traumatic city-set maternal narrative is Carmel Winters's *Snap*. While the focus of this chapter is on Dublin films, it is important to acknowledge the singularity of Winters's work within an otherwise unpromising environment for complex female characters. Nor is *Snap* in any way reliant on its Cork setting for its meaning-making and could as easily take place in any Irish setting. Like the preceding films, it concerns a mother–son relationship, and in this case is structured as a faux-documentary, in which single mother and social outcast Sandra (Aisling O'Sullivan) angrily recounts to camera the story of how her troubled son, Stephen (Stephen Moran), came to kidnap the toddler Adam (Adam Duggan) and hold him in her father's/his grandfather's house. Interwoven with the 'documentary' is a sequence of home-movie images that will ultimately become the key to understanding what drove Stephen to 'snap', as the film confronts mother and son's trauma as victims of sexual abuse. Sandra is a compelling, often foul-mouthed presence, and her narrative is held together by her command of the 'documentary' camera and her insistence that it tell her story. Yet, the film also ends in having Stephen reveal to his mother that she has misunderstood the filmic image, which turns out to tell quite a different story. *Snap* is an elliptical, complex film that is very aware of theories of the camera's gaze (Mulvey, 1975) and of its place in feminist filmmaking.[8] Shot on a miniscule budget, Winters's production enjoyed a limited local theatrical release. This marginalisation of urban female narratives, both in terms of Irish filmmaking practice and thematically, has to be troubling. Contributing to this is the lack of any sense of female spatial agency, even in productions such as *Once*.

These conclusions are particularly concerning given that Dublin has become the locus for the production of cultural representations of contemporary Irish life. It is no longer the case that it is a space without meaning; instead it has become the driver of images of masculinity, whether socially disadvantaged, non-conformist bohemian, or insecure middle class. Often full of angst and striving for a cool that is elusive

Figure 25 Stephen Moran in *Snap*

and constantly deferred, the characters of these Dublin films are defined by the space 'between the canals'; only the coastal suburbs provide an alternative, yet these are complicated by their identification as middle class and bound by traditions of secrecy and conformity. It is thus significant that in *Life's a Breeze*, it is atop a rubbish dump that Nan recounts the truth of her marriage to Emma. Rubbish tips, wastelands and other excremental spaces suggest that the old Dublin of bygone days is just the turn of a corner away from the new global spaces (and non-spaces) that are the legacy of the Celtic Tiger. Yet, it is also significant that this is one of the few sequences in Irish urban cinema to offer a moment of intimacy and friendship between two female characters. That the city has become the locus for discussing Irish male identities is an interesting cultural shift and it is regrettable (and unnecessary) that it seems to have come about at the expense of any equivalent commitment to exploring women's stories on the contemporary screen.

Notes

1 1,007,500 viewers watched the sixth and final instalment on RTÉ, which broke the previous record set by the season premiere of 971,000 viewers (Cronin, 2013). In the UK, it played on Channel 5, with an opening viewership

of 738,000. Newspapers reported that viewers took to Twitter to complain that they needed subtitles to understand the Dublin accents (Hamilton, 2013).

2 So determining of Irish cinema was *The Commitments* that when Harvey O'Brien and I co-edited a collection of essays on the subject, none of which mentioned the Parker film, the publisher insisted on illustrating the volume with an image from it. See Barton and O'Brien (2004).

3 For a detailed account of how the music for *Sing Street* was recorded, see Walden (2016).

4 For a discussion of *Intermission* as a 'fractal' film, see Everett (2005).

5 On popular culture's treatment of Irish American and African American relations, see Eagan (2006).

6 See Sweeney (2016) for more on *Prosperity*.

7 For a detailed discussion of *What Richard Did, Dollhouse,* and other suburban Dublin middle-class films, see Barton (2018).

8 For more on *Snap*, see Vejvoda (2015).

References

Asava, Z. 2013. *The Black Irish Onscreen: Representing Black and Mixed-Race Identities on Irish Film and Television,* Oxford; New York: Peter Lang.

Augé, M. 1995. *Non-places: Introduction to an Anthropology of Supermodernity,* London: Verso.

Barton, R. 2004. *Irish National Cinema,* London and New York: Routledge.

Barton, R. 2009. Kisses (2008). *Estudios Irlandeses,* 4, 157–9.

Barton, R. 2011. Savage. *Estudios Irlandeses,* 6, 196–8.

Barton, R. 2018. Behind Closed Doors: Middle Class Suburbia and Contemporary Irish Cinema. *In*: Workman, S. and Smith, E. *Imagining Irish Suburbia*. London: Palgrave Macmillan.

Barton, R. and O'Brien, H. (eds.) 2004. *Keeping It Real: Irish Film and Television,* London: Wallflower.

Box Office Mojo. 2016. *Sing Street* [Online]. Box Office Mojo. Available: www.boxofficemojo.com/movies/?page=intlandcountry=UKandid=singstreet.htm [Accessed 4 September 2017].

Brady, T. 2014. Boom in the Shot. *Irish Times,* 31 October, p. 6.

Breznican, A. 2007. 'Once' isn't enough: Film gets marketing push. [Online]. *USA Today. Available:* https://usatoday30.usatoday.com/life/movies/news/2007–08–06-once_N.htm. [Accessed 20 August 2017].

Carroll, J. 2007. Once Upon a Time in Dublin. *Irish Times,* 16 March, p. 2.

Courtney, K. 2007. Cul Hibernia? *Irish Times,* 17 March, p. 23.

Cronin, K. 2013. 'Love/Hate' Season 4 Finale Achieves Highest Ratings With Over One Million Viewers. *The Irish Film and Television Network* [Online]. Available: www.iftn.ie/news/?act1=recordandaid=73andrid=4286 612andsr=1andonly=1andhl=love%2Fhateandtpl=archnews [Accessed 27 August 2017].

Crosson, S. and Schreiber, M. 2011. "If Irish Cinema is going to be really great it has to stop worrying too much about being 'Irish cinema": QandA with Lenny Abrahamson and Mark O'Halloran. *In:* Huber, W. and Crosson, S. (eds.) *Contemporary Irish Film, New Perspectives on a National Cinema.* Vienna: Braumüller.

De Certeau, M. 1984. *The Practice of Everyday Life,* Berkeley: University of California Press.

Dyer, R. 2002. Entertainment and Utopia. *In:* Cohan, S. (ed.) *Hollywood Musicals, The Film Reader.* London and New York: Routledge.

Eagan, C. M. 2006. "Still 'Black and 'Proud' ": Irish America and the Racial Politics of Hibernophilia. *In:* Negra, D. (ed.) *The Irish in Us: Irishness, Performativity and Popular Culture.* Durham, NC and London: Duke University Press.

Everett, W. 2005. Fractal Films and the Architecture of Complexity. *Studies in European Cinema,* 2, 159–71.

Gallagher, M. 2012. Multilingual Europeans: Contemporary Ireland and John Carney's Film Once. *In:* Rosello, M. and Károly Marácz, L. (eds.) *Multilingual Europe, Multilingual Europeans.* Amsterdam and New York: Rodopi.

Gant, C. 2016. Development Tale Sing Street. *Sight and Sound,* 26, 12–13.

Ging, D. 2013. *Men and Masculinities in Irish Cinema,* Basingstoke: Palgrave Macmillan.

Hamilton, S. 2013. Love/Hate proves a smash hit in the UK ... but viewers need subtitles. *The Irish Mirror* [Online]. Available: www.irishmirror.ie/whats-on/film-and-tv/lovehate-proves-smash-hit-uk-2090458 [Accessed 27 August 2017].

Hardiman, N. 2011. '*Once* Won't Happen Twice': Peripherality and Equality as Strategies for Success in a Low-Budget Irish Film. *In:* Huber, W. and Crosson, S. (eds.) *Contemporary Irish Film, New Perspectives on a National Cinema.* Vienna: Braumüller.

Holohan, C. 2010. *Cinema on the Periphery: Contemporary Irish and Spanish film,* Dublin: Irish Academic Press.

IMDd. *Between the Canals* [Online]. Available: www.imdb.com/title/tt1787054/ [Accessed 30 September 2017].

Johnston, N. 2014. The Celtic Tiger 'Unplugged': DV Realism, Liveness, and Sonic Authenticity in Once (2007). *The Soundtrack,* 7, 25–38.

Knell, J. 2010. North and South of the River: Demythologizing Dublin in Contemporary Irish Film. *Éire-Ireland,* 1/2, 213–41.

Lynott, L. 2017. Bridget Jones Delivers Top Movie of 2016 – with EUR 100m Spent in Cinemas. *Irish Independent,* 4 January, p. 10.

Massey, D. 1994. *Space, Place and Gender,* Cambridge: Polity.

McDermott, R. 2014. *John Carney Interview – Once Bitten, Twice Wry* [Online]. Available: www.hotpress.com/features/interviews/John-Carney-Interview--Once-Bitten-Twice-Wry/11948913.html [Accessed 20 August 2017].

McLoone, M. 2008. *Film, Media and Popular Culture in Ireland: Cityscapes, Landscapes, Soundscapes,* Dublin: Irish Academic Press.

Mulvey, L. 1975. Visual Pleasure and Narrative Cinema. *Screen,* 16(3), 6–18.

Negra, D. 2013. Adjusting Men and Abiding Mammies: Gendering the Recession in Ireland. *The Irish Review 46,* 23–34.

Pettitt, L. 2004. "We're not fucking Eye-talians": The Gangster Genre and Irish Cinema. *In:* Barton, R. and O'Brien, H. (eds.) *Keeping It Real: Irish Film and Television.* London: Wallflower Press.

Power, K. 2008. *Bad Day in Blackrock,* Dublin: Lilliput Press.

Robinson, T. 2016. Why Sing Street Director John Carney Regrets the Film's Ending. *The Verge* [Online]. Available: www.theverge.com/2016/4/21/11477490/sing-street-john-carney-interview-once-begin-again [Accessed 4 September 2017].

Rockett, K. 2001. (Mis-)Representing the Irish Urban Landscape. *In:* Fitzmaurice, T. and Shiel, M. (eds.) *Cinema and the City, Film and Urban Societies in a Global Context.* Oxford and Malden, MA: Blackwell.

Sweeney, S. 2016. Prosperity: Dublin on the Verge of an Economic Breakdown. *In:* Coulouma, F. (ed.) *New Perspectives on Irish TV Series, Identity and Nostalgia on the Small Screen.* Oxford and Bern: Peter Lang.

Thompson, K. M. 2007. *Crime Films: Investigating the Scene,* London: Wallflower.

Tracy, T. 2007. Once. *Estudios Irlandeses,* 2, 269–71.

Tracy, T. 2014. Interview: Donal Foreman, Writer and Director of 'Out of Here'. *Film Ireland* [Online]. Available: http://filmireland.net/2014/02/17/interview-donal-foreman-writer-and-director-of-out-of-here/ [Accessed 28 August 2017].

Tuan, Y.-F. 1977. *Space and Place: The Perspective of Experience,* London and Minneapolis: University of Minnesota Press.

Vejvoda, K. 2015. Beyond Horror: Surviving Sexual Abuse in Carmel Winters' *Snap. In:* Monahan, B. (ed.) *Ireland and Cinema, Culture and Contexts.* Basingstoke and New York: Palgrave Macmillan.

Walden, J. 2016. *The Sound of 'Sing Street'* [Online]. NewBay Media. Available: www.mixonline.com/news/films-tv/sound-sing-street/428271 [Accessed 4 September 2017].

Conclusion

The intention behind writing this book was to argue for the place of the national within Irish filmmaking. In times past, films were ascribed a national identity through funding. A British-funded film, *The Crying Game* for instance, was British. The less local funding that went into an Irish film, the less Irish it was. The rise of co-production funding complicated this model and the initial response to this shift was to anticipate that its consequence would be the dilution, even eradication, of the local in the face of the global. I hope to have demonstrated that such pessimistic predictions turned out to be ill-founded. Instead, film after film has pursued its own vision of what Irishness means and how it has been constructed historically and in the present. Scattered through *Irish Cinema in the Twenty-first Century* are quotations from filmmakers discussing their own position in relation to the depiction of Irishness in their films. Many, it seems, set out to address questions of national identity formation in their work. Many more were motivated by other concerns, whether it was to escape the older debates (around nationalism, the rural and the Church) that informed the work of earlier generations of Irish filmmakers, or simply to make films that looked and felt like global products. Much of my analysis, therefore, rests on reading the national back into Irish films or weighing it up against the films' embrace of global production practices (in the horror films, for example). I also hope to have resisted the binaries of local/global. If we can more easily define what we mean by the local, then what does the global mean in practice? Does it perhaps mean less recognisably local? In the measure of things, is *Song of the Sea* more local than, say, *Philomena*? Creating taxonomies of Irishness are, in a medium such as film that is inherently global, a waste of energy. More productive is understanding Irish film production as inherently transnational. Even if the funding is entirely Irish, the releases themselves may have as their address all audiences, Irish or other. With the demise of political filmmaking, as a production practice or as thematic intent, address has become less targeted, more diffuse. Even films with a political message, such as *The Wind That Shakes the Barley*, may not reach their target, and audiences may take from them the pleasure of a melodramatic narrative well-told rather than a warning about partition or the Iraq War.

I further hope to have demonstrated how the economic circumstances of the Celtic Tiger, the recession and the recovery have emerged as thematic preoccupations of so many of the productions discussed in these pages. Whether it be the genre films, the rural dramas, or the urban dramas, characters directly reference these events, or the films indirectly respond to them. It may be, as in *Once*, through finding spaces in Dublin that are not inflected by the new architecture of the boom, or in *His & Hers* celebrating an image of the woman in the home that evokes more certain times. The changing structures of Irish life are reflected through a new interest in urban identities, if those remain most commonly white, male and Irish in lineage. Where Irish cinema most closely reflects global concerns is in its dismissal of the establishment. If its representatives do appear – the rural priest, the guard – their influence is most often destabilised and rendered comic, tragic or both. Their former constituents may mock them, but they also appear lost in an unstable world. In the place of the old authority figures, new models step in, notably the urban gangster. But their claims to control their own space are contingent and constantly under threat. Falling back on older, nostalgically realised renditions of Irishness, previously a safety release for periods of social upheaval, is less easily imagined in this new era of unease.

What is problematic is the limited range of characters in these films. I have drawn repeated attention to the marginalisation of women's stories, particularly in films set in contemporary Ireland. Of equal concern is the miniscule attention paid to individuals from the new ethnic communities, and the simplistic depiction of this constituency when it does occur. Similarly, LGBTQ concerns remain marginalised, and overall Irish cinema continues to be identified by its chaste attitude to sex.

This observation threatens to undermine the argument for understanding Irish cinema as arthouse, conventionally viewed as the locus for sexually explicit scenarios and marginalised characters. Again, taxonomies are of limited use, but the prominence of certain auteurs – Lenny Abrahamson, John Carney, John Crowley, Neil Jordan, the McDonagh brothers, Jim Sheridan – all of whom work within arthouse parameters, and all of whom favour a 'writerly' practice, and have humanistic concerns, does still suggest that the dominant model is an arthouse, independent one. This denomination favours their films at festivals and ensures that they reach a wider audience than simply the multiplex-goer.

Accompanying a smiling picture of the new Taoiseach, Leo Varadkar, on the cover of *Time* magazine of 24 July 2017, was a quotation from the interview with him in which he pronounced Ireland to be 'an island at the center of the world'. The wider point concerned Ireland's connectedness to the major global economies. The same might be said about Irish cinema; in most instances, it is defined by the geographical entity that is Ireland, yet it is funded by and speaks to a global network of film producers and consumers. To distinguish itself in that crowded marketplace, it needs to insist on reproducing recognisable identifiers of Irishness and, overall, to tell Irish stories. Whether being too Irish, a concern raised around a number of films discussed here, or even sounding incomprehensibly Irish, is something to be cherished is another matter. Certainly, the more Irish film loses such identifiers, and the more its settings, particularly its urban settings, come to resemble those of any other global city, the less visually recognisable it may be. Yet, even the deployment of these 'non-spaces' speaks to the country's identity as a globalised terrain and is as 'true' a representation as any other.

As a national cinema, there is no sense that the nation it constructs in its documentaries and fictions matches any one person's understanding of what Ireland may actually be. The Ireland of cinema is a protean space, which is made and remade with each production. Even less tangible is the Northern Ireland of cinema, with its landscape still dominated by the Troubles and their legacy. Many of the films set in the North share with certain of the Republic-set productions the understanding that they have a duty to speak to the traumatic inheritance of the past, whether that be miscarriages of justice, clerical sexual abuse, the legacy of violence, or emigration. Even in these very specific local instances, the exploration of trauma, particularly of cultural trauma, is as much outward-looking as inward, which is another identifier of Irishness, and a narrative with resonances for others far beyond the geographic borders of Ireland.

The very instability and porousness of Irish cinema and its narratives are indicative of the fragility of all identity formations in the new global order of uncertainty. Yet, cinema can usefully question, and strengthen, ties of identity and nation. It is an essential component of any country's creative make-up. Irish filmmaking, whether or not it addresses the national, can only survive with support. This means not just financial support but policy interventions that ensure that all its constituents are given the opportunity to speak. Being reactive has its merits, but simply responding to the pressure group of the moment is not enough. For the next generation of writers on Irish cinema to be able to discuss films that represent the evolving nation, then policy-makers need to make certain decisions now. I look forward to that future.

Appendix
Funding for Irish audiovisual content

The responsibility for measuring the value of the audiovisual sector passed from IBEC to the IFB in 2006–7. The model is slightly different in that the IFB figures are based on local spend, whereas the IBEC reports list total income. Given that not all income is spent in Ireland some discrepancies must exist. The Irish Film Board publishes industry figures annually for all projects that receive Section 481 funding (that is, most major projects). The picture, however, is close enough to give a reasonable account of the financial position of the Irish audiovisual sector. Figures are incomplete for the year of the handover, 2006. All figures are in €m. and rounded up.

Table A.1 Funding for Irish audiovisual content, 2000–6

	2000	2001	2002	2003	2004	2005	2006
Animation Local	4.6	5.3	.6.6	8.9	15.3	19.9	
Animation Incoming	4.6	8.2	.12.4	19.2	7.0	24.9	
Animation Total	9.2	13.5	.19.0	28.1	22.3	44.8	23
Film Local	89.2	62.1	.60.3	53.2	44.2	19.3	
Film Incoming	71.3	137.5	67.9	191.1	35.9	14.2	
Film Total	160.5	199.6	128.2	244.3	80.1	33.5	60
TV Drama Local	35.4	44.0	42.9	46.8	59.5	72.7	
TV Drama Incoming	4.4	1.9	0.8	1.0	8.0	1.7	
TV Drama Total	39.8	.45.9	.43.7	47.8	67.5	74.1	155

Source: IBEC: Film and Television Production in Ireland, Audiovisual Federation Review 2006, Dublin: IBEC. IBEC. The Economic Impact of Film Production in Ireland 2000. Dublin: IBEC.

Table A.2 Funding for Irish audiovisual content, 2007–16

	2007	2008	2009	2010	2011	2012	2013	2014	2015	2016
Animation Local	2.8.	6.8	6.8	9.8	18.5	13.8	8.7	15.8	10.7	18.7
Animation Incoming	36.4	21.7	43.2	57.5	62.0	40.5	80.0	69.8	38.9	62.9
Animation Total	39.2	28.5	50	67.3	80.5	54.3	88.7	85.6	49.6	81.6
Film Local	10.4	29.1	16.7	12.9	32.8	21.0	16.9	50.1	20.5	25.2
Film Incoming	11.0.	26.0.	56.4	77.5	87.8	44.9	52.5	42.8	53.7	202.8
Film Total	21.4	55.1	73.1	90.4	120.6	65.9	69.4	92.9	74.2	228.0
TV Drama Local	25.5	25.8	32.1	17.4	21.6	26.2	19.3	23.1	26.0	30.1
TV Drama Incoming	66.3	49.1.	39.9	167.8	55.6	72.4	142.2	221.0	45.6	282.6
TV Drama Total	91.8	74.9	72.0	185.2	77.2	98.6	161.5	244.1	71.6	312.7

Source: IFB/BSÉ, www.irishfilmboard.ie/images/uploads/general/Total_S481_Production_Spend__Trends.pdf. Accessed 4 November 2017.

Index

Note: page numbers in *italic* refer to illustrations.